Belgian Foreign Policy Between Two Wars

Belgian Foreign Policy
Between Two Wars
1919 - 1940

JANE KATHRYN MILLER

BOOKMAN   ASSOCIATES

New York

Preface

As THE TITLE suggests, this study is concerned with the diplomatic aspects of Belgium's foreign policy during the period between the two world wars. It traces the shift from a policy of cooperation with the Allies of 1914-1918 to one of complete independence, showing the effect of internal politics upon foreign relations. One phase—the commercial—has been deliberately omitted, except where, as in the Oslo and Ouchy agreements, there was a clear relationship between it and political developments.

The method pursued has been broadly chronological, although for the sake of clarity a few subjects have been traced to their conclusion before an overlapping topic has been taken up. A chapter on Belgian domestic politics forms the first section of the work, in order to serve as a background against which to watch the varying phases of foreign relations, and to provide an explanation for some of the policies adopted. Then the history of Belgium at the peace conference is presented, and some of the problems immediately connected with the treaty are discussed. Reparations, war debts, and security receive full treatment, bringing the story down to the depression. The gradual change in Belgian policy from cooperation to independence is foreshadowed, explained, and commented on; and its disastrous results are briefly described in the concluding chapter.

The sources on which this study is based are the published debates and documents of the Belgian Parliament, and contemporary newspapers and periodicals. The former provided the factual basis for the study, and gave official interpretations; the latter supplied material for the description of the interrelations of politics, public opinion, and foreign policy. Although except for some material used in the chapters on the Paris peace conference and reparations, no confidential documents have been available, the present study is presented as a contribution to knowledge since it embodies the only extensive study of this phase of Belgian history which has been made since the first world war.

CONTENTS

Belgian Foreign Policy Between Two Wars

CHAPTER ONE

Background: 1830-1918

ON MAY 10, 1940, for the second time in thirty years invading German troops crossed the frontier separating the Reich from Belgium. For over twenty years every Belgian government, no matter what its other policies, had striven to find some method of preventing this disaster, but the march of events had frustrated all efforts to attain security. A brief description of the historical background of the country, and a short account of its internal politics, will help toward an understanding of the problem faced by Belgian statesmen, and of the causes of their failure to solve it.

The small, thickly populated state has not had a long independent existence.[1] By the terms of the treaty of Vienna of 1815, Bel-

---

[1] The standard history of Belgium is still Henri Pirenne, *Histoire de Belgique* (Brussels, 1909-1932), 7 vols. Of the shorter works in English, the most complete is H. Vander Linden, *Belgium, the making of a nation,* translated from the French by Sybil Jane (Oxford, 1920). Emile Cammaerts, *A History of Belgium from the Roman invasion to the present day* (New York, 1921), is less good in its treatment of the more recent period. Leon van der Essen, *A Short History of Belgium* (Chicago, 1915), is a very brief abstract of Pirenne, at times using his very words. R.C.K. Ensor, *Belgium* (New York, 1915), gives an account of the social, economic, and cultural situation at the outbreak of the first war. The best brief history of the nineteenth century can be found in John de Courcy MacDonnell, *Belgium, her king, kingdom and people* (London, 1914.) Modern Belgian politics are best treated in Frans van Kalken, *Histoire de Belgique* (Brussels, 1924) and *La Belgique contemporaine, (1870-1930), histoire d'une évolution politique* (Paris, 1930).

gium was united to Holland, in order to strengthen the latter against France. As a result of unwise policies adopted by King William of the Netherlands, the union was severed by the Belgians in July, 1830, when they took up arms in revolt. After fruitless negotiations, a Dutch army was sent to subdue the rebels, but was forced to retire from Brussels late in September. On October 4, 1830, the provisional government, which had been formed on September 25, declared that the Belgian province formed an independent state.[2] This at once led to the intervention of the Great Powers. Russia, Prussia, and Austria were alarmed at the prospect of a successful insurrection; Great Britain and France were actuated by other considerations. Louis Philippe, recently raised to the French throne as a result of the July revolution, hoped to see his son, the Duc de Nemours, chosen king of the new nation, as a first step towards its incorporation into France. Suspecting this scheme, William of Holland had appealed to the Powers to maintain the provisions of the treaty of Vienna.[3] Lord Aberdeen, British foreign secretary, could not stand by unconcerned while France became master of the Low Countries; at the same time he feared that hasty action would bring on a general war. To avert this disaster, he proposed that representatives of the Powers meet in London to examine the situation. Meanwhile internal affairs in Great Britain were leading to a change of government, and on Novem-

---

A useful handbook to Belgian resources as well as history is Great Britain, Foreign Office, *Handbooks prepared under the direction of the historical section of the Foreign Office, no. 26, Belgium* (London, 1920).

[2] For details of the revolution and the work of the provisional government see Theodore Juste, *Histoire du congrès national de Belgique, ou de la fondation de la monarchie belge* (Brussels, 1861), 2 ed., 2 vols; M. Nothomb, *Essai historique et politique sur la révolution belge* (Brussels, 1876), 4 ed., 2 vols; and Baron Camille Buffin, ed., *Mémoires et documents inédits sur la révolution belge et la campagne de dix-huit jours (1830-1831)* (Brussels, 1912), 2 vols.

[3] For text see Edouard Descamps, *La neutralité de la Belgique au point de vue historique, diplomatique, juridique et politique; étude sur la constitution des états pacifiques à titre permanent* (Brussels, 1902), p. 137.

ber 16, just twelve days after the opening of the conference, Aberdeen, with the other members of the Tory cabinet, resigned his office. His successor, Lord Palmerston, achieved one of the greatest successes of his career at this conference, by frustrating Louis Philippe's plans without causing a war.[4] His first victory was registered on December 20, 1830, when the conference officially recognized the independence of Belgium, and its members pledged themselves not to seek any increase of territory as a result of the new arrangement.

It now remained to secure the assent of the Netherlands to the separation, to delimit the boundaries of the new state, and to determine the share in the national debt of the old kingdom of the Netherlands which each of the succession states should assume. These problems now absorbed the attention of the conference, which spent many months trying to reach an acceptable solution. It will not be necessary to give a detailed account of these negotiations; only those most important to the later history of Belgium will be described here.

A protocol published on January 20, 1831, and generally known as the "Bases of Separation," specified that Belgium would be a perpetually neutral state; Holland would retain control over both banks of the Scheldt at its mouth; the grand duchy of Luxemburg and the duchy of Limburg would be restored to King William; and that Belgium would assume responsibility for sixteen thirty-firsts of the former national debt. The Belgians refused to accept these conditions and, as a gesture of defiance, proceeded to elect the Duc de Nemours for their king. A serious situation was thus

[4] Details can be found in Evelyn Ashley, *The Life and Letters of John Henry Temple, Viscount Palmerston* (London, 1879), I, 223-280; and Stanley Lane-Poole, "Henry John Temple, third Viscount Palmerston," *Dictionary of National Biography* (New York, 1898), LVI, 19-20. In a recent study, W. E. Lingelbach gives Palmerston all the credit for inventing the neutrality formula, which is sometimes ascribed to Talleyrand; William E. Lingelbach, "Belgian neutrality, its origin and interpretation," *American Historical Review*, XXXIX (1933), 52-56.

created, for the British government had given warning that it would regard this choice as a cause for war. Louis Philippe, unwilling to risk a debacle, refused the proffered honor in his son's name. The Belgians then reconsidered their choice, and the conference on its side revised its conditions. On June 4 a second election named Prince Leopold of Saxe-Coburg, husband of the late Princess Royal of England, as the king of the new state; and on June 26, the conference completed its draft of a treaty of eighteen articles, entitled "The Preliminaries of peace between Holland and Belgium."[5]

This treaty stipulated that the questions of Luxemburg and Limburg would be settled by direct negotiations between Belgium and Holland, and that the national debt should be so divided that each country would assume the debts contracted before the union of 1815, and the remainder would be proportionally divided. This arrangement was accepted by the Belgian provisional government, and at once Prince Leopold announced that he would assume the crown offered him a month earlier. The adhesion of Belgium to the conditions was transmitted to the conference on July 12; five days later the Netherlands announced its refusal to accept them.

The tempo of events suddenly accelerated. After taking the oath of office on July 21, King Leopold had begun a visit of his domains when on August 2 he received word that the Dutch considered his accession a hostile act, and had sent troops across the border. He at once took command of the army, but his soldiers were no match for the well-trained Netherlanders, and only the intervention of France, acting on behalf of the conference, saved the country from reconquest—but not from humiliation. Reconsidering their decision of June 26, the Powers drew up a new treaty of twenty-four articles, by which Belgium was given two-fifths of

---

[5] An excellent summary of the negotiations between Belgium and the conference during May and June, 1831, is given in John Hall, *England and the Orleans Monarchy* (New York, 1912), pp. 68-74.

the grand duchy of Luxemburg, but lost Maestricht and nearly all of Limburg. Moreover the debt was divided in such a way as to lessen the share payable by the Netherlands. The latter country was also given full control of the mouth of the Scheldt, though the river was to be open to Belgian ships in peace time. This treaty was not accepted by the Belgian parliament until November 15, after Leopold had threatened to abdicate unless his adopted country conformed to the decisions of the Powers.[6]

The Dutch, having proved their military superiority, refused to recognize the independence of Belgium, notwithstanding an Anglo-French blockade of Dutch ports, which lasted until May 21, 1833, the date on which the government of the Netherlands agreed not to reopen hostilities and to leave the Scheldt open. Meanwhile, until the evacuation of occupied towns by the Dutch army, Belgium retained all of Luxemburg and Limberg. Not until the spring of 1838 did King William inform the Powers that he accepted the twenty-four articles. The Belgians were dismayed. King Leopold tried to get French and British support for his contention that the disputed provinces, having been part of the kingdom since the revolution, should not be returned to Holland. His efforts were fruitless. Limburg and Luxemburg were placed under the King of the Netherlands. On April 19, 1839, the government of the Netherlands at last formally recognized the independence of Belgium. Three treaties were then signed: one between the Powers and the Netherlands, one between Belgium and the Netherlands, and one between Belgium and the Powers. The last, containing the guarantee of Belgian neutrality, was the famous "scrap of paper" of the first world war. Its terms were identical with those of the treaty of November, 1831, which had been favorable to the Netherlands.[7]

[6] Nothomb, *Essai sur la révolution belge,* I, 485-503.

[7] The texts of the three treaties are given in Nothomb, *Essai sur la révolution belge,* II, 213-224.

The history of the new state during the nineteenth century is briefly told. The country, after one severe depression lasting from 1847 to 1854, entered upon an era of prosperity, due in large measure to the intense industrialization that went on after the middle of the century. The various industries, mining, smelting, and iron and steel, were developed; while at the same time the peasants improved their methods and made the best of their small holdings by careful intensive farming.

Political life during the century passed through three periods. During the first, which lasted from the adoption of the constitution on July 21, 1831, until August 12, 1847, when Charles Rogier formed the first Liberal cabinet of ephemeral duration, the activities of the government were directed towards buttressing independence and laying the foundations of national institutions. Two groups—the Catholic conservatives and the Liberals—had combined to carry through the revolt from Holland. The constitution which they framed guaranteed individual liberty, freedom of speech, of religion, of education, and of language. The head of the state and commander-in-chief of the army was the king, who was also entrusted with the executive power, which he exercised through a cabinet responsible to the legislature. This was a parliament composed of two chambers, elected by those citizens paying a direct tax of at least twenty florins. Parliament was given the controlling voice in the government, since it alone had authority to levy taxes and to fix the size of the army.

By 1848 the unity of feeling among the governing classes which had distinguished the early years of independence came to an end. The second period of Belgian political life, marked by a bitter quarrel between Catholics and Liberals, then opened. Henceforth cabinets were recruited from one party, and political antagonism became sharp. Not until after the nation had weathered the difficult years of the Franco-Prussian war, however, did the conflict reach its most serious stage. In 1879 the Liberal ministry successfully advocated an education bill which placed public education under the sole direction of the national authorities, at once eliminating all outside interference, either by clergy or by communes. The Catholic party fought the "godless school" vigorously, receiving support from those who resented the weakening of local government which was an inseparable part of the measure. Although the law was repealed in 1884, the passions stirred up by the issue were still flaming at the outbreak of the first war.

Absorption in the school question tended to blind both parties to a new issue resulting from the rapid industrialization of the country. Long hours, low wages, and unhealthy living conditions made life unbearable for the worker, who, moreover, had no legal means of redressing these conditions, since the high property qualification limited the suffrage, and with it political power, to the middle classes. To remedy this situation a new organization was founded, its advent marking the opening of the third period, in which the working classes fought for their rights, both social and political. In 1879 the Socialist party, based on the ideals later adopted by the Second International, came into being. Its political activity dates from its reorganization in 1885, when it took the name Belgian Workers' Party: in French, *Parti ouvrier belge*, whence it is usually known as the POB. Deriving its chief revenue from well-managed cooperatives, offering recreational and educational facilities at the local *Maison du Peuple*, the party made rapid progress among the more ambitious workers, especially in Wallonia. Less attached to Marxist doctrines than to practical reforms, the party had as its immediate aim universal manhood suffrage, which, its leaders felt certain, would bring in its wake the other desiderata: recognition of the right of collective bargaining, income tax, abolition of child labor, state ownership of public utilities, the eight-hour day — to name only the most outstanding. To achieve manhood suffrage, a revision of the constitution was necessary, and that meant securing a two-thirds majority in parliament, which could only be done if the other parties collaborated. Before the conservative elements in the Catholic and Liberal parties would consent to vote for the democratization of Belgium, the POB had to call a general strike. After four days of rioting, which threatened to develop into revolution, a compromise solution was reached. The conservatives agreed to universal manhood suffrage, provided that the heads of large families, holders of university degrees, and those paying high taxes were granted supplementary votes. On April 18, 1893, by a majority of 119 to 14 a law embodying this compromise was voted.

Universal manhood suffrage gave added importance to a peculiarly Belgian development—the Flemish movement. Since the last days of Roman Empire Belgium had been bilingual. In the days of the barbarian invasions the German-speaking Franks, ancestors of the Flemings, pushed the romanized Belgae south of the natural boundary formed by the impassible *Silva Carbonaria.* In later centuries the forest disappeared, leaving a "linguistic frontier" which cuts across Belgium from north-east to south-west. In medieval times this frontier was no obstacle to the union of the two peoples, and both languages were recognized as official. After the French Revolution, however, when Napoleonic centralization was extended to conquered Belgium, French became the only recognized language. During the fifteen years after the Congress of Vienna when Belgium was part of the Kingdom of the Netherlands, the Dutch language, almost identical with Flemish, was favored. In the course of the revolution of 1830 an attempt was made by the constitutional convention to solve the linguistic problem by making the use of either French or Flemish optional. In practice this meant that as French-speaking officials had led the revolution, French became the ordinary language of administration.[8] At the same time, however, the literary revival of Flemish be-

[8] Shepard B. Clough, *History of the Flemish movement in Belgium, a study in nationalism* (New York, 1930), p. 51.

gan to attract the attention of the educated classes, who had hitherto paid little heed to the language of half their compatriots.[9] By
1856 this literary interest had become strong enough to launch a
movement so vigorous that it could force the nomination of a
parliamentary committee to study Flemish grievances.

The report was kept a state secret, and no reforms followed. A
tragic miscarriage of justice finally caused a change. In 1864 two
Flemish workers were condemned to death and guillotined after a
trial in the French language, of which they understood not a word;
a year later the real criminals confessed their guilt. This outrage
to elementary justice caused the passage of a series of laws tending to give Flemish an equal place with French in administration
and in the courts.[10] Manhood suffrage, by giving the vote to the
previously disfranchised masses of Flanders, strengthened the Flemish movement, which assumed alarming proportions after the
turn of the century. On the eve of the war the country seemed
seriously divided on the question of the conversion of the state university at Ghent into a Flemish-speaking institution. Demands
for administrative separation and for the creation of separate Flemish regiments in the army had also been made, though as yet they
had comparatively few supporters.

Although the country was divided into such sharply opposed
linguistic and social groups, its foreign policy was rarely the object of partisan disputes. The one great preoccupation of the Belgian foreign ministers was to watch carefully over Belgium's neutrality. During the period of uncertainty preceding the signature
of the treaties of 1839, the French government had opened negotiations with the provisional government of Belgium for a tariff

[9] Official statistics in 1914 gave 2,485,384 as speaking only Flemish; 440,-
039 as speaking it in addition to French or German, or both; while 2,230,316
spoke only French, and 462,333 more spoke it together with one or both of
the other national languages. Belgium, Ministère de l'intérieur et de l'hygiène,
Annuaire statistique de Belgique et du Congo belge, 1914, pp. 82-87.

[10] Clough, *Flemish Movement,* p. 101.

union between the two countries. But after 1839 even an economic treaty was considered an infringement of absolute neutrality; consequently in 1845, on the advice of most of the European chancelleries, the negotiations were broken off.

A serious problem for the Belgian government was caused by the French revolution of 1848. In the revolutions of 1789 and 1830 Belgium had followed the lead of France; when the February revolution broke out in France in 1848 many observers believed that again it would spread to the north. Indeed, a party of enthusiastic French revolutionaries actually crossed the border, only to be quietly disarmed by the gendarmerie at the village of Risquons-Tout. The Belgian people remained calm, so that, for the first time, Europe began to believe that Belgium was destined to continue in existence as a sovereign state.

The ambitions of the second French empire, however, were a serious threat to the independence of its northern neighbor. After the outbreak of the Franco-Prussian war Bismarck published Benedetti's draft treaty of 1866, proposing that France receive compensation for Prussian gains in the Seven Weeks' War by annexing Belgium.[11] The British cabinet, already alarmed by the possibility of an invasion of its protégé by one or both of the belligerents, required that both give assurances that they would respect the 1839 pledges. This was done by treaties between Great Britain and both France and Prussia, which stipulated that the signatories would fight together to maintain the treaties of 1839, in the event that the other belligerent failed to respect them.[12] This strong support from England reassured the anxious Belgians. It also strengthened the arguments of the leaders of the Catholic party, who desired to avoid keeping up a large army, for it seemed to bear out their contention that the expense would be unnecessary, since the coun-

[11] Lingelbach, *loc. cit.,* pp. 64-65.

[12] Charles Craven Scott, "Belgian diplomatic relations, 1875-1887; a study in the diplomacy of neutrality" (unpublished doctoral dissertation in Stanford University Library, 1940), p. 55.

try would be defended by the Great Powers who had signed the treaty of neutrality.

The Belgian government, however, realizing that the guarantors would not be likely to defend a state which was not prepared to defend itself, threw all its weight into the struggle for a larger army and more adequate defenses. In fact, in 1878 the Belgian representatives in the capitals of Europe were instructed to make formal statements to the governments to which they were accredited, to the effect that as strict neutrality was and would remain a traditional policy of their government, the latter would see to it that the defenses of the country were strong enough to support this policy.[13]

In spite of this declaration, and the efforts of the Liberals, it was not until 1909 that parliament voted a law reorganizing the army. This had been one of the cherished plans of Belgium's second king, Leopold II, who saw its realization on his deathbed. Unfortunately the new legislation came too late; the army that Leopold's successor, Albert I, led to victory in the world war was still in the throes of reorganization when the German invasion commenced.

As late as July, 1914, the vast majority of Belgians continued to believe that however disturbed Europe might be, the treaties of 1839 would protect them from war.[14] The reaction to the German ultimatum, consequently, was first one of amazement, then one of anger. All parties and groups united to defend their country's rights.

Although its reorganization was still incomplete, the army was able to hold back the invading Germans long enough to enable the French and English staffs to modify their plans and eventually to stop the enemy at the first battle of the Marne. When the Germans,

---

[13] Scott, "Belgian Diplomatic Relations," p. 240.
[14] According to Pirenne, even the invasion of Luxemburg did not dissipate this illusion. Pirenne, *Histoire de Belgique*, VII, 394.

defeated in their original aim of enveloping the French army, attempted to gain control of the Channel ports, Belgian forces rendered a second invaluable service to the Allies, by making a stand at the Yser and there stopping the German advance along the coast.[15]

King Albert set up his headquarters as commander-in-chief of the Belgian army at the town of La Panne, on the only strip of Belgian territory to which the invader had not penetrated. As accommodations there were limited, the government was located at Saint-Adresse, a suburb of Havre, France. The chief work of this government-in-exile was the direction of diplomatic relations; the actual administrative work was carried on by the officials who remained in the occupied territory, under the general supervision of the German military authorities. This state of affairs was inaugurated after the first battle of the Marne, when von der Glotz, Governor-General of the occupied territory, invited officials to return to their departments, giving them written assurances that by so doing they would waive none of their rights as Belgian citizens and would in no way compromise the position of their country as an independent nation. The officials accordingly returned to work, thereby enabling the nation to survive the catastrophe that might otherwise have overwhelmed it.[16]

Equally important for the future was the work of the Commission for Relief in Belgium, which assumed the difficult task of importing food for the population, as the country could raise only 6 per cent of the cereals needed. The food gathered in the markets of the world by the Commission was distributed by the *Comité National,* a Belgian organization, which carried out its work under the supervision of the Commission and the protection of the

[15] See Lt. General Galet, *Albert, King of the Belgians, in the Great War; military actions and experiences set down with his approval* (Boston, 1931).

[16] Brand Whitlock, *Belgium, a personal narrative* (New York, 1919), I, 145. The employees of the Belgian state railways maintained their refusal to work, however, as the lines were used for transporting German troops and supplies.

Spanish, Dutch, and American ministers, who had remained in Brussels after the occupation.[17]

The German government, while ostensibly respecting the rights given to occupied countries under international law as specified in the Hague agreements, in reality treated the Belgians as a conquered people. Levies, ranging in amount from 40,000,000 to 60,000,-000 francs monthly, were exacted from the provinces; any aid given to the Allies—even the assisting of men of fighting age to leave the country—was accounted treason; and Belgian laborers were forced to work for the German government. At the same time "occupation marks" flooded the country with depreciated currency.[18]

Of all the actions of the occupying power, however, none had such lasting results as the support given the extremists of the Flemish movement. While the great majority of Belgians had forgotten partisan, confessional, or linguistic differences in their zeal to defend their independence, there were a few fanatics willing to use any means to advance their cause. The Flemings who thus cooperated actively with the invader were henceforth known as "Activists"; those who refused to accept reforms from the Germans were termed "Passivists." The German authorities moved with caution, first directing their efforts toward rigorous enforcement of all existing laws favoring the Flemish groups, then adding supplementary decrees of their own, and finally, on March 17, 1917, effecting the administrative separation of the Flemish and Walloon provinces.

[17] For an account of the work of the CRB see: George I. Gay and H. H. Fisher, *Public Relations of the Commission for Relief in Belgium; documents* (Stanford University, 1929), 2 vols. The work of the *Comité National* is described in Albert Henry, *Le Ravitaillement de la Belgique pendant l'occupation allemande* (Paris, 1924). Further details can be found in the reminiscences of Brand Whitlock, Mrs. Vernon Kellogg, and Hugh Gibson.

[18] The best general account of Belgium during the war is Henri Pirenne, *La Belgique et la Guerre* (Brussels, 1928). German military government has been described briefly by Adolph Solansky, *German Administration in Belgium* (New York, 1928) and by Charles Delzell, "The Military Occupation of Belgium, 1914-1918" (unpublished Master's thesis in the Stanford University library, 1943).

This action had been preceded by the foundation of a Flemish University at Ghent, which, though long desired by the Flemings, was now boycotted by all but a handful of professors and students.

While the German authorities were supporting Activists in the occupied territory, some Flemish extremists in the Belgian army were carrying on their propaganda among the troops. Discontented soldiers, commanded by officers who did not understand their language, formed a new organization, the Front Party, whose platform demanded administrative separation, the division of the army into Flemish and Walloon regiments, and a Flemish university of Ghent. The severe repressive measures taken by the military authorities caused the "Frontists," as the adherents of the Front Party were called, to engage in secret negotiations with the Activists and even with German military leaders. Before anything could come of these actions, however, the defeat of the Central Powers had begun.[19]

While these intrigues were threatening national unity, the government at Sainte-Adresse was working to enlist the sympathy of the Allies and of the neutrals, without which it would have been impossible to borrow the money necessary to continue fighting. The question of war finance will be discussed later; for the moment only the political aspects of Belgian foreign policy during the war will be considered.

Technically Belgium was not a belligerent, since the treaties of 1839 stipulated that if the country were obliged to take up arms to protect its frontiers it would not lose its neutral status. Consequently, the government at Sainte-Adresse did not sign the Pact of London of September, 1914, by which Great Britain, France, and Russia bound themselves not to undertake separate negotiations with the enemy.[20] The Belgians, nevertheless, spoke of their "allies" and were allotted a portion of the Western Front to defend.

[19] Clough, *Flemish Movement,* pp. 174-217.
[20] Alfred de Ridder, *La Belgique et la guerre* (Brussels, 1928), IV, 194-196.

As far as Belgium was concerned, the most important diplomatic event of the war years was the promise made on February 18, 1916, by the Allies. On that day the governments of France, Great Britain, and Russia declared that:

when the time has come, the Belgian government will be invited to participate in the peace negotiations, and that the hostilities will not be ended until Belgium is reestablished in its political and economic independence and generously indemnified for the damages suffered. They will lend aid to Belgium to assure its commercial and financial rehabilitation.[21]

This statement removed any doubts of allied solidarity which might have arisen as a result of Belgium's decision not to participate in the Pact of Paris. It also, together with President Wilson's seventh point — "the evacuation and restoration of Belgium" — became the basis of that country's claims for special consideration at the Peace Conference.

Although anxious to preserve the independent status of their country in political matters, the Belgian cabinet members desired economic bonds with the Allies. When an inter-Allied conference met in 1916 and worked on plans to continue an economic war against Germany even after the making of peace, some of the Belgian ministers at Saint-Adresse wished to take advantage of the discussions to make an economic treaty with England and France. This scheme was nipped in the bud by King Albert, who insisted that as a constitutional monarch he could not conclude a treaty without the consent of parliament—which of course was unable to convene. His real reason was that he wished Belgium to remain free of any obligations, towards its allies or towards its enemies.[22]

This was not the only occasion when the King acted as a check

[21] Fernand van Langenhove, ed., *Le dossier diplomatique de la question belge, recueil des pièces officielles, avec notes* (Paris, 1917), p. 386.

[22] Allan Nevins, ed., *The Letters and Journal of Brand Whitlock* (New York, 1936), II, 289-290, entry of Sept. 3, 1916. Hereafter cited as Whitlock's *Journal*.

upon his ministers. In January, 1917, when the Allies wished the Belgian government not to answer President Wilson's peace note of the previous December, the King insisted that he could not forget all that America was doing for his people; the cabinet gave in to their ruler, and not only replied, but added a summary of Belgium's special position as a guaranteed neutral.[23]

Again, when the French general staff wished to incorporate the Belgian army with the French, Albert, as commander-in-chief, refused. He considered that his country was fighting in its own right; he would never have consented to a separate peace, but he did wish to limit Belgium's objectives to the fulfillment of its obligations and the reconquest of its independence. For this reason he was not averse to negotiations with the Central Powers to prepare the way for a peace conference, and he permitted his ministers to receive the proposals made through Baron Evence Coppée, Graf Pörring, and Prince Sixtus of Parma.[24] Moreover, he approved the attendance of Camille Huysmans, Socialist deputy in the Belgian parliament and secretary-general of the Second International, at the Socialist Congress in Stockholm, as he believed that by bringing the German Socialists to meet their comrades in other countries, this Congress might be a step toward peace.[25] When these efforts to bring the belligerents together failed, he turned all his energy to the task of preparing his army and uniting his people for the final military campaign. It was with this end in view that he invited the leaders of the opposition—the Socialist Vandervelde, and the Liberals Paul Hymans and Count Goblet—to become members of the cabinet.[26]

With the king carrying the responsibility for major decisions, the cabinet was of secondary importance. Nevertheless there was

---

[23] *Ibid.*, II, 342-343, entry of Jan. 12, 1917; Louis Dumont-Wilden, *Albert I er roi des Belges* (Paris, 1934), p. 167

[24] Emile Vandervelde, *Souvenirs d'un militant socialiste* (Paris, 1939), p. 203.

[25] Désiré Denuit, *Albert, roi des Belges* (Brussels, 1934), pp. 131-132.

[26] Vandervelde, *Souvenirs*, p. 203.

jealousy and dissension among its members, and there were several crises. The most important of these occurred on June 5, 1918, and concerned the question of post-war policy. Premier de Broqueville, who was inclined to minimize the strength of the Flemish movement, disagreed with his colleagues. who wished to grant a large measure of Flemish autonomy. The premier accordingly resigned, to be replaced by Gerard Cooreman, who accepted the office with the proviso that he would be permitted to resign as soon as the government returned to Brussels.[27] The events connected with his resignation on November 12, 1918, caused much controversy at a later period. The facts can be briefly summarized.

During the week preceding the armistice there were disorders in Brussels caused by the mutinous spirit of the German soldiers. To prevent the social upheaval which they feared was imminent, several prominent politicians including the Liberal Janson and the Socialist Anseele, presented themselves at general headquarters, then temporarily located at the château of Lophem. After several long conferences with King Albert several reforms were decided upon. They included concessions to the Flemings, equal suffrage, and social legislation, all to be inaugurated as soon as possible.[28] Cooreman at once resigned, in accordance with his agreement of the preceding August. Later Albert was charged with having been deceived by the Socialists into promising extreme measures of which he disapproved. So persistent was this story that finally, on February 10, 1930, he denied it in a public letter to premier Jaspar.[29]

With the return of the King and his ministers to Brussels in

[27] Denuit, *Albert*, p. 136; Emile Cammaerts, *Albert of Belgium, Defender of Right* (New York, 1925), p. 353; Whitlock's *Journal* II, 438, entry of July 30, 1917; II, 463, entry of Dec. 25, 1917; II, 484, entry of June 6, 1918.

[28] Van Kalken, *La Belgique contemporaine*, pp. 175-176; Paul Emile Janson, "Lophem," *Flambeau*, IX (1926), 257-283.

[29] The charges are strongly urged in Maurice des Ombiaux, *La politique belge depuis l'armistice la grande peur de la victoire* (Paris, 1921), 21-27. The King's letter is given in Cammaerts, *Albert of Belgium*, pp. 299-300.

the last weeks of 1918, the war ended for Belgium, and the reconstruction period began. The following chapter will describe the
work of rebuilding the country, and the political history of the
years preceding the second invasion.

CHAPTER TWO

Belgian Politics, 1918-1939

ON NOVEMBER 22, 1918, in his speech for the opening of parliament, King Albert launched the Lophem program. In an eloquent address, he described his plans and hopes for the future of a prosperous, united Belgium. He promised that his people would be given more democracy, and that loyal Flemings would see the fulfillment of their legitimate aspirations.[1] These royal pledges were the platform of the government of national union, *l'union sacrée,* which had been planned at Lophem. Headed by a Catholic lawyer, Léon Delacroix, it included influential members of the three great parties, among them several who were to take a leading part in politics for the next twenty years.[2]

Emile Vandervelde, minister of Justice, has already been mentioned in these pages. As president of the Second International, he was well known before 1914, but during the war his absorption in the defence of his country had somewhat narrowed his international outlook.[3] One of the founders of the POB, he was "le Patron," its revered chief, until his death in December, 1938. He would

---

[1] Belgium, *Moniteur belge, journal officiel,* LXXXVIII (1918), (Brussels, 1919), pp. 4-7.

[2] For the composition of the ministries from 1918 to 1940, see Appendix.

[3] Cf. Carl F. Brand, *British Labour's Rise to Power: eight studies* (Stanford, 1941), p. 169.

have suffered deeply had he lived through the second invasion, for his patriotism was very real, and as foreign minister he always worked for Belgium's interests. He did not compromise with his Socialist principles, however, and to the end his witty eloquence was at the service of the workers.[4]

The party he represented, while still nominally Marxist—Vandervelde insisted that only a difference in opinion as to the advisability of direct action separated him from the Communists—had become in reality reconciled to the existing order, and concentrated its efforts on improving living and working conditions, not on fomenting revolution. Indeed, the POB could be considered one of the richest capitalists in the country, since it controlled many successful cooperatives, several newspapers, and a banking chain.[5]

The second group represented in the Delacroix cabinet, the Liberal Party, while weak in quantity was strong in quality. Its outstanding leader, Paul Hymans, soon became famous throughout Europe for his diplomatic skill, shown first at the Paris Peace Conference, then on the Council of the League of Nations. Alert, farsighted, tactful, he never lost sight of his country's interests, which he presented with equal clarity and conviction at international assemblies and on the floor of the Chamber. Less fortunate than Vandervelde, he lived to see the second invasion, dying at Marseilles on March 8, 1941, while on his way to the United States.

The Catholic party, with the largest membership in the cabinet,

---

[4] Vandervelde, *Souvenirs,* deals with the early history of the POB, giving little information on the post-war period. Brief character sketches with some biographical information are given in H. K. Norton, "Belgium at Work," *Current History,* XIX (1922), 433, and Antoine d'Alia, *La Belgique intellectuelle, économique, politique* (Brussels, 1923), pp. 275-277. An interesting appreciation by an American Catholic is Albert Lynd, "Death of a Socialist," *Commonweal,* March 17, 1939, pp. 566-568.

[5] Cf. Van Kalken, *La Belgique contemporaine,* p. 180: Great Britian, *Peace Handbooks, no. 26, Belgium,* p. 203; "Chronique," *Revue Générale,* LVIII (1925), 376.

had also its eminent personalities. Although premier Delacroix left little imprint on Belgium's political life, he became famous in international circles by his work on the Reparations Commission. The most colorful of the Catholics was Henri Jaspar, quick, irascible, stubborn; resembling Lloyd George in appearance, if not in character. Despite his temper, Jaspar was a successful diplomat, sharing with Hymans and Vandervelde the credit for Belgium's influence in international conferences. His sudden death in February, 1939, spared him the horrors of the second war.[6]

Charles de Broqueville, urbane, debonair, aristocratic, was another Catholic statesman of importance. Not ordinarily an interesting speaker, he could be forceful on occasion, notably during the thrilling session of August 4, 1914, when parliament ratified the cabinet's decision to defend the country.[7] A clever politician and skillful parliamentarian, he was the most outstanding leader of the right wing of his party during the post war era.

It was fortunate for the nation that such able men were to cooperate in the task of reconstruction. The immediate problem facing them was that of material rebuilding, to which the Belgian people devoted themselves with great energy, assuming a heavy financial burden. So successful were they that when an inter-Allied conference was held at Spa, Belgium, in July, 1920, observers noted the general appearance of prosperity.[8]

Meanwhile a larger share of democracy had been granted the people. It was inconsistent to deny the vote to those who had fought or suffered for their country, but legally it was impossible to grant equal suffrage without amending the constitution—a lengthy and

---

[6] d'Alia, *La Belgique intellectuelle,* pp. 268-270, gives some biographical details.

[7] Whitlock's *Journal,* II, 8-11, entry of Aug. 4, 1914, gives an eye-witness account.

[8] Wallace (Paris) to the Paris Embassy, July 21, 1920, United States, Department of State, *Papers relating to the Foreign Relations of the United States, 1920* II, 402. Hereafter cited as *For. Rel.*

complicated process. Under the circumstances the constitution was tacitly set aside, and all parties agreed that the next election would be on the basis of equal manhood suffrage.[9] The vote was also given to wives or widowed mothers of soldiers or civilians killed in the war, and to women sentenced by the Germans for patriotic actions. The parliament thus elected reflected the temper of the times. By reason of the suppression of the plural vote, the Catholic party lost its majority, and the Socialists made large gains at the expense of both Catholics and Liberals.[10] These changes caused a shift in the cabinet which gave the Socialists a larger representation. The new cabinet carried out such democratic reforms as the abolition of the property qualification for deputies and senators, the payment of salaries to deputies, and the extension of eligibility to the Senate.[11] It was, perhaps, easier to carry through these reforms than to solve the problems arising from the war. Possibly the most urgent of these was the housing question; returning refugees found themselves homeless, with no materials at hand for reconstruction. Ceilings on rents had to be imposed in order to prevent unreasonable rates, and every effort was made to provide for the construction of new buildings. Want of adequate shelter aggravated the misery and discontent of the working classes, already suffering from unemployment.[12]

The spring of 1920 was characterized by an epidemic of strikes, notably in the zinc factories, where unhealthy conditions pre-

[9] Chambre, *Annales,* April 10, 1919, p. 801. The measure was voted unanimously and greeted with prolonged applause. The vote in the Senate was similar.

[10] Henry Carton de Wiart, "Les grands partis belges et les élections," *Flambeau,* IV (1921), pp. 155-156.

[11] Belgium, Constitution, *La Constitution belge revisée,* 1921 (*Brussels,* 1923), pp. 1-22.

[12] Conditions in pre-war Belgium are thoroughly described in B. Seebohm Rowntree, *Land and Labour, Lessons from Belgium* (London, 1911); post-war conditions are fully described in Ernest Maheim, ed., *La Belgique restaurée; étude sociologique* (Brussels, 1926), a study made under the auspices of the *Institut Solvay.*

vailed.[13] To prevent further troubles several necessary measures were quickly adopted, among them the eight-hour day, a progressive income tax, an inheritance tax, and compulsory old age insurance.[14]

In general these reforms were well received in all parts of the country. It was not so, however, when the Flemish question was taken up. Some Walloons associated everything Flemish with treasonable wartime Activism, and did all in their power to delay much needed legislation. Those Flemings, the majority, who had repudiated Activism during the war, were exasperated at this, and were impelled by their resentment to identify themselves more and more with the movement. Moreover the trial of certain Activists and the heavy sentences imposed tended to create "martyrs."[15] In retreating from Belgium the Germans boasted that they were leaving behind them a seed which would one day bear fruit.[16] That seed was Flemish nationalism; its fruit was ready for the picking in 1940, and had been ripening for many years.

During the first years following the Armistice the movement, though strong, was not dangerous. Many influential Flemings hoped to achieve their ends by working with the older parties, and aimed only at reasonable changes. The most important of these groups was that, which, under the leadership of Frans Van Cauwelaert, formed the Flemish wing of the Catholic party, and by sheer weight of numbers, swayed the party at decisive moments. The Socialist party also had a large Flemish section under the leadership of Anseele and Huysmans. The Liberals were with-

---

[13] Chambre, *Annales,* May 7, 1920, II, 1061, and July 9, 1920, II, 1988. So strong was the discontent that on July 29, 1920, when the Chamber was about to open a debate on a veterans' bonus, an unruly crowd invaded the Chamber, halted the proceedings, and attacked some of the deputies. This was typical of the disturbed spirit of the times. Chambre, *Annales,* July 29, 1920, II, 2242-2244.

[14] Louis Piérard, *Belgian Problems since the War* (New Haven, 1929), pp. 76-77, credits these and other reforms solely to the POB; the left wing of the Catholic party was equally interested, and gave full support.

[15] Clough, *Flemish Movement in Belgium,* pp. 220-222.

[16] Roland de Marés, "La crise belge," *Revue de Paris,* April 1, 1939, p. 663.

out an important Flemish section, as liberalism was almost entirely confined to Wallonia. Catholic and Socialist Flemings united to achieve such common aims as that all teaching in the public schools should be given in the mother tongue of the students; that the University of Ghent should be a Flemish-speaking institution; that conscripts should be free to enter either Flemish- or French-speaking regiments; that the defendant should be allowed to choose the language in which his trial would be conducted. Before the end of Albert's reign these aims and more had been attained.

The extremists among the Flemish nationalists were not well organized. The most coherent group was the Front Party, named for the soldiers' party formed in the trenches during the war, and later expanded to include some former Activists, their sympathizers, and new converts who felt that the older parties were not strongly backing the Flemish cause. Their chief demands were autonomy for Flanders, the abolition of French as a secondary language in the public schools, the development of the port of Antwerp, and an independent foreign policy.[17]

The Frontists leaders, all young men, included Herman Vos, Gustaf Declerq, and Ward Hermans. Hermans' activities during the war were such as to force him to remain in Holland until a general amnesty bill was passed. Declerq was one of Belgium's "Quislings" in the second war. Vos, a soldier in the trenches during the 1914-1918 war, was his party's constant and bellicose representative in the Chamber.

Agitation for Flemish "rights" began in May, 1919, when Van Cauwelaert opened a four-day discussion in the Chamber. The order of day adopted at the end of the debate promised redress of grievances at an "opportune moment."[18] This opportune moment was slow in arriving. On January 20, 1920, a parliamentary committee

[17] Clough, *Flemish Movement in Belgium*, pp. 222-231.
[18] Chambre, *Annales*, May 14, 1919, II, 904-910; **May 15**, II, 911-937; **May 21**, II, 951-974; May 22, 975-1000.

was appointed with authority to report on every aspect of the question.[19] This delaying action did not stop all debate on the subject and there were consequently many stormy sessions that spring.[20] It was over a year before a new cabinet headed by Carton de Wiart secured the passage of a law providing for the use of Flemish in administrative offices in the provinces of Antwerp, East and West Flanders, and Limburg, and the districts of Brussels and Louvain.[21]

In the interval premier Delacroix' position had been weakened by a serious split in his cabinet due to the action of the Socialists. On August 16, 1920, it became known that some French munitions destined for General Wrangel had been stopped at Antwerp by order of the Belgian government, which had received information that the shipment was really going to Poland, then at war with Russia. Lively protests were issued by the French foreign office, and Hymans hastened back from his vacation to explain to his colleagues the folly of antagonizing Belgium's closest friend, on the eve of the signing of a treaty of alliance. The Socialists carried the day, however, and the order was not revoked. On August 28 Hymans sent in his resignation as minister for foreign affairs, and a month later his Liberal colleague Paul Emile Janson, who had remained in office at King Albert's request, followed his example.[22] The

---

[19] Chambre, *Documents,* Jan. 20, 1920, doc. no. 53.

[20] On one occasion the President of the Chamber threatened to apply a gag rule to the subject. On another, a near riot was caused when a Socialist deputy quoted the Frontist paper, *Ons Vaderland,* which was exhorting Flemings to start a Sinn Fein movement in order to win independence. Chambre, *Annales,* Feb. 17, 1920, I, 368 and March 2, 1920, I, 444.

[21] Chambre, *Documents,* Aug. 5, 1920, doc. no. 504, and July 14, 1921, doc. no. 470, pp. 1420-1425. The opponents of the bill called it the "von Bissing law," referring to the separation attempted by the German governor general. Sénat, *Annales,* Aug. 11, 1920, pp. 875-885.

[22] France, Ministère de la guerre et des affaires étrangères, *Bulletin périodique de la presse belge,* no. 33, Nov. 7, 1920, pp. 2-3. Hereafter cited as BPB. In 1936 the precedent of refusing to transship munitions was cited against the Socialists during a debate on non-intervention in Spain; Chambre, *Annales,* Nov. 21, 1936, p. 191.

weakness of premier Delacroix, who was unable to hold his cabinet together, led eventually to his resignation in November. His successor, Henry Carton de Wiart, had carried out diplomatic missions at Washington and The Hague during the war, and one of his brothers was the King's political secretary. The new premier was a prominent member of the Catholic left wing, and was perpared to continue the reform legislation.[23]

At this juncture the POB was weakened by internal dissension. On December 12, 1920, a group of very active Socialists who had banded together as "Les Amis de l'Exploité" were read out of the party at the annual congress. A week later they were joined by three comrades who became their leaders, Jaquemotte, Massart, and Everling. Such was the foundation of the Belgian Communist Party.[24] Jaquemotte was for long their representative in the Chamber, where his ready answers won the admiration, and his obvious sincerity the respect, of even his most conservative colleagues.[25]

With his strongest opponents thus divided, Carton de Wiart was able to carry out his program with a reasonable amount of success. Not only did he finally get the administrative separation bill through Parliament; he also completed the work of constitutional revision, which had been dragging along for two years; and vigorously continued the work of reconstruction.[26]

This last named item was expensive, and the resulting high taxes were unpopular. The conservatives wished to handle the situation

[23] Cf. d'Alia, La Belgique intellectuelle, pp. 267-268. Whitlock admired the "big, handsome, well-groomed minister" whom he called the best of the Belgian politicans, and with whom he had a strong personal friendship; cf. Whitlock's Journal, III, 8, entry of August 6, 1914; II, 482, entry of May 27, 1918, and elsewhere.

[24] Charles Massart, La Belgique socialiste et communiste (Paris, 1922), pp. 128-138.

[25] Cf. the tributes paid him in the Chamber at the time of his sudden death in October, 1936. All stressed his probity and devotedness to the workers; Chambre, Annales, Oct. 27, 1936, p. 348.

[26] Ibid., Oct. 19, 1921, III, 2675.

by restricting the social services, while the Socialists and left wing Catholics advocated reducing the time of military service. The Flemings also supported the proposals for limited service, for they were afraid that the army might be used to assist France in a preventive war against Germany, to which they were strongly opposed; and in addition, they felt that their large families bore the brunt of conscription.

The agitation for a shorter period of military training made much headway until it was temporarily checked by the incident of the *fusil brisé*. On October 16, 1921, at a meeting presided over by Anseele, minister of public works, the local Socialist youth organization was presented with a banner representing a soldier breaking his gun over his knee. Patriotic feeling was outraged, and Devèze, the Liberal defense minister, refused to remain in the cabinet with Anseele. Carton de Wiart asked for the latter's resignation, and at once received that of all his Socialist colleagues. The matter was discussed in the Chamber, where feeling ran very high.[27]Thereupon Carton de Wiart, feeling that the case should be presented to the voters for consideration, dissolved Parliament. The Socialists lost seats in the ensuing elections, but remained the second largest party. The Liberals refused to participate in the new cabinet and the tripartite coalition which had ruled since the Armistice came to an end. The ministry which took office on December 16, 1921, under Colonel Theunis, was composed only of Catholics and Socialists.[28]

The new premier was a business man rather than a politician; and though a Catholic in religion, he was not affiliated with any party. He had served as one of the Belgian financial experts at the Paris Peace Conference, and later was a member of the Reparations Commission, before accepting the portfolio of finance in the Carton de Wiart ministry. He kept this responsibility during his premiership, and represented his country at the economic and at the

---

[27] Chambre, *Annales,* Oct. 19, 1921, pp. 2674-2696.
[28] Paul Tschoffen, "Le parti catholique," *Flambeau,* IV (1921), 166-170.

political conferences called during the next few years to deal with
the reparations problem. Philip Snowden, Chancellor of the Exchequer, wrote of him that he was "one of the ablest men I have met
among foreign statemen. . . . Since the London conference M.
Theunis has left politics to devote himself to business. This must
have been a great loss to Belgian politics, for he was one of the most
astute diplomatists in Europe, and carried great influence at international gatherings."[29]

Theunis was faced with a serious financial situation. Belgium
had experienced a brief period of semi-prosperity in 1919-1920,
but the too rapid reconstruction, the failure to receive expected
reparations, and the unfavorable balance of trade, soon ended this
deceptive boom.[30] By May, 1921, the budget deficit had climbed
from the 474,000,000 francs of 1920 to 683,000,000 francs.[31]

In October, 1922, Theunis could report that some headway had
been made against the depression. The franc had risen from 15.96
to 11.74 to the dollar. The number of unemployed had decreased
from 210,000 in 1921 to a more normal 48,000 in the spring of
1922, and this figure was reduced to 30,000 by the following
September. At the same time steel production had gone up to sev-
enty-six percent of the prewar output, and the textile industries
showed a comparable improvement.[32]

In spite of this economic improvement, Theunis had a difficult
time, due to a renewal of the language conflict. This time it was
the creation of an all-Flemish university at Ghent which nearly
turned the cabinet out of office. The personal influence of King
Albert alone prevented a political crisis.[33] In July, 1923, the bill

[29] Philip Snowden, *An Autobiography* (London, 1934), II, 679.
[30] Chambre, *Annales*, Dec. 21, 1921, I, 35; Sénat, *Annales*, Dec. 22, 1921, p. 17.
[31] Chambre, *Annales*, May 20, 1921, II, 1293.
[32] Chambre, *Annales*, Oct. 24, 1922, II, 1841.
[33] A bill, not emanating from the cabinet, was rejected by the Senate. Albert
refused to accept the subsequent resignation of his ministers because they had
not sponsored the bill. He suggested that a new measure be drafted, and submitted to the approval of all party leaders before being made public. This

taking the first steps toward the inauguration of a purely Flemish-speaking public university was passed.[34]

During these post-war years the Socialists and the Flemings were drawn closer together: the democratic element in the Flemish group was favorable to many points of the Socialist program, and the occupation of the Ruhr united the two parties in a common distrust of French imperialism. This sentiment motivated the rejection of a Franco-Belgian commercial treaty, on February 27, 1924, which caused another ministerial crisis.

However, as none of the party leaders was willing to face the dangerous financial problem caused by the rapid fall of the franc, Theunis returned to office with his third cabinet. During this third term of office Theunis was instrumental in working out the Dawes plan and in securing its adoption at the London conference.

With post-war problems at least temporarily settled, the major issues of Belgian politics during the next few years were primarily domestic. The regular parliamentary elections of April, 1925, showed that the Socialists were growing in strength, chiefly at the expense of the Liberals. As the Socialists had gained nineteen seats—a difficult feat under proportional representation—Vandervelde was the obvious choice for premier, but as there was no majority, he had to form a coalition. He tried for ten days before admitting his inability to win the support of either Catholics or Liberals. In turn de Broqueville, Aloys Van de Vyvere, and Max tried unsuccessfully to organize a cabinet. At last on June 17, the Catholic Vicomte Poullet appeared before Parliament as head of a Catholic-Socialist coalition in which Vandervelde was deputy premier and minister for foreign affairs.[35]

was done, and a serious crisis averted. Hubert Langerock, "The Flemish demand for Autonomy," *Current History*, XVIII (1923), 789.

[34] Chambre, *Annales*, July 27, 1923, III, 2475; Sénat, *Annales*, July 18, 1923, II, 1220.

[35] Chambre, *Annales*, May 22, 1925, and *Indépendance Belge*, April, May, June, 1925.

The new cabinet, which received a formal vote of confidence on July 2, was faced with the ever-recurring financial problem. The reconstruction plans drawn up immediately after the war, when Germany was counted on to supply huge reparations payments, had been very expensive. The costs were met by the Belgian treasury, and as the prospect of immediate receipts from Germany receded, the Belgian franc began to slip. To strengthen the currency, loans were raised in the United States, raising the total foreign debt to 18,425,000,000 francs. At the same time there was heavy short-term borrowing on the home market.[36] To remedy this state of affairs, in September, 1925, Janssens, the minister of finances, launched a stabilization program. He planned to consolidate the public debt, and to balance the budget by reducing expenses and raising taxes.[37] Of course these measures were unpopular and were not voted at once. The franc kept sliding downward, until in March, 1926, it reached the low level of 3.97 cents. Janssens, at his wits' end to provide a remedy, mentioned the word "inflation." At once there was near panic. Capital fled the country, the franc fell to lower depths, the government was forced to resort to borrowing by the week to meet its current expenses. Under the circumstances public opinion demanded a return to *l'union sacrée,* and on May 20, 1926, Henri Jaspar was able to organize a cabinet. Its chief figure was the minister without portfolio, Emile Francqui, who took office only at the urgent request of the King.[38] Although head of Belgium's largest bank, the *Société Générale,* he was more popular than millionaires usually are, for during the war he had been head of the *Comité National de Secours et d'Alimentation,* a position where he acquired a justly deserved reputation as a patriot and an

[36] Louis Franck, *La stabilisation monétaire en Belgique* (Paris, 1927), p. 23; George Theunis, "Belgium Today," *Foreign Affairs,* IV (1926), 270.

[37] G. de Francisci-Gerbino, "La réconstruction financière de la Belgique; un nouveau project d'amortissement de la Dette Publique," *Flambeau,* VIII (1925), 35.

[38] Denuit, *Albert,* p. 241.

organizer. In the cabinet his task was the rehabilitation of public credit, for which he was given quasi-dictatorial powers.[39]

He needed them: within seven months the government would have to raise 8,000,000,000 francs just to redeem its short-term loans. Francqui met a desperate situation with strong measures. He asked for, and received, 2,100,000,000 francs in additional taxes, floated a 534,000,000 franc loan in London, funded the national debt, stabilized the franc at 175 to the pound sterling, and restored the gold standard.[40] When this program was carried through, in November, 1926, he resigned.

The coalition government lasted until November, 1927, when the Socialists resigned after vainly trying to persuade defense minister de Broqueville to reduce the time of military service to six months. Again King Albert acted, with the suggestion that the matter be submitted to a mixed military commission, which would receive confidential information from the army and then decide on the policy to adopt.[41] The compromise was acceptable to the Liberals, and, what was more important for its success, to the Flemings. In return for their votes the latter were promised further concessions.

The Flemish movement had grown in numbers and in boldness in the decade since the Armistice. In the debate on conscription, Staf Declercq, leader of the Front party, went so far as to say: "Yes indeed, we want the death of Belgium. . . . We do love our country, but it is Flanders, and not Belgium."[42] While the majority

[39] Marcel-H. Jaspar, "Chronique des mauvais jours: les élections du 5 avril et le ministère Poullet-Vandervelde," *Flambeau*, XI (1928), pp. 320-341.

[40] Henry L. Shepherd, *Monetary Experience of Belgium, 1914-1936* (Princeton, 1936), pp. 147-182.

[41] Cammaerts, *Albert*, p. 348.

[42] Chambre, *Compte Rendu Analytique*, Dec. 1, 1927, pp. 25-26. The *Compte Rendu Analytique*, hereafter cited as the *CRA*, is a summary of the parliamentary debates, published the very night of the meeting. There are two editions, one French, one Flemish, but the language used by the speaker is always indicated. The *Annales* contain the stenographic text of the speeches, corrected—and occasionally ampli-

of Flemings did not harbor such antipatriotic ideas, it is quite possible that they used the anxiety created in the mind of the average Belgian by such statements to bring their own platform to realization. On November 7, 1928, a law was enacted that soldiers would be placed in regiments where their mother tongue was used, and that both languages would be on an equal footing in the military academy. Then came an amnesty bill, releasing all Activist prisoners, and permitting those in exile to return.[43]

The Front party now assumed the name of Flemish Nationalist party, and won several seats in the election of May, 1929. The Catholics, largest party but not commanding a majority, allied with them to form a ministry. This of course implied further concessions, which were soon adopted. Premier Jaspar announced this policy to the Chamber on December 10, 1929, and later introduced bills reforming the procedure in criminal cases, and completing the process of making the University of Ghent a Flemish-speaking institution. This latter measure caused much controversy, but in April, 1930, it at last was enacted into law.[44]

In November, 1930, King Albert again averted a cabinet change, this time by refusing to accept the resignation of his ministers on the ground that there had been a hasty action, and without debate he had nothing to guide him in his choice of a premier.[45] When the king's position became known, the Jaspar ministry was given a vote of confidence, and remained in office for another six months. On May 21, 1931, during a stormy debate on military credits, the Lib-

fied—by their authors. Speeches are given in the language in which they were delivered, and all official remarks, directions of the President of the House, descriptive asides, etc., are given in both languages. Cf. Chambre, CRA, March 8, 1933, p. 169, Avis de la Direction.

[43] Ibid., Dec. 10, 1928, pp. 19-20.

[44] Sénat, CRA, Apr. 2, 1930, p. 270.

[45] Sénat, CRA, Nov. 11, 1930, p. 5; Chambre, CRA, Nov. 18, 1930, p. 9. Albert also said, "In accepting purely and simply the Cabinet's resignation, I should establish the most dangerous precedent in the normal working of the political institutions which, for a century, have secured the country's existence." Cammaerts, Albert, p. 349.

eral ministers suddenly resigned, because Jaspar seemed prepared to cut down military expenditures to please the Flemings.[46]

After a month of uncertainty, on June 11 Jules Renkin announced that he had formed a Catholic ministry, which derived much of its strength from Flemish support. This had to be paid for, but only after long debate and a shake-up in the cabinet was complete administrative separation enacted, and a stringent law requiring the use of Flemish in all schools in Flanders passed.[47] This left the premier free for a time to concentrate on the financial situation of the country. The depression had by this time reached such proportions that it dwarfed all other issues, and continued to do so for at least four years.

On September 7, 1932, Renkin called a special session to authorize the floating of a short-term loan and the renewel of a loan of $1,000,000 in Treasury bonds. These expedients did not improve matters, and the Socialist victory in the municipal elections of October 9, 1932, was interpreted to mean that the people were dissatisfied with the existing government. On October 18 Renkin resigned, and four days later Parliament was dissolved,

In the general election of November 27, 1932, the Socialist success in the municipal elections was repeated, though the Catholics also made important gains at the expense of the Liberals and Flemish nationalists.[48] The new legislature was not in sympathy with de Broqueville's proposal to default on the debt payment to the United States, and he resigned. A few days later he returned, and was able to carry through his policy.[49] The following May 16 he was given full power to control expenditure by decree. A policy of rigid economy was adopted, and by the end of the year there was some improvement.

[46] Chambre, CRA, May 21, 1931, p. 345.
[47] Chambre, CRA, March 2, 1932, p. 375; Sénat, CRA, May 25, 1932, p. 385, June 21, 1932, p. 455; July 12, 1932, p. 657.
[48] Sénat, CRA, Dec. 27, 1932, p. 9.
[49] BPB, no. 111, Jan. 17, 1933, pp. 9-10.

At once the Flemish nationalists resumed their agitation, one going so far as to proclaim in parliament: "What do we want? Purely and simply the destruction of Belgium."[50] The mass of the people, however, were loyal to their country, and showed it clearly, when on February 18, 1934, the sorrowing nation learned of the tragedy of the eve. While out on a solitary walk, King Albert had fallen to his death. At once the whole nation, Socialists, Liberals, and Catholics, Walloons and Flemings, united in a tribute of homage to the memory of the "Soldier King," and a pledge of loyalty to his son and successor.[51]

Leopold III faced a difficult task. Without the prestige that long years of constant and wise service had given his father, he had to grapple with problems of vital importance. Foremost among them were the perennial language quarrel, the economic situation with its attendant social and political complications, and looming in the background, the threat of war.

The new king and his ministers first turned their attention to the economic problem. Conservative in outlook, premier de Broqueville and his colleagues, both Liberal and Catholic, believed that deflation was the best means of ending the depression. The Chamber disagreed, and a change of ministers resulted.[52] The new cabinet members were two ministers without portfolio, Van Zeeland and Igenbleek, prominent bankers, whose special function was to advise on economic affairs. When the government refused to abandon its deflationary policy they resigned, causing a cabinet crisis.[53]

There was some difficulty in forming a new ministry. Henri Jaspar's attempt failed when King Leopold rejected his choice because it included too many bankers and manufacturers. The men

---

[50] Chambre, *Annales,* May 12, 1933, p. 344.

[51] *Ibid.,* Feb. 19, 1934, p. 1067.

[52] Chambre, *CRA,* June 6, 1934, p. 563.

[53] *Cf.* Louis Piérard, "Les arrêtés-lois du gouvernement de Broqueville," *Europe Nouvelle,* XVII (1934), 880; B. R., "Réforme bancaire en Belgique," *Europe Nouvelle,* XVII (1934), 870-871.

selected by George Theunis were approved by the King on November 18, although they also were largely business men.

Theunis himself had done well in business since he left politics nearly ten years before, and his colleagues included such men as Camille Gutt and Emile Francqui. Although the Socialists and Flemish Catholics attacked the composition of the cabinet, they did not seriously oppose the grant of special powers which on December 5, 1934, was voted by Parliament.[54] The reason is to be found in the bad financial state of the *Boerenbond* and the *Banque du Travail,* the savings banks of the Catholics and Socialists respectively.[55] Once these institutions had been saved from bankruptcy by loans from the currency reserve, attacks on the government increased, and on March 19, 1935, Theunis resigned.[56]

Paul van Zeeland, his successor, was vice-governor of the National Bank, and an international authority on finance and economics. A young man of forty-two, he had been a prisoner in Germany during the war, then the first Fellow appointed by the Educational Foundation of the Commission for Relief in Belgium to study in the United States. Later he rose to be director of the Institute of Economic Science at the University of Louvain. An ardent disciple of Thomistic philosophy, he was a leader in the young progressive wing of the Catholic party.[57]

When he appeared before Parliament to describe and explain his policies, conservatives of all parties felt some hesitancy about

[54] Chambre, *Annales,* Dec. 5, 1934, p. 125.
[55] Georges Rotvand, "Problèmes Belges," *Europe Nouvelle,* XVIII (1935), 397.
[56] Chambre, *Annales,* March 19, 1935, p. 684.
[57] For further details see Verax, "Silhouettes étrangères, M. Paul van Zeeland," *Revue des Deux Mondes,* XXXII (1936), pp. 520-532; Richard Dupierreux, "La nouvelle équipe de M. van Zeeland," *Europe Nouvelle,* XVIII (1935), 308, and Henri Laurent, "Belgium under a new leader," *Current History,* XLII (1935), 482-483. The first article is strongly in favor of van Zeeland; the second, by a Socialist, gives more moderate praise; the third, by a professor from the Liberal University of Brussels, describes him as a clever, but not statesman-like, politician.

accepting him. There were two reasons for their attitude. First, the cabinet was composed of young men, two of whom, Paul-Henri Spaak and Henri de Man, were advocates of changes in the Socialist platform. The three "elder statesmen"—Jaspar, Hymans, and Vandervelde—who were ministers without portfolio, would probably be unable to restrain the zeal of the younger men. Secondly, there were misgivings about adopting a policy which included such innovations as devaluation, drastic banking reform through governmental regulation, and the establishment of an Economic Administration to coordinate the work of the different departments.[58] The debate on the ministerial program was therefore a dramatic struggle. For forty hours, with scarcely a break, van Zeeland defended his program, first in one house, then in the other. He finally was approved, in the Chamber by a vote of 107 to 54, with 12 abstentions, in the Senate by 110 to 20, with 19 abstentions.[59]

A decree establishing a new monetary unit, the belga, was at once promulgated, and devaluation had become a fact. The operation was highly successful; not only was there a marked increase in foreign trade, but production increased sixteen percent during the period between February and November, 1935, and unemployment decreased by one-third, in spite of the fact that some 20,000 Belgian workers who had been expelled from France swelled the numbers of men seeking positions.[60]

Van Zeeland had been given almost dictatorial powers for one year. It is possible that he could have succeeded without them, for he met with surprisingly little opposition during the first months he held office. By taking three outstanding Socialists into his cabinet

[58] Chambre, *Annales*, March 29, 1935, pp. 688-698.
[59] *Ibid.*, March 29-30, 1935, pp. 688-753; Sénat, *Annales*, March 29, 1935, pp. 319-324; March 30, 1935, pp. 333-338.
[60] Philippe Schwob, "Les dévaluations, la production, et les échanges," *Europe Nouvelle*, XVIII (1935), 1207; Shepherd, *Monetary Experience of Belgium*, p. 228, Sénat, *Documents*, Dec. 12, 1935, doc. no. 27, pp. 49-51; H. de Man, "La résorption du chômage," *Europe Nouvelle*, XIX (1936), 425.

he had disarmed criticism from that quarter, and as one of their foremost publicists wrote, ". . . a great party like the POB has nothing to gain by separating itself from the national community in difficult times."[61]

His program of strict government of banks, and of housing projects to benefit the poor, pleased the POB.[62] The development of a new movement within the old Liberal party also helped the premier. The young neo-Liberals repudiated *laissez faire* as an outmoded doctrine, and advanced a new theory of state supervision which they claimed was the real inspiration of van Zeeland's reforms.[63]

It was not from the older parties, then, that van Zeeland met with opposition, but from three extremist factions broken off from his own Catholic party; the VNV, the Dinasos, and the Rexists.

The *Vlaamsh National Verbond,* better known as the VNV, was founded in October, 1933, by Staf Declercq, the former Frontist. This new party had as its goal the formation of a Flemish speaking national state, under the rule of the house of Orange. It was to contain all those of Netherlandish stock, including the Flemings of Northern France. This party soon absorbed all the Flemish Nationalists.[64]

---

[61] Louis Piérard, "La Belgique, terre de compromis," *Flambeau,* XVIII (1935), 657.

[62] In 1934 the Belgian Socialist party officially adopted Henri de Man's "Plan du Travail," a detailed program for bringing the Socialist state into being. For its text see "Le plan du travail de Man," *Europe Nouvelle,* XVII (1934), 286-291; a commentary is given by a Belgian Socialist, Louis Piérard, "Un plan quinquennal belge," *Europe Nouvelle,* XVII (1934), 5-7. During the occupation de Man tried to put his plan into action by collaborating with the Nazis. He escaped to Spain before the liberation.

[63] Marcel-Henri Jaspar and Henry Janne, "Les jeunes libéraux belges,"*Europe Nouvelle,* XIX (1936), 848.

[64] *BPB* no. 113, April 5, 1934, p. 15. Edgard de Bruyne, "Le Mouvement" *Revue Générale,* CXXXVII (1937) 451-472.

A few of them, however, joined Joris van Severen, who in 1933 set up the *Verbond van Dietsch Solidaristen,* usually known as Verdinaso, or Dinaso. Completely outfitted with all the familiar totalitarian trappings: green shirt, militia, youth organizations, and leader, Dinaso introduced a fascist element into the Flemish movement, by working for a "Flemish state based on corporative principles." The other important difference between the two organizations was that van Severen planned the formation of what he called a "Thiois State," to include Holland, Flanders, Wallonia, Frisia, and Luxemburg, while Declerq would exclude all French-speaking peoples.[65] Dinaso remained relatively small, however, since those who favored breaking up Belgium wanted complete separation from all French-speaking persons, and those who were attracted by fascism turned to another new party, the Rexists, founded by Léon Degrelle.

Much more widely publicized than Dinaso or the VNV, following a dynamic leader with a gift for emotional oratory, the Rexists rapidly became a factor to be reckoned with. In 1931 Degrelle became director of the Rex publishing company, a Louvain institution devoted to the furtherance of Catholic Action. Full of initiative, the new director expanded the activities of the company, by founding in 1932 two weeklies, one, *Rex,* devoted to literary and artistic subjects, the other, *Vlan,* a political paper. Two years later he bought out the publishing firm and acquired the two papers, which he combined to form a single political journal, *Rex.* With it he intended to work for the renovation of the Catholic party, but his attacks on its leaders and on its policies led to his expulsion. He then organized a party of his own, also called Rex, which in the parliamentary elections of May, 1936, won 21 seats in the

---

[65] Désiré Denuit, "En Flandre avec les Dinasos," *Revue Générale,* CXXXIV (1935), 48; Pierre d'Ydewalle, "Au delà du flamingantisme: le Verdinaso," *Revue Générale,* CXXXVII (1937), 696.

Chamber.[66] Degrelle capitalized on a feeling of disgust at the fumbling ineptness of the politicians in their handling of the depression, and loudly warned of the danger of a Communist uprising if a better economic and political system were not adopted. To avoid becoming embroiled in the linguistic quarrel he promised regional decentralization under the Coburg dynasty, and by adroit quotations from Papal encyclicals he tried to win the confidence of the Catholics.

The Rexist seats in the May, 1936, elections had been won at the expense of the Catholic party, and as the Socialists and Liberals who likewise supported van Zeeland, also lost seats, the cabinet resigned. On June 13, after King Leopold personally intervened, van Zeeland formed his second ministry.[67] During the interim a series of strikes occurred which were suppressed only after martial law was proclaimed. This violence, coupled with the success of the Communists in the May elections when they had polled 143,000 votes and won 9 seats, alarmed the Belgian public. Degrelle, with his anti-Communist platform, would have reaped the benefit of this fear, but for three events. This first was the reorganization of the Catholic party, which finally bowed to the inevitable, and set up a completely autonomous Flemish wing under Frans van Cauwelaert. The "Catholic Union" thus formed was attractive to many of the Flemish population, and in recognition of this fact Degrelle and Declercq at once allied their organizations.

The second cause was more spectacular: it was the discovery of a secret interview which took place on September 27, 1936, between Degrelle and Hitler. The loss of popularity which this news brought to Degrelle was proved on October 23, the date set for a monster Rexist rally to overthrow van Zeeland. Instead of the

---

[66] André Buttgenbach, "Le mouvement rexiste et la situation politique de la Belgique," *Revue des Sciences Politiques,* LIX (1936), 515-517.

[67] *Indépendance Belge,* June 12, 1936.

60,000 who were expected to demonstrate, a bare 5,000 appeared on the streets, many just through curiosity.[68]

The third cause of Degrelle's failure was King Leopold's active leadership of his people, especially in foreign affairs. On October 14 he presided at the historic cabinet meeting where he proposed a complete reorientation of Belgian foreign policy.[69] This plan was welcomed by many of his subjects, who forthwith abandoned Degrelle and returned to their traditional party allegiance.

From this time on the security of Belgium was the most absorbing question in politics. The Flemish issue, the Rexist agitation, social and economic problems, all were considered primarily in regard to their effect on the safety of the nation. The first indication of this new departure came in April, 1937, when all the Rexists on the Brussels list resigned, in order to force a by-election. Degrelle announced his candidacy, and challenged the premier to run against him. Van Zeeland accepted the challenge, and contested the seat.[70] The Rexist-Flemish alliance suffered a severe blow on the eve of the election when Cardinal van Roey, in a resounding *coup de crosse*, flatly denied that his previous silence meant approval. In a formal statement the Cardinal declared that "Rexism is a danger to the country and to the Church," and rebuked any Catholic who voted for Degrelle, or even cast a blank ballot.[71]

Van Zeeland's victory was a foregone conclusion. All Belgians understood that; they also realized that the important point was the size of the vote Degrelle polled. He expected 100,000 votes. He received only 69,242, of which 15,840 were interpreted as the

[68] *Ibid.*, October 24, 25, 1936.
[69] See below, chapter IX.
[70] Chambre, *Annales*, March 9, 1937, pp. 898-899.
[71] *Indépendance Belge*, April 10, 1937.
[72] *Ibid.*, April 12, 1937; Robert Leurquin, "Les Bruxellois contre la dictature," *Europe Nouvelle*, XX (1937), 374.

result of his alliance with the VNV.[72] Although Degrelle continued his political career, Rexism was dead.[73]

Premier van Zeeland remained in office only five months after his victory. His political enemies accused him of drawing a salary as Vice-Governor of the National Bank while serving as minister in de Broqueville's cabinet. The bank had a rather unusual method of pensioning its officers, which gave some color to the charge, and although van Zeeland received a strong vote of confidence he resigned. He believed that as an official investigation had been opened into the workings of the bank, he ought to sever his connection with the government.[74]

It was not easy to form a new ministry. The Liberals would not serve under the Socialist de Man; the Socialists opposed the Catholic Pierlot; and the Catholics rejected the Socialist Spaak. King Leopold therefore called a conference of the heads of all parties. They accepted a compromise which raised to the premiership Paul-Emile Janson, the first Liberal to hold that office in over fifty years.[75]

Janson was faced with the problem of balancing the budget in spite of the difficulties caused by the recession. Once again there was conflict between the partisans of deflation and of inflation, which led to the resignation on May 13, 1938, of the Catholic ministers. Three days later Spaak formed a tripartite coalition which

[73] In the communal elections of 1938, the Rexists polled only one-third as many votes as they had received in 1937, and in the parliamentary elections of April, 1939, the number of Rexist deputies was reduced from 21 to 4, and of Senators from 8 to 1. Robert Leurquin, "Après les elections communales belges; le Rexisme et le nationalisme flamand refoulés." Europe Nouvelle, XXI (1938), 1187; Flambeau, XXII (1939), 468.

[74] The vote in the Senate was 121 to 6, with 17 abstentions; in the Chamber, it was 130 to 34, with 21 abstentions; Chambre, Annales, Sept. 8, 1937, p. 105. Only Rexists and members of the VNV voted against van Zeeland; the abstentions came from the 8 Communists and from those who disapproved of the system practiced by the bank.

[75] Chambre, Annales, May 18, 1938, p. 1637, and Indépendance Belge, Nov. 1, 1937.

tried to combine a program of economy with the social services desired by the POB.[76]

The new premier represented the younger Socialists who abandoned the internationalism of Vandervelde and his generation and took as their ideal what they called *Socialisme national,* or nationalistic socialism, not to be confused with the German National Socialism which they abhorred. Spaak coined this term in February, 1937, during an important interview he gave as foreign minister. He said that since 1900 socialism had been changed by the impact of the war, of communism, and of fascism. Nationalistic socialism is not opposed to religion, nor has it any sympathy with communism. It seeks the welfare of all citizens without attempting to change the structure of the state.[77] This new type of socialism, friendly to religion and to private property, was formally adopted by the POB on February 22, 1937, in spite of the disapproval of Vandervelde.[78]

During the summer and early autumn months of 1938 Belgians felt that the threatening aspect of international affairs ruled out the usual political manoeuvering. But the expense of the mobilization in September unbalanced the budget, and once more raised the question of deflation. To complicate the situation, there were differences of opinion about the recognition of Franco's regime in Spain. The fall of the ministry on February 9, 1939, was not due to either of these issues, however, but to the Flemish question.[79] The appointment of a former Activist, Dr. Adriaan Martens, to the state-controlled Academy of Arts and Sciences in November,

[76] *BPB,* no. 129, June 9, 1938, p. 18.

[77] *Indépendance Belge,* Feb. 9, 1937.

[78] *Le Peuple,* Feb. 23, 1937.

[79] Jules Garson, "La situation politique en Belgique," *Revue Politique et Parlementaire,* CLXXIX (1939), 293. A qualified observer writing at the time stated that "the most serious internal problem of the country is the maintenance of a peaceful relationship between these two racial groups, a situation which politicians both inside and outside the country seem ready to exploit"; Thomas H. Reed, "Final Report," *Belgian American Foundation,* Sept. 3, 1937.

1938, aroused strong opposition, and eventually Spaak resigned.[80]

A serious crisis ensued. The veteran Jaspar made a valiant attempt to form a cabinet, but the Socialists refused their collaboration.[81] On February 22 Pierlot assumed the premiership, but the new cabinet did not survive the rejection of finance minister Camille Gutt's plans for reducing the deficit.[82] After fruitless attempts to find an acceptable leader, King Leopold decided to call a general election. The situation was serious, as no party was willing to make concessions; the Socialists refused to accept deflation, the Liberals would not join the cabinet as long as Martens remained in the Flemish Academy, and the Catholics refused either to change their financial program or to remove Martens.[83]

Leopold expressed his mind on the subject in an open letter to Pierlot in which he denounced the political mistakes of the past years and asked for unity "in the face of international problems which may arise in the next few years."[84]

In the election of April 2 the Catholic and Liberal parties made such large gains, at the expense of Socialists and Rexists, that they controlled a good majority. The king called on Pierlot to form a cabinet, and as Martens had resigned from the Academy, the Liberals felt free to support him. Pierlot at once asked for and received special powers in order to guarantee the defense of the

---

[80] Chambre, *Annales,* Jan. 31, 1939, 435-457.

[81] Two days later Jaspar died on the operating table.

[82] Chambre, *Annales,* Feb. 23, 1939, p. 646.

[83] A French observer wrote at this time: "It is feared . . . that the ministerial crisis has already assumed the characteristics of a national crisis, a 'crise de régime.' For if the king does not succeed in appeasing the racial conflict . . . it is not clear how the normal play of parliamentarianism can function in the kingdom." "La crise belge," *Europe Nouvelle,* XXII (1939), 247.

[84] *Flambeau,* XXII (1939), 351. The idea of writing open letters to justify his actions or to inaugurate a policy had begun with Leopold I, and was often used by Albert; Louis de Lichtervelde, "Albert I er", *Revue Générale,* CXXXI (1934), 267.

nation and its economic recovery.[85] The authority thus granted was used to make further additions to the frontier defences.

When the war broke out the Socialists accepted an invitation to form a *union sacrée,* and on September 5,1939, Spaak, Balthazar, Wauters, Soudan and de Man joined the cabinet, the first named taking over the portfolio of foreign affairs from Pierlot. In January, 1940, there was a slight reorganization, and among others de Man and Wauters were dropped. The "Government of National Concentration" thus formed was in office when the Germans invaded Belgium. Four of the number, premier Pierlot, foreign minister Spaak, finance minister Gutt, and minister of colonies Vleeschouwer managed to escape to London, where they established a "government-in-exile" to represent Belgium until its liberation.

This rapid summary of Belgian politics during the twenty years separating the two great wars is a necessary background for the presentation of the story of the country's foreign policy. The first scenes of the story are laid at the Paris Peace Conference.

[85] E. Rouland, "La crise politique en Belgique," *Journal des Economistes,* CIX (1939), 182-183, Chambre, *Annales,* April 25, 1939, pp. 30-35 and April 26, pp. 37-87, Sénat, *Annales,* April 22, 1939, pp. 32-35 and April 28, pp. 38-90.

CHAPTER THREE

Belgium at the Peace Conference

As THE Allied armies advanced in the autumn of 1918, Belgian hopes ran high. The nation was not only to be freed from German domination, it was to be generously indemnified for wartime suffering, and it was to be fully restored to its pre-war economic condition. Nor were Belgian expectations limited to the economic field: both government and people felt that in order to be safe from a second invasion from the east, Belgium should obtain from the peace conference the revision of the treaties of 1839. Such revisions, by abrogating the obligatory neutrality imposed by the Powers, would permit the nation to protect itself by alliances. Many also believed that the Dutch province of Limburg, and the grand duchy of Luxemburg, shorn from Belgium in 1839, should be returned, on the ground that the little grand duchy had submitted too easily to German aggression, and that the Netherlands had permitted the escape of the fleeing Germans through Limburg. Moreover, since control of the approaches to Antwerp by neutral Holland had prevented the arrival of British reinforcements in 1914, it seemed logical to many Belgians that the peace conference should at least open the lower Scheldt to warships, even if it did not go so far as to give their country sovereignty over the whole of the river by transferring to it the Dutch province of

Zeeland. Such hopes of territorial aggrandizement were certainly too optimistic, and were destined to be frustrated.

If the hope for more territory was the most extravagant of those entertained, the hope for reparations was the most important. A small nation of little over seven million inhabitants, Belgium had been obliged to borrow nearly a billion dollars from its allies during the war. A considerable part of this sum, or approximately $341,362,821.00, had been turned over to the Commission for Relief, to be used in supplying food for the occupied territory; the remainder was used for military needs.[1] The Belgian government counted on a large indemnity to cover these loans. It also expected reimbursement for all the damage suffered on account of the invasion, damage officially stated by Premier Delacroix to cover the following items:

War contributions	(gold francs)	2,500,000,000
Cost of national defense		5,000,000,000
Disabled, widows, pensions, etc.		870,000,000
Destruction of railways, shipping, ports		3,700,000,000
Other injury to public property		1,000,000,000
Losses in tax returns		1,500,000,000
Injury to laboring classes		225,000,000
Penalties exacted by Germany		1,000,000,000

(gold francs) 15,795,000,000[2]

This statement referred only to the claims of the government; private claims were believed to amount to another twenty billion francs.

Whether the figures were deliberately exaggerated in order to

[1] Gay and Fisher, *Public Relations of the Commission for Relief in Belgium,* II, 215-216.

[2] David Hunter Miller, *My Diary at the Conference of Paris, with Documents* (New York, 1924), III, 98-99, doc. no. 121.

provide a good basis for bargaining, or whether they were merely the result of the optimism of the first flush of victory, is hard to determine. In any case, the claim was too large. On May 6, 1919, the Division of Economics and Statistics of the American Commission submitted to the Reparations Commission its estimate, which placed all Belgian damages, public and private, at $4,525,000,000, or approximately 23,000,000,000 gold francs.[3] Although this was only about 65 per cent of the official figure, it was an accurate computation, to judge by the amount actually spent for reconstruction.[4] Whatever the exact amount of material destruction, no reparation could restore the 46,000 dead or the 50,000 permanently disabled. Considerations such as these, coupled with their oft-stated and well founded conviction that their loyal observance of treaties had caused all the damage and suffering, motivated the Belgian people in their demands and spurred on their delegates to press these demands at Paris.

In their negotiations they could count upon public opinion in the Allied countries. World sentiment had been profoundly shocked by the German invasion, and by the Imperial Chancellor's cynical reference to the "scrap of paper." There was general agreement that whatever countries might be responsible for causing the war, Belgium was not only innocent, but even heroic. This attitude was reflected in official statements. The moderate peace proposals of Pope Benedict XV, like those of the Socialist conference of 1915, included the liberation and compensation of Belgium. The people of the United States had from the first been deeply sympathetic, and the British government had made the invasion of Belgium the official cause of Britain's entrance into the war. In a confidential

[3] Philip Mason Burnett, *Reparations at the Paris Peace Conference from the standpoint of the American Delegation* (New York, 1940), I, 1131-1133, doc. no. 341.

[4] According to the report made in 1932, when the "Office des régions dévastées" was liquidated, over 23,226,000 gold francs was spent on reconstruction. Sénat, *CRA,* July 19, 1932, p. 551.

Foreign Office memorandum drawn up by Sir Eyre Crowe in 1916, many of the most extreme Belgian demands were approved, among them a treaty of permanent alliance with France and Great Britain, the annexation of Luxemburg, and generous indemnification.[5]

Not only was public opinion favorable, but the Allied governments had formally promised to insure the restoration of Belgium —the governments of France, Great Britain, and Russia in the declaration of Sainte-Adresse, made on February 14, 1916, and the United States, through President Wilson, in the seventh of the Fourteen Points. An official commentary on the Fourteen Points, published in October, 1918, expressly stated that

in the case of Belgium there exists no distinction between legitimate' and 'illegitimate' destruction. The initial act of invasion was illegitimate and therefore all the consequences of that act of the same character. Among these consequences may be put the war debt of Belgium.[6]

In a note of May 18, 1917, Balfour, the British foreign secretary, sent Secretary of State Lansing a copy of his statement on foreign policy made to the Imperial War Council: "I take it that whatever we fight for, we fight for the restoration of Belgium to her old limits and her old condition of independence and prosperity."[7]

[5] David Lloyd George, *The Truth about the Peace Treaties* (London, 1938), I, 33. The British government felt, moreover, that the defense of Belgium was necessary to the security of the island kingdom. The memorandum stated: "It will remain a vital British interest after the war, as it was before it, to prevent Germany from obtaining access to the Belgian coasts. Recent events have shown conclusively that that interest is not effectively safeguarded by treaties providing for Belgian neutrality under international guarantees; we submit that Belgian independence will be better secured by substituting a treaty of permanent alliance between Belgium, France, and ourselves, in the plan of the present safeguards. It is understood that Belgium herself would welcome such an alliance." Quoted in David Lloyd George, *Memoirs of the Peace Conference* (New Haven, 1939), I, 12.

[6] Charles Seymour, ed., *The Intimate Papers of Colonel House, arranged as a narrative* (Boston, 1928), IV, 156-157.

[7] Balfour to Lansing, May 18, 1917, United States, Department of State, *Papers Relating to the Foreign Relations of the United States, The Lansing Papers, 1914-1920* (Washington, 1940), II, 29.

As the war progressed to a victorious conclusion, the Belgian government reminded its allies of their promises. During the Armistice negotiations Hymans wrote to Colonel House:

It must be understood that by 'restoration' is meant that Germany will be obliged to indemnify Belgium for all the damages of every nature that it has suffered as a result of the war.[8]

At the same time he tried in vain to have the phrase "all damages caused by the war" inserted into the Armistice agreement, so that from the outset the claim of his government for indirect damages would be accepted by the Allies and by Germany.

Premier Delacroix had drawn up a document showing how the claims against Germany could be met. This plan, communicated to the Allies on January 2, 1919, provided that Belgium would surrender its claims against Germany to the Allies, in return for raw materials. In this way Delacroix hoped to revive the economic life of the nation, as well as to provide for speedy restoration.[9]

There were, however, two good reasons why this plan was relegated to obscurity: none of the Allies would surrender valuable raw materials for hypothetical German payments, and none was overeager to build up the industrial life of a possible competitor.[10] Moreover, before securing the adoption of plans for payment, the Belgian delegates found that they must first direct their energies to the difficult task of persuading the Great Powers to admit the justice of their claim to complete reparation.

Those selected for the task were fully equal to it. Paul Hymans, head of the delegation, was an accomplished diplomat, who later ably represented his country on the League Council. Probably none

[8] Burnett, *Reparations*, I, 406, doc. no 34.

[9] Miller, *Diary*, III, 98-99, doc. no. 121.

[10] *Cf.* Lloyd George's remark that "Belgium was a very near neighbor and the competitor of Scotland which had an enormous debt," Ray S. Baker, *Woodrow Wilson and World Settlement, written from his unpublished material* (New York, 1922), II, 389.

of his countrymen could have succeeded as well as he, for he combined perseverance, tact, and intelligence with true patriotism. The technical side of financial questions was put in the capable hands of Jules Van den Heuvel, who was given a seat on the Reparations Commission. Emile Vandervelde, leader of the Socialist party, was a member of the committee which planned the labor clauses of the treaty, but he had comparatively little to do with the financial and political side of the negotiations.

On January 18, 1919, the Peace Conference officially opened. During the first few days the delegates from the smaller states received the impression that the methods of the Congress of Vienna would be adopted, and that they would have no voice in the proceedings. The Belgians were especially indignant at the idea of such cavalier treatment. At the second plenary session, on January 25, when the announcement was made that the five Great Powers were to have two members on every commission, while the nineteen other countries together were to choose five, Hymans protested vehemently. So violent, indeed was his speech, that the Great Powers were forced to change their plans.[11] The "Powers with Special Interests"—that is, the smaller nations represented at the conference, met on January 27 to nominate their delegates to the commissions. In recognition of the special part Belgium had played in the war, it was given membership on every commission.[12]

[11] Miller, *Diary,* IV, 65-68, doc. no. 230.

[12] U.S. *For. Rel., Paris Peace Conference,* III, 447-455. Hymans' speech had attracted the attention of some of the Americans present, and on January 27 several of them met in Shotwell's room "to discuss the case of Belgium, which had been badly mismanaged in these early sessions of the Conference, giving the Belgians a feeling that the Great Powers, and especially America, on whom so many hopes had been placed, were not standing by Belgium in its demands." James T. Shotwell, *At the Paris Peace Conference* (New York, 1937), p. 150. *Cf.* also Baker *Woodrow Wilson,* II, 390; Bernard Baruch, *The Making of the Reparation and Economic Sections of the Treaty* (New York, 1920), p. 34; Edward M. House and Charles Seymour, eds., *What Really Happened at Paris, the Story of the Peace Conference* (New York, 1921), p. 280; Charles Haskins and Robert Lord, *Some Problems of the Peace Conference* (Cambridge, 1920), pp. 48-71. Later House,

The problems to be solved by the Reparations Commission were among the most important facing the Conference. The questions of evaluation of damages, financial capacity of enemy states, and measures of control and guarantees were referred to three subcommittees of financial experts. The Americans on the first subcommittee were agreed that the Belgian claim to reparations rested on an entirely different basis from the other Allied claims. This basis was the fact that a lawful state of war had never existed between Belgium and Germany, because the invasion had constituted a violation of international law, being a breach of a treaty binding Germany. As early as January 3, 1919, Frank L. Warrin, one of the American secretaries, had written:

The contemplated restoration of Belgium thus necessarily includes in the broadest sense compensation for damages of every kind suffered by person or property in Belgium, whether direct or consequential, due to the acts of the invading forces, upon a basis much broader than that accepted for the indemnities receivable by other Allied Powers.[13]

This argument was presented at the February 13 meeting of the subcommittee by John Foster Dulles, on behalf of the American delegation. Hughes of Australia, an aggressive Britisher, retorted that if this argument were admitted, Germany could be assessed for all the war costs of Great Britain, which had entered the war in defence of Belgian neutrality.[14] Hymans and his colleagues, of course, wished to confine the argument to the justification of their own claims, lest otherwise the German debt be raised to such astronomical figures that full payment would be impossible; in that case

Shotwell, Lamont, Miller, Davis, and Haskins proved particularly friendly. Wilson was less well disposed towards the Belgians, and at a later period Lansing showed himself definitely hostile, above all when the negotiations with Holland opened.

[13] Miller, *Diary*, III, 102-113. *Cf.* also Miller's memorandum of February 6, 1919, in *ibid.*, V, pp. 123-124; and the memorandum of Paul D. Cravath, December 12, 1918, in *U. S. For. Rel. Paris Peace Conference*, II, 185.

[14] Baruch, *Making of the Reparation Sections of the Treaty*, p. 23 ; pp. 300-301.

each state would be given a pro-rata share in what could be raised by the debtor, and Belgium's portion would be woefully inadequate to meet the estimated costs of reconstruction. Consequently Van den Heuvel supported Dulles in opposing the inclusion in the reparations bill of full costs for any other power.[15]

The question was hotly debated during the month of February, and after bitter arguments the Commission voted to exclude war costs for all nations. Hymans brought all the pressure he could command to have Belgium's war costs recognized, but with both Lloyd George and Clemenceau against him, he fought a losing battle.[16] The Americans on the Reparations Commission then tried to come to his aid by creating a special category of damages applicable only to Belgium. On April 7, at a meeting of the Council of Four to consider the report of the sub-committee on categories of damage, Vance McCormick, an American expert, made valiant efforts to have included among the categories of damage to be paid by Germany, "damages in violation of international agreements." Lloyd George firmly opposed this, and insisted that when all the clauses relating to reparations had been worked out, the Belgian delegates might be allowed to state their case, but that it would not be taken up earlier. The Prime Minister also resisted the claims for reimbursement of the now worthless occupation marks which had been forced upon the inhabitants of Belgium and northern France by the German authorities. The French were less interested in this matter than were the Belgians, and Lloyd George's opposition was sufficient to block the feeble attempt made by the French minister

---

[15] Lloyd George, *Truth About the Treaty,* I, 488-489; Miller, *Diary,* XX, 270; Burnett, *Reparations,* II, 330-333, doc. no. 458. With war costs excluded, except for Belgium, that country would receive 24 per cent of the German payments; with war costs for all countries included, Belgium would receive only 1.7 per cent.

[16] Burnett, *Reparations,* I, 27-28.

of finance to force Germany to redeem the marks at par.[17] These
and other decisions regarding war costs, categories of damage, and
redemption of the marks were taken by the Council of Four on
April 7, 1919, but they were not made public until the end of the
month.[18]

Meanwhile Hymans had been trying to get recognition of his
government's claim to priority of payment. Without specifying
any amount, the Allies had practically admitted the justice of this
request, yet once the conference met no one seemed willing to aid
in attaining it.[19] Late in February Colonel House suggested that
Belgium be given a priority claim of $500,000,000 on the first
German payments, to make possible the negotiation of a reconstruction loan. On February 27 Balfour replied that the British government would accept this plan in principle; the following day
Klotz, the French minister of finance, agreed to the proposition on
condition that priorities apply also to indemnification for stolen
property.[20] This was one step forward, but it was by no means a
complete success, as the British had only agreed "in principle"—
a familiar diplomatic device for politely rejecting a proposal.

This problem was thenceforth linked with that of damages. On

[17] Minutes of the Council of Four, IC-170K, April 7, 1919, *U. S. For. Rel.,
Paris Peace Conference,* V, 52-54. Lloyd George was almost venomous in his
attack on the Belgium claims, *cf.* George A. Riddel, *Lord Riddell's Intimate
Diary of the Peace Conference and After, 1918-1923* (New York, 1934), p. 43.

[18] Although the report was not published, the Belgians got wind of
what was going on, since on April 4 King Albert pleaded his country's
case before the Big Four. *Cf.* Burnett, *Reparations,* I, 831. Lloyd George, *Truth
about the Peace Treaties,* I, 424, does not mention King Albert's action on the
reparations question, but speaks only of his having supported the British view on
the Rhineland problem. André Tardieu, *Truth about the Treaty* (Indianapolis,
1921), pp. 223-224, does not speak of Albert's connection with the Rhineland
dispute, but describes his attempt to secure Belgium's reparations claims. The
minutes of the meeting of the Council at which King Albert spoke are not available, and the only mention is the passing reference in Burnett cited above.

[19] House and Seymour, *What Really happened at Paris,* pp. 279-280.

[20] Seymour, *Intimate Papers of Colonel House,* IV, 353; Burnett, *Reparations,*
I, 633, doc. no. 149.

April 23 the Belgian delegation was given a hint by Loucheur, the French minister of reconstruction, that the Reparations Commission was preparing an adverse report on these issues. Hymans at once protested against such action, and appealed directly to the Council of Four.[21] In the note accompanying his list of demands, Hymans, after rehearsing again the basis upon which they rested, pointed out that the list of categories of damages adopted by the Council of Four did not correspond to the list drawn up by the Reparations Commission, and that the new list implied that his country would lose its special claim to full reparation. He then named four categories of special damages which he proposed should be exacted from Germany: expenses for food; expenses for administration and other services carried on outside Belgium during the occupation; expenses incurred in carrying on the war, and in repairing war damages; and expenses incurred in redeeming the German marks forced upon Belgium. He asked, moreover, that Germany be forced to return the works of art removed during the war.[22]

On April 25 the Belgian delegates were notified that the Council of Four had decided to give them a special hearing on April 29, when they could present their case. At once premier Delacroix and Louis Franck, minister of colonies, made a flying trip to Paris to arrange with Hymans and his colleagues the exact extent of any concessions that might have to be made, and to support them to the limit of their power. Reinforced thus, the Belgian delegates set out for what proved to be a long and stormy session.

Hymans read the note he had drawn up at the direction of his government. It laid down two conditions *sine qua non*: indemnity for all war expenses, including that entailed in the procurement and distribution of food for the population, and a two and one-half billion franc priority on German payments. If these could not be

[21] Paul Hymans. *Fragments d'histoire, impressions et souvenirs* (Brussels, 1940), p. 162.

[22] Miller, *Diary*, XVIII, 81-84.

granted, the whole question would have to be referred to the Belgian parliament. As Hymans pointed out, this might mean that his country would not sign the treaty. Lloyd George retorted that such a move would involve separate negotiations between Belgium and Germany. Nevertheless Hymans did not give way; he was in a strong position, for the Italian delegation had already left the conference, and no one wanted a further demonstration of disunity among the Allies. Twice the meeting recessed when the discussion became too violent; finally, however, a provisional agreement was reached whereby the desired priority was granted, and the Allied leaders promised to recommend to their parliaments the transfer to Germany of Belgium's war debt. On their side the Belgians withdrew their demand for the inclusion of the claims of the civil population as a special category of damage.[23]

Hymans at once telegraphed Brussels for approval, but the cabinet was not satisfied. On May 1 three ministers—Jaspar, Franck (who had just returned from a similar trip), and Renkin—went to Paris to urge Hymans not to sign the treaty. Hymans and his two colleagues, however, feared that such a refusal would entail the economic breakdown of their country.[24] Nevertheless, they were willing to try to obtain better terms, and to this end they asked for a conference with the experts. At this meeting Hymans proposed that the Allies waive all claims to repayment of their war loans to Belgium, and make Germany liable for them; that they also postpone the date of the first payment on post-war loans until the first install-

[23] This account of the Meeting of April 29 is based on three sources: Council of Four, "Minutes," I. C. 177D, April 29, 1919 [Paris, 1919], hereafter cited as IC; Hymans, Fragments d'histoire, pp. 160-163; and Vandervelde, Souvenirs, p. 285. Describing the scene six years later, the report of the foreign affairs committee of the Belgian Chamber thus referred to the session: "Qui ne se souvient que ce fut seulement après deux suspensions de séance et l'intention manifeste de nos délégués de se retirer à la dernière heure du Congrès de Versailles, qu'on fit droit à ce double revendication, pourtant si légitime?" Chambre, Documents, July 14, 1925, doc. no 64.

[24] Hymans, Fragments d'histoire, pp. 165-166.

ment of German reparations had been applied to reconstruction; and that until Belgium should have received all that was due, it be guaranteed 15 per cent of all German payments. The experts agreed that the second demand might be conceded; they were silent on the others.[25] That night Hymans wrote to House, repeating the statements made at the meeting. There was a veiled threat of a refusal to sign the treaty in his concluding sentence:

If after allotment of $200,000,000 on the first German payments we could obtain a fair percentage, 15 per cent on all subsequent payments until Belgium has covered certain categories for dommages [sic] the whole arrangement could be presented to the country as an acceptable solution.[26]

The following day the decision of the experts was communicated to the Council of Four, who accepted it with some modifications. They retained the suggestion that the Allies waive their claims to repayment from Belgium, but instead of trying to collect the debt by including it in the reparations, the Council sanctioned an issue of German government bonds to the amount of the debt, the proceeds of the bonds to be accepted by the Allies in lieu of direct Belgian payments. The demand of 15 per cent of future reparations was refused.[27] Immediately after this meeting Hymans left for Brussels to describe the situation to the Crown Council, a body consisting of all the present and former cabinet ministers, presided over by the King. The Council unanimously decided to accept the arrangements.

On June 24 the final texts of the agreements between Belgium and the Allied and Associated Powers regarding priorities and the

---

[25] IC 179B, May 1, 1919.

[26] Hymans to House, May 2, 1919; Burnett, *Reparations*, I, 1113, doc. no. 328.

[27] IC 180D, May 2, 1919. According to his biographer, it was at this session that Wilson remarked, "In the case of Belgium we were dealing with a sick person. The sum involved was not large, and it was hardly worth while contesting." Baker, *Woodrow Wilson*, II, 390.

Belgian war debt were approved by the Supreme Council. By the terms of the first treaty, Belgium was to receive, beginning May 1, 1921, a priority of 2,500,000 gold francs on the first cash payments made by Germany. This priority was to be without prejudice to Belgium's proportionate share in the balance of the reparations payments, and was to be amortized at the rate of one-thirtieth annually. The second agreement specified that the Belgian war debt was to be paid out of a special German bond issue, to be delivered to the reparations commission. Wilson, Clemenceau, and Lloyd George undertook to recommend to their governments the acceptance of these bonds to the amount of the debt, at 5 per cent interest.[28]

The Belgians found their former enemies much more ready to see their point of view than were many of the Allies. In his speech of May 7, 1919, Brockdorff-Rantzau, head of the German delegation, while rejecting many of the Allies' claims stated clearly: "We repeat the declaration which was made in the German Reichstag at the beginning of the war. Wrong has been done to Belgium and we wish to redress it."[29] Moreover, both in the German foreign office draft proposal, and in the "Observations on the Report of the Commission of the Allied and Associated governments on the responsibility of the authors of the war," the German envoys recognized the Belgian claims to full indemnity, and expressed regret that any justification of invasion had ever been attempted. In addition, the draft proposal contained an offer to assume responsibility for the repayment of the loans the Allied governments had made Belgium, but this was offered as a concession, not as of right.[30] No answer to this German counter-proposal was ever published, for by the end of May, 1919, it was obvious to the Belgians that the im-

[28] Burnett, *Reparations,* II, 211-213, doc. no. 437; II, 213-214, doc. no. 438.
[29] Plenary Session of May 7, 1919, *U. S. For. Rel., Paris Peace Conf.,* III, 417.
[30] Alma Luckau, *The German Delegation at the Paris Peace Conference* (New York, 1941), pp. 96-97, 294, 348-349.

portant thing was to secure a German promise to pay, without quibbling over "rights" and "concessions."

While these financial negotiations were under way, certain political claims were also being put forward by Hymans. The chief of these were the abrogation of the treaties of 1839, and the rectification of the Belgian frontiers in order to improve the defense of the country. In fact, these two demands were very closely bound together, as on the one hand the abandonment of neutrality would make imperative the possession of a well-defended boundary; and, on the other, only the abrogation of the treaties, including the neutrality clause, would enable Belgium to achieve the freedom of the Scheldt, union with Luxemburg, and repossession of Dutch Limburg.[31]

The members of the Belgian government had decided early in the war that obligatory neutrality no longer safeguarded their country's interests, and in June, 1915, included its suppression among their official war aims.[32] On July 27, 1917, at the close of an Allied conference at Paris, the Belgian foreign minister stated his desire for revision in these terms:

The international status established in 1831-1839 to guarantee the security of Belgium has lapsed because of the violation of the collective treaty by two of its signatories. It must be revised. To this effect it is desirable that the powers who have remained faithful to their engagements should call together their representatives to study with Belgium the stipulations of the new treaty which should replace the old . . . and to deliberate on our claims.[33]

In September, 1918, Hymans charged the Belgian ministers in London, Paris, and Rome to make the following declaration:

The Belgian government is opposed to the re-establishment when

[31] For a complete statement of the Belgian argument from strategic necessity, see Miller. *Diary,* IV, 426-432, doc. no. 298.
[32] *BPB,* no. 17, Nov. 4, 1918, p. 6.
[33] Miller, *Diary,* IV, 426, doc. no. 298.

peace comes of the regime of permanent neutrality which in the past has shackled its liberty of action without assuring peace to the country.[34]

The Allies agreed that revision was in order, and a commission was set up in London to negotiate the necessary treaties.[35] This commission made no contribution to the peace conference, and after November, 1918, seems not to have been mentioned.

Like the Allies, the vast majority of Belgians were also convinced of the wisdom of this policy, as is evident from the editorials of newspapers of all parties, from the Liberal Walloon *Nation Belge* to the Flemish Catholic *Het Vaderland*.[36] In his famous speech from the throne of November 22, 1918, King Albert openly expressed the mind of his people on this point:

Victorious Belgium, freed from the neutrality imposed upon her by the treaties whose foundations were shaken by the war, will rejoice in complete independence. These treaties, which determine her position in Europe, did not protect her from a most criminal attack. Reinstated in all her rights, Belgium will govern her destiny according to her needs and aspirations, in full sovereignty. In the international order founded on justice which is about to begin, she will assume the position befitting her dignity and her rank.[37]

Only one important group challenged this position: the reactionary wing of the Catholic party, led by the veteran Charles Woeste. He maintained that Belgium should not easily relinquish the neutrality which had brought such speedy succour from France and England. Woeste had few supporters in this matter, however; parliament was overwhelmingly in favor of abandoning obligatory neutrality.[38]

The stand taken by the Belgian government in this question was not contested by any of the signatories of the treaties of

---

[34] Chambre, *Annales,* Jan. 20, 1926, I, 652.
[35] *BPB,* no. 17, Nov. 4, 1918, p. 6.
[36] *Ibid.,* no. 18, Dec. 3, 1918, pp. 3-4.
[37] Belgium, *Le Moniteur Belge, journal officiel,* LXXXVIII, 7, Nov. 23, 1918
[38] Chambre, *Annales,* Dec. 11, 1918, I, 23-27.

1839, but claims to territorial changes, which would be chiefly at the expense of the Netherlands, aroused the hostility of that nation, and received no support from other sources. The Belgian government, consequently, had to steer a devious course. On the one hand, a claim to complete freedom of the Scheldt was made in a note to the Allies.[39] On the other, an attempt was made to reassure the Netherlands, when, in July, 1916, Baron Beyens, Belgian minister of foreign affairs, gave formal assurances to van Weede, Dutch minister at Sainte-Adresse, that "the government of the King energetically disapproves of the intrigues directed against the integrity of Netherlands territory."[40]

Some sections of Belgian opinion were, however, more outspoken than the government in this matter: the *Comité de Politique National,* whose membership was largely drawn from the conservative Catholics, was particularly active in propagandizing for annexations of Dutch territory, above all of Dutch Limburg and Zeeland. There were, however, several Catholic leaders unfriendly to this policy, partly for political reasons, since they had to consider the wishes of the large and influential Flemish section of the party, which was solidly opposed to any gains at the expense of the Netherlands. The Socialists also were unfavorable to any annexations, as they adhered to the principle of self-determination.[41]

By the time the Peace Conference opened, the Belgian government was definitely committed to an annexationist policy. Consequently, on January 17, 1919, the Allies were presented with three closely reasoned notes containing a summary of Belgium's political

[39] Miller, *Diary,* IV, 435-436, doc. no. 298.

[40] Sénat, *Documents,* July 27, 1926, doc. no. 233, p. 843.

[41] Robert Cedric Binkley, "Reactions of European Public Opinion to Woodrow Wilson's Statesmanship from the Armistice to the Treaty of Versailles," (Unpublished doctoral dissertation in Stanford University library, 1927), pp. 100-130; Mary Margaret Moore, "Public Opinion in Belgium in 1919," (Unpublished master's thesis in Stanford University library, 1942), pp. 139-140.

claims, supported by arguments drawn from international law and history. In the first of these notes the story of the signing of the treaties of 1839 was retold. Stress was laid on the fact that the treaties had been imposed on both Belgium and Holland, and that the former had accepted them only to prevent war.

All these conventions were forced upon Belgium as upon Holland. The Belgo-Dutch treaty, like the others, was not the result of free negotiations between these two states. . . . The system has failed, and the motives that determined the Belgians to accept the treaties of 1839 have ceased to exist.[42]

Recognizing that Holland must have some compensation for the sacrifices asked, Hymans suggested three alternatives: the cession of German territory, for instance, Prussian Guelderland or East Frisia; a colonial acquisition; or a guarantee of peaceful possession of its present colonial holdings. There was also a hint that Dutch refusal of proffered compensation would severely strain relations between the two countries.

In conclusion the note stated the Belgian political demands: first and foremost, complete independence, unlimited by obligatory neutrality; secondly, freedom of the Scheldt, in war as in peace, with control over the navigation of the river, if not complete sovereignty over its banks; thirdly, a canal through Limburg, joining Antwerp to the Meuse. Such a canal would be of great commercial value in peace, and a good defensive bulwark in war. The grand duchy of Luxemburg should not be allowed to remain neutral and disarmed, thus inviting German aggression, nor should its economic ties with the Empire be allowed to subsist. The German territories of Eupen and Malmédy, and the little strip known as "Neutral Moresnet," were added to the claims, apparently as an afterthought.[43]

---

[42] Miller, *Diary,* IV, doc. no. 298, p. 428, italics in the original.
[43] Miller, *Diary,* IV, doc. no. 298, pp. 432-441. "Neutral Moresnet" was the name given a triangular scrap of land which, through an error in describing

The second note was an attempt to prove the legality of the projected treaty revision. Belgium argued that as it had lost the advantages resulting from the treaties, it should be freed from the servitudes imposed by them. The procedure suggested in the note was a small international conference consisting of those signatories of the 1839 conventions which had not violated their pledges, that is, France, England, Belgium, and the Dutch Netherlands.[44]

The third note gave the historical arguments for the desired changes. The background of the territorial claims was reviewed as far back as the Conference of London of 1830. The history of the control of the Scheldt was traced back to the Treaty of Münster, 1648, which had closed the river to international commerce.[45]

The American legal experts, David Miller and J. B. Scott, who examined the memoranda, supported their conclusions. They even went beyond them by stating that in their opinion Holland had violated the 1839 treaty by allowing the German army to retreat through Limburg on November 12, 1919, thus saving it from surrender.[46] Charles Haskins, the well-known historian, and member of the American commission, likewise studied the notes with an approving eye. He found that "Holland's policy [regarding navigation of the Scheldt] has been essentially negative and selfish, injuring Antwerp for the benefit of Rotterdam, and her exclusive rights should be abolished." But while advocating the cession of Dutch Zeeland, he was opposed to Belgian acquisition of Dutch Limburg.[47]

The British foreign office also favored the proposed changes, though with some reservations. Downing Street preferred direct

boundary limits, was not assigned to any nation in the distribution of territory made at the Congress of Vienna. For further information see Charles Hoch, *The Territory of Moresnet* (Cambridge, 1882), translated by W. W. Tucker from *Un Territoire oublié au centre de l'Europe* (Berne, 1881).

[44] Miller, *Diary*, IV, 441-450, doc. no. 299.
[45] *Ibid.*, IV, 451-467, doc. no. 300.
[46] *Ibid.*, IV, 482-495, doc. no. 304.
[47] *Ibid.*, V, 3-8, doc. no. 306.

Belgo-Dutch negotiations to action by the Powers at the peace conference. The British were aware, moreover, of the incompatibility of the cession of either Dutch Flanders or Zeeland with the principles of self-determination.[48]

As to the French, two years earlier they had recognized that Belgium had the right to annex Luxemburg, provided the population consented.[49] In addition, the French experts who studied the situation in a pre-Armistice survey, admitted the justice of the claim to the lower Scheldt and to improved transit facilities from Antwerp to the Rhine.[50]

The people and government of Holland, however, were strongly opposed to any aggrandizement of Belgium at their expense. They had housed and fed thousands of Belgian refugees during the war, at a time when the Allied blockade made it difficult to procure enough food to mainatin the Dutch population.[51] Moreover, the lands now claimed had been part of the Netherlands for nearly three hundred years, and were inhabited by Dutchmen who had no desire to change their allegiance. Queen Wilhelmina's government had, it believed, fulfilled its treaty obligations, which nowhere included a clause requiring that the river be improved to the eventual detriment of Rotterdam.[52] These considerations caused the Dutch negotiators to maintain an intransigent attitude throughout the discussions; no Belgian diplomat ever succeeded in drawing from them any statement which might remotely have resembled recognition of his country's claims.

---

[48] *Ibid.,* V, 30-34, doc. no 316.

[49] Gabriel Terrail [Mermeix], *Le Combat des Trois, notes et documents sur la conférence de la paix* (Paris, 1922), p. 192.

[50] France, Ministère des affaires étrangères, Comité d'Etudes, *Travaux* (Paris 1918), II, 79.

[51] Details are given in A. J. Barnouw, *Holland under Queen Wilhelmina* (New York, 1923), pp. 178-188.

[52] Batavus, *Belgian ports and Dutch waterways* (London, 1919), and A. A. H. Struycken, *Holland, Belgium and the Powers* (The Hague, 1919) contain succinct statements of the Dutch position, which it is difficult to find in English.

As the doctrine of self-determination of peoples was one of the cardinal points of Wilson's policy, it would be to Belgium's advantage to show that the populations of the coveted regions desired a change of sovereignty. Nevertheless Hymans was forced to admit that the sentiment in Dutch Flanders was strongly opposed. On the other hand he did insist that many Luxemburgers wanted union with his country, as did also the people of Limburg.[53] The American minister at The Hague supported this last assertion by independent testimony to the existence on the part of "not a few Limburgers" of a desire to be incorporated into King Albert's realm.[54] Colonel House and Wilson could have checked this statement had they listened to the deputation from the province which vainly haunted their antechambers to present their petition to become Belgians.[55]

In their efforts to gain the political demands, Hymans and his colleagues relied on the support of the members of the American delegation, especially of Colonel House. He was willing to cooperate with them, but felt with the British that the matter ought to be discussed outside the peace conference.[56] This was not what Hymans wanted, and at length, on February 11, he was invited to present his case to the Supreme Council. At this meeting he stated Belgium's desire for abrogation of the treaties of 1839, control of the mouth of the Scheldt, and annexation of Limburg, and also brought up the transfer of two German territories, the administrative district of Malmédy, and "Neutral Moresnet," to Belgium.[57] The following day the Supreme Council, at Balfour's suggestion, set up a committee of experts, known as the Commission on Belgian Affairs, or the Commission of XIV, to consider and advise on the

[53] Miller, *Diary*, I, 103, entry of February 1, 1919.

[54] *Ibid.*, V, 10-11, doc. no. 311, January 21, 1919.

[55] Chambre, *Annales*, June 10, 1920, II, 1525.

[56] Miller, *Diary*, I, 104, entry of February 2, 1919; and 111-112, entry of February 6, 1919.

[57] Council of Ten, "Secretary's notes of a conversation," *B. C.* 28, February 11, 1919. [Hereafter cited as *BC*.]

matter of Malmédy, Moresnet, and the possible rectification of the Dutch-German frontier. The questions of the Scheldt, the Ghent-Terneuzen Canal, and the communications between Antwerp and the Rhine and Meuse Rivers were referred to the Commission on Ports, Waterways and Railways.[58]

When the Commission on Belgian Affairs met, there was some doubt in the minds of its members as to its exact duties. The matter was referred back to the Supreme Council, which decided that since the peace conference could not ask neutral Holland to make any cessions of territory, the work of the commission was limited to the practical study of determining what German land could be given Holland in exchange for whatever the latter might be induced to relinquish. It was also decided that the commission should examine the question of Belgium's neutral status as established by the treaties of 1839, and make recommendations to the Supreme Council in that regard.[59]

The commission completed this latter task first. On March 7 it issued a report, approved two days later by the Supreme Council, stating that the treaties of 1839 ought to be revised; that all the signatories, including Holland, should participate in the revision; that the purpose of the revision was to free Belgium from limitations on its sovereignty, and to remove the dangers to the country resulting from the neutrality treaties. The report further adopted the argument, advanced by Hymans, that by preventing the re-

[58] *BC* 30, February 12, 1919. This commission never actually considered these questions, as they were so closely related to the problem of the 1839 treaties, which was not solved; Miller, *Diary*, XII, 18, and 337. Moreover, the Belgian delegates were opposed to discussion of these matters in the Commission of Ports, Waterways and Railways; Miller, *Diary*, I, 112, entry of February 6, 1919. This opposition was probably due to a fear lest the Scheldt might henceforth be considered international if discussed in an international commission, and Belgium still had hopes of acquiring complete sovereignty over both banks. *Cf.* Wilson's complaint that Belgium sought not absolute freedom of the Scheldt for all, but unrestricted control, in Baker, *Woodrow Wilson*, II, 310.

[59] Miller, *Diary*, X, 4-13, February 25, 1919; *BC* 40, February 26, 1919.

lief of Antwerp, by rendering impossible the defense of the Meuse, and by enabling Germany to use the Grand Duchy of Luxemburg as a base of operations, the treaties had seriously hampered the defense of the country.[60]

A second report, adopted and transmitted to the Central Territorial Commission on March 16, dealt with territorial changes directly affecting Belgium. The commission unanimously decided to unite to that kingdom Moresnet and the circles of Malmédy and Eupen, although no claim had been made for the last named. The circles were only to be ceded if a majority of the population did not sign written protests in registers opened in Eupen and Malmédy for that purpose.

The second half of the report related to territorial compensations which might eventually have to be made to Holland in return for the cession to Belgium of Dutch Flanders and Limburg. After examining the various solutions suggested by Hymans on February 11, the commission adopted the view that Holland's compensation should be taken not in East Frisia, as was first thought, but in Prussian Guelderland and Cleves. A draft article was framed, providing for a commission to determine the exact modifications of the Dutch-German frontier, which Germany was to bind itself in advance to accept. By the terms of another proposed article, Germany was to renounce all title to the circles of Kleve, Mors, Geldern, Kempen, Rees, and Borkum in favor of the Allied and Associated Powers, though the inhabitants of these districts were to be allowed to declare their wishes as to their future allegiance.[61]

The Central Territorial Commission ignored these drafts, and in their place substituted a new, less definite clause, by which Germany was bound only to adhere to any convention that might be drawn up in future to replace the treaties of neutrality.[62] Although Hymans

[60] Miller Diary, X, 176-184, March 8, 1919.
[61] Ibid., X, 192-210. In the annotation by P. W. Slosson, ibid., XIX, 50, a different version is given.

and Tardieu both appeared before the Council of Four on April 16 to plead for the retention of the articles drawn up by the Commission of XIV, their arguments were vain.[63] The Council approved, instead, the work of the Central Territorial Commission; and the articles it had framed were incorporated in the treaty, despite strong German protests against any cessions to Holland.[64]

The Commission on Belgian Affairs had recommended that the Netherlands participate in the revision of the treaties of 1839, since it had been party to them. Consequently Pichon, French minister of foreign affairs, transmitted an invitation from the Allies to Stuers, the Dutch minister at Paris. Not until April 4 was an answer received, to the effect that Holland would take part, but only on the understanding that the negotiations would be conducted not by the peace conference, but by the powers directly concerned.[65] As the Belgians were eager to have the matter taken up as soon as possible, the Council of Ten agreed to set an early date for the special conference, which would be composed of the five ministers of foreign affairs of the great powers, and representatives of Belgium and of the Netherlands. Later The Hague was informed that this group would meet on May 19, 1919, in Paris.[66]

At this meeting, Jonkheer van Karnebeek, the Dutch foreign minister, strongly opposed the Belgian claims. He insisted that while his government was willing to negotiate a revision of the

---

[62] Ibid., XVI, 54, April 17, 1919; Chambre, *Annales*, II, 1438, August 8, 1919. Germany was also forced to consent to the establishment of international control of the Rhine River; the Dutch government, possibly fearing for Dutch sovereignty, and with the Belgian claims in mind, protested strongly; Miller, *Diary*, XII, 6, 18-21, protest and note of March 26, 1919; also XII, 251-253, note of June 23, 1919.

[63] Tardieu, *Truth About the Treaty*, pp. 222-223.

[64] Luckau, *German Delegation*, pp. 323-324.

[65] Belgium Ministère des Affaires Etrangères, *Documents diplomatiques relatifs à la revision des traités de 1839* (Brussels, 1929), p. 9, docs. no. 3 and 4 [Hereafter cited as *D. D. Rev.*]

[66] Council of Five (Foreign Ministers), "Secretary's Notes of a Conversation," F. M.-18, May 20, 1919. [Hereafter cited as *F. M.*]

treaties so as to free Belgium from neutrality, the *status quo* must otherwise be maintained. "The Netherlands government could under no possible circumstances contemplate any territorial concessions." He believed, moreover, that direct Belgo-Dutch negotiations would be more satisfactory than a conference.[67] The next day Hymans rejected this last suggestion, but said he would agree to conversations between experts from the two countries. He stated, furthermore, that while his government did not desire aggrandizement for its own sake, nevertheless, in order to insure the future of an independent Belgium, certain arrangements would have to be made which might necessitate territorial readjustments. The principal changes desired were four: full sovereignty over the whole course of the Scheldt and its lower dependencies: the right to base the left pivot of the Belgian defense system on the river; control of the locks regulating the flow of water from Flanders; and the creation of an Antwerp-Moerdijk canal, together with protection of the locks regulating the flow of water from Flanders; and the construction of a Rhine-Scheldt-Meuse canal.[68] The demand for complete annexation of Limburg had been dropped; only protection of Belgian interests there remained.

Van Karnebeek asked for time to study these points and to prepare an answer. The Council having acceded to this request, it was June 3 before the next discussion took place. On that occasion the Dutch foreign minister gave a categorical refusal to any proposition to talk over proposals "tending either upon grounds of defense, or for economic reasons, to withdraw certain territories from Dutch sovereignty in order to transfer them to Belgian sovereignty." He then asked that the other matters be the subject of direct Belgo-Dutch negotiations. With regard to the communications between Antwerp and Moerdijk, he remarked that although they were in good condition, his government was not averse to arranging for further improvements. He also suggested that the existing system of joint regulation of certain phases of Scheldt navigation be extended to cover the technical questions raised by modern inventions and improvements in shipping. He closed by a plea for friendly direct negotiations between the two countries directly interested, at the same time expressing his willingness to submit the solution thus reached to the League of Nations.

In reply, Hymans merely repeated that his country desired to be freed from the whole of the system established by the treaties of 1839, not merely from obligatory neutrality. He concluded by reminding the conference that the Supreme Council had already decided that the revision he so strongly advocated should be carried through. To his mind the best method was a commission of all the powers.

In view of the conflicting attitude of the two governments, the conference then adjourned to allow the great powers to discuss the conflicting proposals.[69]

This they did the following day. Tardieu, one of foreign minister Pichon's advisers, pointed out that they were faced with two questions, one of matter and one of method. They were unable to act on the former, as Holland could not be forced to cede territory. On the question of method, he favored that advocated by Hymans.

Balfour, the British foreign secretary, agreed with Tardieu. He desired, however, that while Holland and Belgium carried on their negotiations directly, the great powers should remain in the background, only intervening in case the smaller nations could not agree, and at all events participating in the final settlement. He proposed the following resolution:

Having recognized the necessity of revising the treaties of 1839, the Powers intrust to a commission comprising a representative of the United States of America, Great Britain, France, Italy,

Japan, Belgium, and Holland, the task of studying the measures which must result from this revision and of submitting to them proposals implying neither transfer of territorial sovereignty nor creation of international servitudes. The Commission will ask Belgium and Holland to present agreed suggestions regarding navigable streams in the spirit of the general principles adopted by the Peace Conference.

Secretary of State Lansing opposed this resolution, as he considered that the matter was purely economic, and interested only Belgium and Holland. He favored direct negotiations between these two states. He believed that if there were points on which unanimity could not be reached, they could be referred to the arbitral decision of an umpire. Finally, however, after much discussion, Lansing was induced to accept the resolution, since it so clearly excluded all cessions of territory.[70]

When notified of the Council's decision, Hymans replied that his government, while adhering to the resolution, understood that: the procedure indicated must not have for effect the prevention of the examination and adoption of all measures indispensable to the suppression of the risks and disadvantages to which, according to the conclusions formulated by the Powers on May 6 last, Belgium and the general peace may be exposed by the treaties of 1839. Neither must it interfere with guaranteeing to Belgium her free economic development as well as her entire security.[71]

On their side the Dutch interpreted the decision as meaning that no measures would be taken unless the delegates from both governments were in full agreement regarding them.[72] The implications in this idea went further than the Council had intended, and Pichon felt obliged to explain that the commission was not supposed to limit itself to registering the solutions reached in the direct negotiations, but would, if necessary, take part in the dis-

---

[70] *FM*-22, June 4, 1919. It was Lansing's attitude at this meeting which caused a revulsion of Belgian feeling against the United States. *Cf.* Whitlock's *Journal,* II, 583, entry of Dec. 30, 1919.

[71] Hymans to Pichon, June 14, 1919, Miller, *Diary,* XVIII, 507.

[72] Van Karnebeek to Pichon, June 19, 1919, *D. D. Rev.,* p. 10, doc. no. 8.

cussions in order to adjust any differences which might threaten to disrupt good relations.[73]

The negotiations between Belgium and the Netherlands began on July 29, 1919, and lasted until March 23, 1920. At first the Belgian delegates, MM. Segers and Orts, tried to win two conces sions from the Dutch—one, a military convention providing for common defense of Limburg, and the other, a grant of complete freedom of navigation on the Scheldt both in peace and in war. The Dutch government refused to grant the former, in spite of the fact that the Commission of XIV agreed with the Belgians that organized defense of the Limburg gap would have to be planned by the two nations in concert. The request for complete freedom of the Scheldt did not receive the approval either of the great powers or of the Dutch government.

A second phase of the negotiations opened when, disappointed in their desire to secure good strategic boundaries, Segers and Orts tried to obtain a definite guarantee of armed support in case of another German attack. The Dutch were willing to subscribe to a guarantee fixed by the League Council. This was acceptable, provided that France and Great Britain would give a provisional guarantee to cover the period until the Council was in a position to act. Great Britain, however, would not accede to this unless Belgium would return to the regime of obligatory neutrality. As this was quite opposed to the prevailing sentiment in Belgium, the whole plan of guarantee fell through.[74]

In the third and final phase of the negotiations, a treaty plan that seemed satisfactory to all concerned was elaborated. It can be briefly summarized. Two political clauses abrogated the articles of the 1839 treaty which required Belgium to observe perpetual neutrality, and the articles stipulating that Antwerp could not be used

[73] Pichon to van Karnebeek, June 26, 1919, *ibid.,* pp. 10-11, doc. no. 9.
[74] Segers in the Belgian Chamber, Chambre, *Annales,* June 10, 1920, II, 1525-1530.

for military purposes. A series of fluvial clauses provided for unlimited navigation of the Scheldt in time of peace, a permanent
commission to oversee the maintenance and improvement of the
Scheldt channel, and the construction of the long desired canals
connecting Antwerp with Moerdijk and with Ruhrort.[75] This treaty
was submitted to the Commission of XIV on March 23, 1920, with
every prospect of its being approved.

While it was under consideration, the Dutch delegates unex-
pectedly brought up a claim to sovereignty over the Wielingen
Pass, the southermost of the three channels leading from the Scheldt
estuary into the North Sea. If this claim could be successfully maintained, the Belgian port of Zeebrugge would be completely cut off
from the sea except through Dutch waters, so that in time of war
sea-borne reinforcements could not reach Belgium. During the
World War the Dutch foreign office had made no protest when
German submarines made use of the pass, and in a note to the
British government expressly stated that it claimed no more than
the right of passage in the Wielingen.[76] Under these circumstances
the Belgian cabinet, with the support of parliament, refused to
allow negotiations on the treaty to continue until the Wielingen

[75] Segers in the Belgian Chamber, Chambre, *Annales,* June 11, 1920, II, 1577-
1583.

[76] The Belgian argument that the Dutch government, far from claiming
sovereignty over the pass during the war, had refused the responsibility, is borne
out by the facts given by Hymans to the Chamber on June 11, 1920: On August 7, 1914, Davignon, then Belgian foreign minister, telegraphed Fallion, his
minister at The Hague, directing him to ascertain where the Dutch minefields
began. In reply, Fallion said he had seen both the minister of foreign affairs
and the minister of marine, and had been assured that the Dutch were only
laying mines in the waters to the right of a line drawn from the farthest corner
of Belgian Zeeland to the North Sea. Moreover, in May, 1916, the government
of the Netherlands sent maps showing the limits of Dutch territorial waters
to the British government; these maps showed the Wielingen as within the
Belgian waters. Finally, in June, 1917, the Dutch government sent a note to the
Belgian legation at The Hague stating that the capture of a Belgian fishing
smack by the Germans in the Wielingen Pass could not be considered as a violation of Dutch neutrality, the ships having been taken "sans aucun doute en eaux
territoriales belges." Chambre, *Annales,* June 11, 1920, II, 1583.

issue was settled.[77] As both parties remained adamant, the commission was dissolved. No further action was taken at Paris on the abrogation of the 1839 treaties, and when the peace conference ended, the status of Belgium in international law was still unsettled.

On still other points the pride and ambition of Belgium were frustrated. Since the history of the country's relations with the League of Nations will be treated in a later chapter, it is enough to mention here that Belgium was refused a permanent seat on the Council, and that the request that Brussels be made the home of the League was rejected. Belgian colonial hopes were also temporarily thwarted. During the war troops from the Belgian Congo played an important part in the conquest of German East Africa. It was naturally hoped that they had won for the mother country at least part of this territory, but the coveted mandate went instead to Great Britain. Hymans protested, for a time with no success. At length, on June 23, 1920, Orts and Lord Milner reached an agreement whereby Great Britain surrendered to Belgium the mandates of Ruanda and Urundi, among the most fertile, healthy, and populous in the former German colony.[78]

Belgium, then, received from the Peace Conference comparatively few of the advantages which its people had been led to believe would naturally accrue to the country whose resistance to invasion had been such a powerful stimulus to the morale of the Allies. Instead of full reparations, a priority of only two and one-half billion gold marks, to begin only in 1921, and eventually to be repaid with interest; an indefinite promise regarding freedom from the war debt to the Allies (a promise which was not kept by the United States, the largest creditor); no assistance in the important negotiations with Holland; not even a colonial mandate until Great Britain ceded part of German East Africa—

[77] Hymans in the Chamber, Chambre, *Annales,* May 26, 1920, II, 1219-1221.
[78] Lloyd George, *Truth about the peace treaties,* I, 552; and Moore, "Public Opinion in Belgium," p. 181. Questions concerning the colony alone are outside the scope of the present work.

such were the disappointments the peace treaty held for Belgium.

Wounded in their pride, disappointed in their hopes for material gains, the Belgian people reacted strongly against the treaty. During the first months of 1919 there was comparatively little interest shown in the peace conference; it seemed to be taken for granted that Belgium would receive full reparations, revision of the treaties of 1839, and perhaps territorial acquistions. The first doubt arose when it became known that Belgium was considered a small power, and was allotted only two delegates. At once there was a protest, the Socialist daily, *Le Peuple,* even going so far as to threaten that "The Council of Ministers will send a strong protest and if justice is not done, the question of Belgium's abstention from the Conference of Paris will be raised."[79] The wound was reopened when the personnel of the chief commissions was announced, with the smaller nations receiving very limited representation. And in early May, when the terms of the treaty were published, Belgian indignation became angrily vocal.

The general discontent was caused less by the failure to receive Dutch Zeeland and Limburg, than by the reparations settlement.[80] The Socialists, the Walloons, and the Flemings all had consistently opposed annexations at the expense of the Netherlands, though in this they were motivated by different considerations; while the extreme nationalists, who favored annexations, were more effective at organizing demonstrations than at influencing their fellow citizens.[81] Adequate reparations, on the other hand, was considered vital by all groups. On May 4, the very day that the Crown Council

---

[79] *Le Peuple,* January 17, 1919. The Belgian protest was successful. At a meeting of the Council of Ten on January 17, the Belgian delegation was increased to three, despite the disapproval of Lloyd George. On this occasion Secretary of State Lansing effectively presented the Belgian case. U. S. *For. Rel., Paris Peace Conference,* III, 601-604.

[80] Binkley, "Reactions of Public Opinion," p. 123.

[81] *BPB,* no. 20, February 13, 1919, p. 7. In the elections of November, 1919, the *Comité de Politique National,* the extreme nationalists, polled only 1.05 per cent of the total vote cast; Binkley, "Reactions of Public Opinion," p. 120.

voted to accept the treaty, thousands of Belgians paraded through the large cities, expressing their desire for complete reparations. The newspaper criticisms of the treaty stressed the same point, though a few minor papers, such as the *Flandre Libérale*, were satisfied.[82]

In parliament considerable dissatisfaction was expressed. On May 14 the Socialist deputy Mechelynck interpellated the government on the financial and economic consequences of the peace treaty. He described the feelings of his countrymen when they learned that the King would preside over a council of state to deliberate on the treaty, and to decide whether or not his representatives would sign it. There was even a rumor abroad that the government might choose to withdraw its delegates from Paris if the nation were not given better terms. After the decision of the council had been taken, the foreign affairs commissions of both Senate and Chamber had been convoked. The discussions in these commissions had been secret, but it had become known that the treaty was not given full approval, and that the premier had not been in a position to give all the information desired. This secrecy alarmed the country, and caused the spread of disquieting rumors. Consequently Mechelynck was asking for precise information.[83]

In reply premier Delacroix gave a fairly complete summary of the financial clauses of the treaty in so far as they concerned Belgium. These clauses, as agreed upon by the Allies on May 2, were release from the war debt, reparation for damages with priority of payment up to two and one-half billion francs, payment in kind to replace confiscated livestock and coal, and the right to

<hr />

[82] *BPB*, no. 21, July 21, 1919, pp. 2-3.

[83] Chambre, *Annales,* May 14, 1919, I, 895-896. Among the rumors that had circulated was one that the Allies theatened to cut off Belgium's food supply if the signature was not forthcoming; Whitlock's *Journal,* II, 559, entry of May 3, 1919. The Belgians were almost pathetic in their expressions of injured feelings. One Deputy said: "Once more I express regret that at the Peace Conference more consideration and respect were not shown to Belgium." Sénat, *Annales,* March 12, 1919, pp. 129-134.

liquidate the property of enemy aliens. In spite of the fact that Germany had not been forced to redeem the marks introduced into Belgium during the war, the premier continued,

After having carefully weighed all this, I have reached the conclusion that our public credit has emerged from this war in a privileged position, but that the state of our Treasury is frightful, and disturbing. . . . Gentlemen, what ought we to have done? There could be no question of our slipping out and refusing to sign the treaty. That would have been unjust. Could we leave out of consideration the enormous difficulties of the other States, to which I have alluded? It would have been unworthy of us; could we, in the face of the Germans, separate ourselves from our Allies? It would have been a fault against good taste; it would have been a fault belying our political and economic interests.

After developing this last point, he ended with a plea for greater economy, higher taxes, and hard work:

From now on we will receive no more help. What I have announced for all Belgium I now announce for the workers. They must revive every means of raising Belgium from the category of those who receive assistance.[84]

The other speakers on the matter were of one mind that the treaty must be signed, and that a thorough discussion of the terms would be premature at that point. The Catholic deputy Segers, while friendly toward the Allies, presented a long list of political, commercial, and financial demands which he expected the completed treaty to satisfy—demands ranging from a special customs arrangement with France and Great Britain, to increase in the territory of the Belgian Congo.[85] The Liberal, Van Hoegarden, complained of the economic sections of the treaty. He believed that they ought to be studied carefully, because "the life or the

[84] Chambre, *Annales,* May 14, 1919, I, 896-897.
[85] Chambre, *Annales,* May 14, 1919, I, 899.

death of Belgium depends on the application of the treaty. . . . [Reparations] are a question of Belgium's very existence."[86]

Vermeersch, speaking for the Socialists, echoed these sentiments, dwelling particularly on his country's need for special treatment in the economic sphere. After recalling the promises of Sainte-Adresse, he described the high tariff walls raised against Belgian goods by the Entente governments. "This is not the way that the Allies will contribute to the restoration of Belgium."[87] The debate closed with a final protest from Charles Woeste, veteran leader of the conservative wing of the Catholic party, who insisted that Hymans' formula describing the treaty as giving Belgium "des conditions honorables et satisfaisantes" was inacceptable. "Honorable" the terms were, but not "satisfactory," for they did not provide sufficient safeguards in case of a future German aggression.[88]

This speech closed the discussion, which was not reopened until the treaty was presented to parliament for ratification the following August. Meanwhile the decision of the Council of Five to exclude from examination by the Commission of XIV any measures that would imply territorial transfers or the imposition of international servitudes aroused much resentment in the country.[89] The fact that Belgo-Dutch negotiations were in progress, however, precluded an extended debate on the subject.

The debate on ratification was brief and somewhat formal. By this time it was obvious that Belgium was not in a position to reject the treaty, defective as it seemed in many respects. The discussion opened with a speech by Woeste, who began his remarks by saying:

[86] *Ibid.*, May 14, 1919, I, 899-902.

[87] *Ibid.*, May 14, 1919, I, 902-904.

[88] *Ibid.*, May 14, 1919, I, 904.

[89] *BPB*, no. 21, July 17, 1919, pp. 4-5; Chambre, *Annales,* August 8, 1919, II, 1458. A detailed account of Belgian reactions to the treaty is given in Moore, "Public Opinion in Belgium," pp. 182-199, which contains an analysis of practically the entire Belgian press for this period.

In reading the treaty, I cannot but maintain the opinion I expressed at the Crown Council when the minister of foreign affairs told us the principal clauses of the treaty relating to Belgium. I then said at once that we must vote for the treaty; it contains no clause contrary to Belgium's honor, but in spite of that it is not completely satisfactory. . . . The treaty as it has been drawn up has many undesirable aspects, and contains the germ of formidable conflicts.

Among these he listed the uncertain and badly drawn boundaries, and the minorities problem. He feared that in the future, when the influence of the Great Powers would have waned, these questions would cause trouble. Then, speaking from a purely Belgian point of view, he discussed the articles he found faulty: the reparation settlement, the unsolved Belgo-Dutch question, and the failure to provide a substitute for the guarantees of 1839. He criticized the repudiation of neutrality by the government, making observations that fifteen years later were finally endorsed by his fellow citizens:

Belgium remains a small country, surrounded by great neighbors; she is not protected from future vicissitudes, and, indeed, the case could arise when we might, under the guarantees of which I have just spoken, call for assistance from France, England, and the other Great Powers which were associated with them and which, if it were necessary, would again join them, or so we hope.[90]

With these reservations he voted for ratification.

Bertrand, the official spokesman of the Socialists, described his comrades' point of view. They favored ratification, first of all because it would end the war, secondly because they would not vote against a treaty which at least partially provided for the restoration of their devastated country, and finally because the treaty created permanent organizations which promised to develop into a true league of peoples. Of course the Socialists were disappointed at the inadequacy the reparations promised to Belgium, and in the

[90] Chambre, *Annales,* August 8, 1919, II, 1456-1457.

decision to locate the seat of the League at Geneva instead of at Brussels. His statement of the party's position on the larger issues raised by the treaty is interesting:

From the international point of view the treaty obliges us to formulate express reserves, notably with regard to the guarantees surrounding the popular consultations provided for, the organization of the League of Nations, disarmament, the colonial question, the mode of making reparations payments.

But whatever the importance given these reserves, they cannot make us forget that the peace treaty guarantees the complete liberation of the country, that it restores to France the provinces wrested from her by force, that it brings about the resurrection of Poland, and that, through the League of Nations and the permanent conference for the regulations of labor, it sets up organizations which through the efforts of democracy and the working classes of all lands will be vivified, improved, and developed.[91]

His Socialist colleague, Jules Destrée, echoed these thoughts in a speech that summed up the opinion of many of his fellow countrymen:

With regard to Belgium the treaty is not that work of justice and reparation that we rightfully expected, and we cannot say we are satisfied with it. Nevertheless, we accept it for lack of a better, with the hope that our great allies will realize that they still have duties towards us, and that Germany herself, returning to a saner understanding of things, will admit that Belgium has not even asked from her all she had a right to obtain.[92]

It is remarkable that whatever their complaints, not a single Belgian Socialist protested that the treaty was too hard on Germany. After these brief declarations from leaders of the Catholic and Socialist parties, the Chamber unanimously voted for ratification.[93]

The speeches in the Senate ten days later were almost identical. This time, however, the government presented its side of the case,

[91] Chambre, *Annales,* August 8, 1919, II, 1461-1462.
[92] *Ibid.,* August 8, 1919, II, 1464.
[93] *Ibid.*

deputing Van den Heuvel, who had been a delegate to the conference, and a member of the reparations commission, to explain the financial settlement. He stressed especially the impoverishment of Germany and the consequent impossibility of exacting full reparations. The claims dropped by Belgium were those for war expenditures, for damages asked by private citizens for their failure to make their usual profits from business, and for reimbursement for the marks introduced into the counry by the invaders.

This explanation did not satisfy the majority of the Senators, who maintained their objections to the reparation settlement, as well as to the territorial clauses of the treaty. Nevertheless they, too, voted the ratification.[94]

Outside of parliament there was also very real dissatisfaction with the treaty, though it was not widely advertised abroad. But with the realistic spirit characteristic of their nation the people turned their energies away from fruitless criticism to the hard work needed for reconstruction. At the same time the government devoted itself to the task of cooperating with the Great Powers in the business of putting the treaty into operation.

[94] Sénat, *Annales,* August 19, 1919, pp. 558-561; 566-670.

CHAPTER FOUR

Unfinished Business

AFTER the adoption of the treaty of Versailles, there remained
no small amount of unfinished business, including two items which
concerned Belgium. The first, stemming directly from the treaty,
was the delimitation of the new Belgo-German boundary, with all
the associated problems; the second was the revision of the treaties
of 1839, which had been a major Belgian aim at the conference.
The present chapter will deal with these two topics, both of which
though otherwise unrelated, were results of the war.

It was manifestly impossible for the statesmen who had negotiated the peace treaty to supervise its execution, since each had
already a heavy responsibility in the government of his own country. It was likewise obvious that circumstances demanded that
there be some authority vested with power both to oversee the
application of the treaty and to settle disputed questions. Accordingly, recourse was had to a device that had succeeded before in
carrying out the decisions of international conferences, namely,
a council or conference of Ambassadors. In this case it was to consist of the Ambassadors of the Great Powers accredited to the
French government, and was to be presided over by the French
minister of foreign affairs or his delegate.

When the Belgian government learned of the existence of this
council, it at once requested to be admitted to membership, on the

ground that Belgium, as one of the occupying powers, and as a neighbor of Germany, was vitally interested in the enforcement of the treaty.[1] The Quai d'Orsay supported this claim, provided that this representation was accorded only when matters in which Belgium was directly concerned were to be treated.[2] The cabinet at Brussels understood this to mean that its representative would be invited to participate in the conference whenever the discussion turned on any questions arising from the treaty.[3] This interpretation was not admitted by the council, which decided that if Belgium wanted what amounted to full membership, it must apply to the governments of the Great Powers.[4] The Powers, when consulted, repeated the answer of the conference, that a Belgian delegate was to be invited only when the interests of his country were directly involved.[5]

The first such occasion was brought about by the transfer of the cantons of Eupen, Malmédy, and Moresnet from German to Belgian sovereignty. As early as August 4, 1919, Graf von Lersner, head of the German delegation at Paris, had protested against the action of the Belgian authorities in the cantons. He particularly objected to the measures taken by the officials of the state railway administration to speed the transfer of control over the Eupen-Malmédy railway.[6]

Unsuccessful in his attempt to restrain the Belgians in this instance, von Lersner renewed his protests when the registers were opened for the "popular consultation" provided for by the treaty. In a series of notes addressed to Clemenceau, von Lersner de-

---

[1] Jacquemyns to Clemenceau, Nov. 23, 1919, American Commission to Negotiate Peace, "S-H Bulletin," 1450, Dec. 5, 1919. [Hereafter cited as SH.]

[2] Conference of Ambassadors, "Notes of a Meeting," CA-3, Feb. 2, 1920, pp. 7-9. [Hereafter cited as CA.]

[3] Gaiffier to Millerand, Feb. 25, 1920, CA-16, March 4, 1920, Appendix F.

[4] CA-16, March 4, 1920, pp. 19-20.

[5] CA-17, March 6, 1920, p. 20, and Millerand to Gaiffier, Appendix I.

[6] Von Lersner to Clemenceau, Aug. 1, 1919, SH-620, Aug. 4, 1919; same to same, Aug. 5, 1919, SH-674, Aug. 11, 1919.

scribed the manner in which the German government believed that the consultation ought to be carried out. According to Berlin, there were several measures which should be taken in order to secure a fair vote. First, all persons living in Eupen and Malmédy on November 11, 1918, not merely those resident there on August 4, 1914, should be eligible to vote. Secondly, registers should be opened in every commune, not only in the two towns of Eupen and Malmédy. Thirdly, the inhabitants should be asked definitely to choose between Germany and Belgium, not merely to say whether they thought all or part of the territory should be German. And lastly, the plebiscite should be conducted under the auspices of the League, and should be secret—in other words, there should be a true plebiscite.[7]

In reply the Belgians appealed to article 34 of the treaty, which nowhere used the word "plebiscite," but simply stated that "in Eupen and Malmédy registers were to be opened in which the inhabitants might record a desire to have any part of the ceded territory remain under German sovereignty."[8] On November 10, 1919, this argument was adopted by the Supreme Council.[9] Again von Lersner remonstrated, and added to his former protests complaints against the exactions of the army of occupation. The Belgians again based their stand on the letter of the treaty.[10] The conference supported them, and did not reply to the German note.

A further attempt by the German government to prevent the cession of Eupen and Malmédy was made in the spring of 1920. A series of complaints was forwarded to the Ambassadors' con-

---

[7] Von Lersner to Clemenceau. Oct. 3, 1919, *SH*-1014, Oct. 7, 1919.

[8] Guillaume to Dutasta, Oct. 14, 1919, *SH*-1093, Oct. 18, 1919.

[9] Council of Heads of Delegations, "Notes of a Meeting of the Heads of Delegations," *HD*-88, Nov. 10, 1919, p. 22; Clemenceau to von Lersner, Nov. 10, 1919, *SH*-1264, Nov. 11, 1919.

[10] Rolin Jacquemyns to Dutasta, Jan 8, 1920, United States Embassy, Paris, comp., "ESH Bulletin," 452, May 13, 1920. [Hereafter cited as *ESH*.]

ference, repeating the protests against the method of consulting the people, and charging that Belgian officials were exercising undue pressure to induce the inhabitants of the territory not to sign the registers, even going so far as to expel those who insisted on signing.[11] A railway strike which broke out in Eupen in April did not improve matters. The Brussels government, claiming that the strike was incited by the German *Vereinigte Landmannschaften*, arrested the union leaders.[12] The German government insisted that the strike was a spontaneous outbreak resulting from the lower standard of living consequent upon the occupation, and from dissatisfaction with the actions of the Belgian authorities.[13]

In reply to the German charge of undue pressure, Baron Gaiffier, the Belgian ambassador at Paris, while admitting that one official had been overzealous, declared that only the leaders who had fomented the strikes had been expelled from the territory. Otherwise, he said, the measures complained of were simply precautions to prevent fraudulent voting, such as stamping the identity cards of voters so that they could not sign the register in the other canton. These explanations were satisfactory to the conference, and the discussion there was closed.[14] Although the German government continued to protest to the conference and to the Supreme Council, apparently these bodies did not consider an answer necessary, for there is none on record.[15]

[11] Göppert to conference, Mar. 21, 1920, *ESH*-451, May 12, 1920; same to same, May 2, 1920, *ESH*-449, May 13, 1920; Göppert to Clemenceau, May 9, 1920, *ESH*-448, May 12, 1920; same to same, May 15, 1920, *ESH*-447, May 21, 1920. That there was some truth in the German complaints is evident from Delacroix' statement to the Chamber; Chambre, *Annales*, May 11, 1920, II, 1067.

[12] *CA*-46, May 29, 1920.

[13] Göppert to Millerand, April 19, 1920, Great Britain, *Parliamentary Papers*, 1921, Cmd. 1325, p. 82, doc. no. 107.

[14] Millerand to Göppert, June 4, 1920, *ibid.*, p. 83, doc. no. 151.

[15] Göppert to Millerand, July 6, 1920, Great Britain, *Parliamentary Papers*, 1921, Cmd. 1325, pp. 161-167, doc. no. 184; same to same, July 14, 1920, *ibid.*, pp. 173-174, doc. no. 192.

In spite of this setback, the German foreign office did not despair of achieving its object. On April 21, 1920, even before the final decision of the conference of Ambassadors, Baron Sthamer, German chargé in London, had addressed a note to the Secretariat of the League of Nations, presenting the same complaints that the German government had made to the Ambassadors and asking for the intervention of the League. The matter was referred to the Council, and Matsui, the Japanese member, was named to study the matter. In his report, after summing up the various German arguments, he reached the conclusion that the League was not competent to deal with the question. The Council unanimously adopted this conclusion.[16]

By the terms of article 34 of the treaty of Versailles, the League was to decide upon the permanent status of the cantons of Eupen and Malmédy. In August, 1929, the Belgian government asked that a short Council session be held in Paris the following September for the purpose of giving a final decision.[17] Accordingly the Council met in Paris on September 16 to hear the report drawn up by da Cunha, the Portuguese member. His findings were that the "popular consultation" had been held in accordance with the terms of the treaty, and that the result might be accepted as a genuine indication that there was no strong objection on the part of the inhabitants to being permanently under Belgian sovereignty.[18] The Council adopted this report without debate, and passed a resolution confirming the transfer of the cantons to Belgium.[19]

The German government did not accept this decision, maintaining that the Council was not competent to decide, and that the matter should be referred to the Assembly.[20] In 1928 premier

[16] League of Nations, *Council Minutes,* V session, Rome, May 14, 1920, pp. 6-7; May 14, Annex 37, pp. 65-111.
[17] *Ibid.,* VIII session, San Sebastian, Aug. 4, 1920, p. 51
[18] *Ibid.,* IX session, Paris, Sept. 16, 1920, p. 7 ; annex 97, II, 51-57.
[19] *Ibid.,* IX session, Paris, Sept. 16, 1920, p. 35.
[20] *Ibid.,* X session, Brussels, Oct. 20, 1920, p. 5; XI session, Geneva, Nov. 29, 1920, p. 17.

Jaspar claimed that the German government itself carried the question directly to the Assembly in September, 1921. If so, no record of such an appeal was kept, the only mention of the case in the proceedings either of the Assembly or its committees, is in the "Report of the Activities of the Council" presented by that body to the Assembly, which was adopted without debate. The short section of the report dealing with the matter received no attention.[21] On December 6, 1920, after the German chancellor and his minister of foreign affairs had publicly criticized the legality of the transfer of Eupen and Malmédy, the representatives of France and Great Britain in Berlin had joined the Belgian minister there in protesting against this action.[22] With the failure of the appeal to the League, official German protests against the loss of the cantons came to an end for some years.

This does not mean, however, that the German people or their government were reconciled to losing these two prosperous districts. Henceforth different methods to regain them were employed. Stresemann, the great German minister of foreign affairs, used peaceful means. During the Locarno negotiations in 1925, he vainly tried to have the cantons excepted from the territory to be guaranteed by the pacts.[23] His intention in so doing was probably to facilitate the private discussions which for some time had been going on regarding the provinces.

In March and April, 1925, Hjalmar Schacht, head of the Reichsbank, held several conversations with the Governor of the National Bank of Belgium in an effort to regain the cantons by exchanging them for a favorable settlement of the marks claim. This offer was firmly rejected by King Albert and premier Theunis. The following

---

[21] Sénat, *CRA,* March 14, 1928, p. 249, and League of Nations, Assembly, *Official Journal, Records of the Second Assembly,* Plenary meetings, Sept. 8, 1921, pp. 83-84.

[22] Chambre, *Annales,* Dec. 8, 1920, I, 123.

[23] Eric Sutton, ed., *Gustav Stresemann, his diaries, letters, and papers* (New York, 1935-1940), II, 217. [Hereafter cited as *Stresemann.*]

December Schacht tried again, this time approaching Delacroix, former premier, and at the time, the Belgian delegate to the Reparations Commission. Premier Poullet and foreign minister Vandervelde, to whom the matter was referred, after consulting the King gave a categorical refusal.

The following spring and summer Belgium was in the throes of a severe financial crisis, and Emile Francqui, minister of finances, needed money to fund the floating debt. Schacht once more approached Delacroix. This time things seemed more promising for the Germans, but in late July King Albert got wind of the matter. He at once notified premier Jaspar of his formal opposition to the projected bargain. When the ministers were informed they took the same stand.[24] Believing that this setback was at least partly due to the attitude of the Quai d'Orsay, Stresemann discussed it with Labouleye, the French chargé in Berlin. From him he learned that Briand would regard any change in the Belgo-German boundary as a modification of the treaties of Versailles and Locarno, and additional payments by Germany as interfering with the Dawes Plan. Although Stresemann quoted Parker Gilbert, the Agent General for Reparations, in refutation of the latter statement, he was unable to change Briand's attitude.[25] This was probably due to French fears that any revision of Germany's western boundary, however slight, might eventually lead to a retrocession of some parts of Alsace and Lorraine. Stresemann realized this, and in a conversation with the British ambassador in Berlin tried to show that the apprehension was unfounded. He stated:

The constant reserves I make about the western frontier apply much more to Eupen-Malmédy than they do to Alsace-Lorraine. As regards the latter, if it was offered back to Germany tomorrow, I

[24] G. A. Detry, "La Belgique et les papiers de Stresemann," *Revue Belge des Livres, Documents, et Archives de la Guerre,* VIII (1932), 498-500. Stresemann stated that Delacroix opened the negotiations, and that they fell through because the Belgians demanded too much; *Stresemann,* II, 432-433.

[25] *Stresemann,* II, 426.

would not accept it. It would create difficulties for us, like Ireland for England. As regards Eupen-Malmédy, it is not impossible that we shall arrive at an arrangement with the Belgians under which, for financial considerations, they would hand us back the district. It is not one of any considerable importance.[26]

In September, 1926, when Briand and Stresemann held their famous meeting at Thoiry to try, by friendly conversation to improve relations between their respective countries, Briand accepted the German point of view on the matter. He said that he personally had no objections to the suggested retrocession, but that the Belgians were not of one mind on the subject.[27]

After this, the idea of regaining Eupen-Malmédy by a financial bargain was apparently dropped. Henceforth the methods used were less peaceful. Astute propaganda kept alive the pro-German feeling in the cantons. Some of the inhabitants were even given the impression that the Saar plebiscite would settle their future status, as well as that of the population of the valley. In March, 1934, Hymans officially denied this, in an unequivocal statement of the government's position:

These territories are incorporated into Belgium in virtue of the treaty of Versailles. Their frontier is the Belgian frontier, and the Belgian frontier is recognized, consecrated, and guaranteed by the Rhenish pact, which Germany freely proposed, negotiated, and signed.[28]

Meanwhile the authorities in Brussels had been obliged to justify to their fellow-citizens the treatment given the inhabitants of the new acquisitions. In 1919 the Socialist party strongly criticized the manner in which the population of the annexed cantons had been consulted. The Socialist deputy, Camiel Huysmans, although favor-

[26] Edgar Vincent D'Abernon, *An Ambassador of Peace; pages from the diary of Viscount d'Abernon (Berlin, 1920-1926)* (London, 1929-1930), III, 222, entry of Feb. 3, 1926.

[27] *Stresemann*, III, 32.

[28] Sénat, *CRA*, March 13, 1934, p. 252.

ing the acquisitions of the Walloon areas in Malmédy, asked for a
true referendum instead of "the parody to which we have committed ourselves."[29] His colleague Louis Piérard went even further, and began a public investigation of conditions in the provinces. Although he uncovered some abuses, the net result of the inquiry was to convert the investigator to the government's policy.[30]

The administration of Eupen and Malmédy after their incorporation into Belgium is really part of that country's internal history. Here it is sufficient to state that from 1919 to 1921 the cantons
were rather harshly treated as annexed territory. There was a change
for the better when, in September, 1921, General Baltia was appointed High Commissioner, with almost complete legislative and
executive powers.[31] This regime continued until May 1, 1929, when
the cantons were incorporated into the arrondissement of Verviers.
From that time on, the inhabitants enjoyed all the rights—and
duties—of Begian citizens, with a few minor exceptions, such as
remaining under the German social code for pensions, which was
a benefit rather than a drawback.[32] Even Marc Somerhausen, deputy from Verviers, who openly worked for the return of his native
province to Germany, admitted in parliament that "the regime of
the redeemed provinces is one of liberty, of equality, and of tol-
erance, and I think that among all the minorities formed after the
treaty of Versailles and protected by the League of Nations, there
are few which rejoice in a regime as liberal and as generous."[33]
Nevertheless, the inhabitants were not won over entirely, for they
did not forget the abuses of the first years, and they were dissatis-

---

[29] Chambre, *Annales*, Dec. 8, 1920, I, 134.

[30] Chambre, *CRA*, May 4, 1920, I, 955-961.

[31] Chambre, *Documents*, 1920-1921, p. 1397, doc. no. 456. A short account
of the whole subject is given by Robert H. George, "Eupen and Malmédy,"
Foreign Affairs, V (1927), 332-335.

[32] Louis de Lichtervelde, "Les cantons de l'est," *Revue Générale*, CXXXVIII
(1937), pp. 156-172.

[33] Chambre, *CRA*, March 15, 1927, p. 359.

fied with the solution given to such problems as that of local government.

In addition to the difficulty resulting from the popular consultation in Eupen and Malmédy, the Belgian government had to meet the German protests regarding the eastern boundary of the ceded territory. By the terms of article 35 of the treaty, a delimitation commission composed of seven representatives—one German, one Belgian, and five appointed by the Supreme Council—was to determine the new Belgo-German frontier, "taking into account the economic factors and the means of communication." The chief problem facing the commission was the disposal of the Kalterherberg-Raeren railway. After much discussion, the commission finally awarded Belgium the railway, together with a strip of German Montjoie, since otherwise both passenger and freight trains would be stopped three times in thirty-six kilometers to pass through the customs.[34] In vain did the German government protest to the Supreme Council.[35] Equally unavailing was the appeal to the League; the League Council decided that it was not competent to act on the matter, the Conference of Ambassadors having been made the official executor of the treaty.[36] This conference, to which Germany next turned, referred the matter to its technical Geographic Committee, which, on May 20, 1920, reported that economic factors fully warranted the decision taken by the delimitation commission.[37] The conference accepted this report, stipulating that Germany should receive adequate compensation for the additional strip of territory it was obliged to cede.[38] The Belgian government accepted the con-

[34] Gaiffier to Cambon, April 26, 1920, *CA*-35, May 1, 1920, p. 23, Appendix N.
[35] Göppert to Millerand, April 16, Great Britain, *Parliamentary Papers,* 1921, Cmd. 1325, pp. 77-78, doc. no. 102.
[36] League of Nations, *Council Minutes,* V session, Rome, May 15, 1920, Annex 37, I, 67.
[37] *ESH*-494, May 25, 1920, pp. 22, Appendix C.
[38] *CA*-47, June 5, 1920, pp. 16-22.

dition, and at once took over the railway.[39] Evidently the compensation was satisfactory to the German government, and the Belgians were faithful in carrying out their promises, for no further objections were raised on this score.

The second issue opened by the invasion of Belgium, and left undecided by the peace conference, was that of the revision of the treaties of 1839, which obstinately resisted settlement. A description of the treatment of this question at Paris in 1919 and 1920 has already been given. After the negotiations broke down in the spring of 1920 because of the Dutch claim to sovereignty over the Wielingen Pass, the Belgian government, with the approval of parliament, decided not to continue the discussions until the Netherlands' claims were withdrawn.[40]

The following autumn Van Vredenbergh, the Dutch Minister at Brussels, asked premier Delacroix to visit The Hague in order to talk over with foreign minister van Karnebeek the prospects of settling the difference. Delacroix replied that before taking such a step he must have two assurances, first, that the government of the Netherlands would put a stop to the official encouragement given Belgian traitors who had found asylum in Holland, and second, that the Wielingen problem would receive a satisfactory solution. He also hoped for a military agreement with Holland, to counterbalance the convention with France.[41] As the Dutch refused to give these assurances, the visit did not take place.[42]

Segars, who had been one of the Belgian plenipotentiaries in the negotiation with van Karnebeek at Paris, suggested in December, 1920, that the matter could be reopened if both parties would agree to a compromise giving Belgium the Wielingen, the

---

[39] Gaffier to Cambon, June 8, 1920, ESH-550, June 10, 1920; ESH-756, July 24, 1920.
[40] Chambre, Annales, May 26, 1920, II, 1225.
[41] Whitlock's Journal, II, 633-634, entry of Sept. 15, 1920.
[42] Ibid., II, 634-635, entry of Sept. 24, 1920.

Netherlands the lower Scheldt, and ships of both nations the same treatment in war and in peace.[43] It may have been this suggestion which impelled the Dutch government to give Van Vredenbergh instructions to ask the aid of Brand Whitlock, the American minister, in bringing about a solution. Whitlock gladly accepted the charge, and approached foreign minister Jaspar. The latter was very cooperative and hopeful, for he felt that Belgium's withdrawal of the earlier territorial claims would facilitate matters. He suggested that Van Vredenbergh see him in person to discuss the situation.[44] Nothing came of this plan, however, nor does the question appear to have been taken up again until the following September, when Jaspar discussed it with van Karnebeek, when the two men met in Switzerland. The conversation was wholly general and no attempt was made to reach agreement on details, but Jaspar found it very promising.[45]

Nevertheless the next conversations on the subject were delayed for nearly seven months, until the two statesmen met again during the economic conference at Genoa.[46] Again several months elapsed before the topic was broached, this time at Geneva, whither the foreign ministers had gone for the regular meeting of the League Assembly.[47]

The Wielingen question was the greatest stumbling block to a solution, and failure to agree on this point rendered the negotiations fruitless. The Belgian deputies from Antwerp were restive at this non-success, as their city needed the improvements for its maritime communications which the treaty was expected to bring. At their insistence further preliminary discussions were held, and finally official negotiations opened in 1924, with de Ruelle repre-

---

[43] Chambre, *Annales,* Dec. 1, 1920, I, 66.

[44] Whitlock's *Journal,* II, 645-646, entries of January 11 and 12, 1921.

[45] *Ibid.,* II, 705-706, entry of September 6, 1921.

[46] Sénat, *Annales,* June 13, 1922, p. 618.

[47] *Ibid.,* December 27, 1922, I, 243.

senting Belgium and van Zuylen Holland. On April 3, 1925, van Karnebeek and Hymans signed the long-desired treaty.[48]

Its first clause formally abrogated two clauses of the Belgo-Dutch treaty of 1839: article VIII, which imposed perpetual neutrality on Belgium, and article XIV, which stipulated that Antwerp should not be used for military purposes. These clauses were not the subject of much controversy between the two governments, because the real points of interest in the treaty were the articles dealing with canals and rivers. The Belgian desire for a change in the regime governing the upkeep of the lower Scheldt was satisfied by the clauses appointing a mixed commission to superintend maintenance and improvements. Other important concessions made by the Netherlands were its promise to build a canal connecting Antwerp with Moerdijk on the Rhine, and to permit the construction on Dutch territory of the Rhine-Meuse-Scheldt canal provided for by the treaty of Versailles. These waterways, as well as an improved Liège-Maestricht canal, were to be administered by a mixed commission. The question of the Wielingen Pass was expressly reserved for the moment.[49]

As soon as this draft was agreed upon, the British and French governments, as signatories of the 1839 collective treaty of guarantee, were notified, in order that they might take action. The rights of Austria and Germany in this matter had been nullified by their violation of Belgian neutrality, as they had admitted in the treaties of Versailles and St. Germain. Since the Soviet government had not been recognized, Russia, the other signatory, was ignored. A short convention was drawn up by which the governments of France and Great Britain in their turn formally abrogated the neutrality of Belgium. This agreement was not signed until May 22, 1926, as some further Belgo-Dutch negotiations were in progress.[50]

[48] Chambre, *Documents,* May 27, 1926, p. 36, doc. no. 306.
[49] *D. D. Rev.,* pp. 11-23, doc. no. 11.
[50] Arnold Toynbee, ed., *Survey of International Affairs,* 1925 (London, 1926), II, 170; *D. D. Rev.,* pp. 24-25, doc. no. 11.

These negotiations were due to dissatisfaction in the Netherlands, where the treaty had not been given a warm welcome, because it was interpreted as unduly favoring Belgium. In response to this criticism, the government of the Netherlands asked that certain points be defined in such a way as to make ratification easier.[51] The result was the adoption, on May 18, 1926, of a protocol whereby the Belgian government assumed a larger share in the expenses connected with the navigation and improvement of the Scheldt.[52] These arrangements were quickly ratified by the Belgian parliament, which recognized that although their country was not receiving the territorial acquisitions once hoped for, the treaty at least improved the transportation situation, and settled Belgium's status in international law.[53]

In the Netherlands the case was different. The great shipping companies, especially those located at Rotterdam, felt that their interests would suffer if Antwerp's communications with the North Sea and the mouths of the Rhine were improved, and forthwith they created a political crisis to complicate matters. The treaty passed the Second Chamber by the narrow margin of three votes, but before it was submitted to the First Chamber, the opposition grew even stronger. Although van Karnebeek, foreign minister, pleaded that ratification would lead to a closer understanding with Belgium, and pointed out that at least two decades would elapse before the proposed canals would be ready for operation, the treaty was rejected.[54] This repudiation rendered ineffectual all the agreements reached with the other signatories of the 1839 agreements.

The matter rested for two years, until in April, 1928, Jonkheer Beelaerts van Blokland, Karnebeek's successor as foreign minis-

[51] Chambre, *Documents,* February 10, 1926, doc. no. 168.
[52] *D. D. Rev.,* pp. 23-24, doc. no. 11.
[53] Vandervelde's speech, Chambre, *Annales,* July 17, 1926, II, 2326-2329.
[54] Manfredi Siotto-Pinto, "Le régime internationale de l'Escaut," *Académie de Droit international, recueil des cours,* XXI (1928), pp. 355-359; Robert H. George, "The Scheldt Dispute," *Foreign Affairs,* VI (1927), 155-157.

ter, declared, in answer to an interpellation in the Estates General, that he intended to reopen the negotiations, and to sign a treaty within the year. Hymans, then Belgian foreign minister, at once notified him that Brussels desired to see this plan carried through as soon as possible, and asked to be informed of the bases on which van Blokland was preparing to negotiate.[55] It was, no doubt, somewhat disappointing to Hymans to learn that before taking up the question with the Belgian diplomats, the Netherlands government intended to have it thoroughly studied by experts—a procedure which would cause further delay.[56] The Dutch technical studies were, however, completed in time for Hymans and van Blokland to take up the question when they met in Geneva for the meeting of the League Assembly in September.[57] The conversations between the two foreign ministers on this occasion seemed to promise a satisfactory conclusion, but further technical investigations were considered advisable before formal negotiations could be opened.

The chief difficulty was connected with the waterways leading from the Scheldt to the Rhine. Van Blokland was naturally reluctant to accede to Hymans' desire for a Rhine-Scheldt canal that would avoid the dangerous Hellegat pass, and thus insure Belgium the easy access to the sea promised by the treaty of 1839. If such a canal were found to be absolutely necessary, van Blokland insisted that it should be constructed as far to the west as possible. The Belgians retorted that this would fail to eliminate the danger at the Hellegat, since van Blokland's plan called for a canal that would reach the mouth of the Rhine just at the entrance to the dangerous pass. Hymans continued to insist that the more east-

---

[55] Belgian memorandum, June 14, 1928, *D. D. Rev.,* p. 25, doc. no. 12; Chambre, *CRA,* July 6, 1928, p. 585.

[56] Note of the Netherlands government, June 28, 1928, *D. D. Rev.,* pp. 25-26, doc. no. 13

[57] Chambre, *CRA,* December 20, 1928, p. 125.

erly Moerdijk canal would be imperative. It was finally decided to refer the point to a committee of experts.[58]

On October 23, 1928, the negotiations were resumed with the presentation of a note from the government of the Netherlands containing the plan proposed by the Dutch for the negotiations. Articles VII and XIV of the Belgo-Dutch treaty of 1839—the articles stipulating that Belgium should remain perpetually neutral and that Antwerp was not to be used as a naval base—were to be considered abrogated. No surrender was to be made, however, on the navigation questions. A slight concession as to improvements on the lower Scheldt was hinted at, but article IX of the treaty of 1839 was not to be changed; that is, the Dutch government maintained that there was no need for a canal to join Antwerp to the Rhine. In return for the slight concessions that actually were offered, namely the abrogation of the neutrality clause and release from the restrictions on Antwerp—by which Holland lost nothing—the Dutch government desired that the Juliana canal, designed to join the lower Rhine to the Meuse, should be built partly through Belgian territory.[59]

While willing to negotiate on the minor points in this note, Hymans rejected the major propositions in a lengthy memorandum presented on January 12, 1929, to the Dutch foreign minister. Arguing from the notes exchanged between the Netherlands and the Great Powers in 1831 and 1832, Hymans concluded that the purpose of the Powers at that time had been to secure for Belgium easy access to the lower Rhine, not to specify the exact route such access had to follow. Accordingly he claimed that permission to construct a new canal was a right, not a favor.[60]

[58] Note of the Belgian government, January 12, 1929, *D. D. Rev.*, p. 27, doc. no. 15.

[59] Note of the Netherlands government, October 23, 1928, *D. D. Rev.*, p. 26-27, doc. no. 14.

[60] Note of the Belgian government, January 12, 1929, *D. D. Rev.*, pp. 27-34, doc. no. 15.

Van Blokland disagreed with this interpretation of the intentions of the statesmen of 1831. He refused, moreover, to accept the statements made in a supplementary Belgian note of February 28, 1929, showing the dangerous conditions of the existing ship communications between Antwerp and the Rhine, and the vital necessity of the desired canal.[61] And, finally, he refused to accept the concessions Hymans offered, such as the assumption of a greater share of the expense of the joint waterways, and guarantees of employment to Dutch pilots. Van Blokland held that because he had not asked for these in his note of October 23, they could not be accepted in exchange for Dutch concessions.[62]

After this very exasperating reply, Hymans made one last attempt to persuade van Blokland of the justice of the Belgian position, and then apparently gave up the struggle.[63]

No further efforts were made until the economic crisis of 1930 drew the smaller nations together. Belgium and the Netherlands in particular entered into more cordial relations, and in 1931, the Dutch government itself re-opened the question by suggesting semi-official discussions. In his reply Hymans pointed out that no surrender was possible on the Belgian demands that the system of providing for the upkeep of the Scheldt be revised, or that connections between Antwerp and the Rhine be improved. These conditions were accepted by the Dutch. Frans van Cauwelaert, an influential Flemish deputy, was named by the Belgian government as its representative, and Baron van Zuylen, who had been one of the plenipotentiaries in the negotiations in 1924-1925, was sent from The Hague. Although van Zuylen admitted the soundness of many of the Belgian claims, the state of Dutch public opin-

[61] Note of the Belgian government, February 28, 1929, *D. D. Rev.*, p. 34, doc. no. 16.

[62] Note of the Netherlands government, May 7, 1929, *D. D. Rev.*, May 7, 1929, p. 35, doc. no. 17.

[63] Note of the Belgian government, May 28, 1929, *D. D. Rev.*, 34-35, doc. no. 18.

ion prevented the signature of an agreement. In April, 1932, these fruitless negotiations were broken off.[64] With the spread of the depression, and the rise of Hitler to power in Germany, more important problems arose to absorb the attention of the two parties. When Belgium and Holland were invaded in May, 1940, the treaties of 1839 had not been revised.

[64] Sénat, *CRA*, May 31, 1932, p. 391; March 8, 1934, p. 245.

CHAPTER FIVE

Reparations

A VERY important aim of Belgian foreign policy in the years immediately following the war of 1914-1918, was to collect reparations from Germany. It was of major significance to the entire people, for the reconstruction of their economic life was largely dependent on these receipts.

The most immediate use for the money was to meet the expenses resulting from the physical reconstruction of the country. Reliable authorities have stated that 100,000 houses and 1200 public buildings were destroyed during the war, causing a housing shortage that demanded attention at once.[1] At the same time measures had to be taken to speed the general economic recovery. For this the canals and railroads had to be restored to their former efficiency, and 250,000 acres of arable land that had been flooded or otherwise rendered unproductive had to be reclaimed. Moreover, practically all the great iron and steel works which were the mainstay of industry had been dismantled, if not destroyed, by the Germans.[2]

The Belgian government at once set to work on the formidable task confronting it. By a decree-law of October 23, 1918, amended

[1] Mahaim, ed., *La Belgique restaurée, étude sociologique,* p. 117.
[2] *Ibid.,* p. 201.

by a law of May 10, 1919, provision was made for the reconstruction of the devastated areas. The organization of this work was long and difficult; only in July, 1932, nearly fourteen years after the cessation of hostilities, and eight years before the second invasion, was it possible to liquidate the "Office des Régions dévastées." During these fourteen years over 23,226,000,000 gold francs were spent for reconstruction.[3] This sum, as well as the heavy war expenses incurred by Belgium, was chargeable to Germany.

For an understanding of the work done by the Belgian representatives at the various conferences which met during the years following 1919 to deal with reparations, two facts must be kept in mind.[4] First, the Belgian people and their government felt that Belgium had been assigned a share in the German payments quite inadequate to meet the costs of reconstruction; consequently they insisted that their diplomats make no further concessions on this point either to the Allies or to Germany. Such an intransigent policy harmonized with the attitude of the French, but differed from that of the British, who realized the economic troubles that the ruin of Germany would entail. The second fact to be remembered is that Belgium was determined to obviate any possibility of a second German invasion. This policy of security called for a close union between the two powers which could assure its success: France and Great Britain. As a result, Belgian diplomats, while insisting upon all their country's rights to reparation under the treaty, never lost sight of the importance of maintaining the Anglo-French entente, which they believed essential to the security of their fatherland. In the following pages this double aim

---

[3] Sénat, *CRA,* July 19, 1932, p. 551.
[4] The broader aspects of the complicated reparation problem have been dealt with by qualified expert economists; this study will be concerned with the question only from the Belgian standpoint, and will stress the political and diplomatic side of the negotiations.

will be seen motivating Belgian policy throughout the reparations negotiations.

These negotiations passed through three phases: the first, from 1919 to 1924, was one wherein the French government, often seconded by the Belgians, refused to relax any of its demands for full reparations. The second phase, inaugurated by the Dawes plan, was one of comparative good feeling, wherein Germany repaid the Allies with money borrowed from the United States. The Young Plan, which its sponsors hoped would usher in an era of greater prosperity and stronger good feeling, marked instead the end of prosperity and peace, and the beginning of depression and ill-will. During this third phase, reparations receded from the realm of reality, even before March, 1936, when they were officially repudiated by Hitler.

The two principal tasks confronting the Allies during the first period were those of fixing the amount and modality of German payments, and of agreeing on the percentage to be allotted to each of the creditors. Although a reparations commission had been set up by the treaty to perform the first task, the Allied governments soon took matters into their own hands, and attempted to reach an acceptable political solution, without too much regard for expert economic opinion.

The first of the conferences at which the Allied statesmen grappled with the problem met from April 19 to 26, 1920, at San Remo. Here Jaspar, the Belgian premier, and Hymans, his minister for foreign affairs, assumed the role which their country's interests required, and which henceforth they were to fill so well: that of endeavoring to adjust conflicting British and French policies in order to preserve the entente.[5]

They pointed out to the other delegates the three essential fac-

[5] Chambre, Annales, May 4, 1920, I, 953-954. Whitlock ironically said of this attitude: " . . . the Belgians love that role and always try to play it, or pretend to play it, at their conferences." Whitlock's Journal, II, 661, entry of May 1, 1921

tors necessary to bring about a final settlement; namely, the fixing
of the amount to be paid, the commercialization of the debt,
and a close understanding among the Allies.[6] Unfortunately
these essentials were notoriously elusive, as future events were
to show.

Lloyd George and Millerand, premier of France, met twice at
Hythe, England, to prepare a common policy for the inter-Allied
conference which was to open at Spa, Belgium, in July. During
the second series of talks at Hythe, the two premiers reached an
agreement whereby 55 per cent of the reparations receipts was al-
located to France, 25 per cent to Great Britain, and 6 per cent to
Serbia. When this news reached the Allied financial representatives
then in session at Boulogne to discuss this very matter of apportion-
ment, a serious crisis arose. All the remaining creditors, for whom
this agreement destined only 14 per cent, were greatly dissatisfied.
The issue was eventually referred to a group of financial experts
who were instructed to report their findings on July 2 to an Allied
conference at Brussels.[7]

At this meeting the already thorny situation was further complicated by Italy, which advanced a claim to 20 per cent of the
receipts. This demand received British support, to the dismay and
alarm of the Belgians.[8] They protested vigorously, but fruitlessly,
until King Albert personally intervened to support them. Only
then did Millerand and Lloyd George lower their percentages
from 55 and 25 per cent to 52 and 22 per cent respectively. This
insured 20 per cent to Italy, while making it possible to place
Belgium's share at 8 per cent, and to respect the priority so hardly
won at Paris.[9] These arrangements were ratified at Spa the following
week. The chief work of this last named conference, however, was

[6] Henri Jaspar, "La Belgique et la politique occidentale depuis le traité de
paix," *Revue Belge*, II, (1924), 391-392.
[7] Whitlock's *Journal*, II, 613-614, entry of June 29, 1920.
[8] Riddell, *Intimate Diary*, p. 210, entry of July 2 and 3, 1920.
[9] D'Abernon, *An Ambassador of Peace*, I, 56-57.

the elaboration of plans for German disarmament and the presentation of a demand for more coal deliveries.

On July 9 the Germans agreed to the disarmament program laid down by the Allies; that is, they promised to disband the volunteer military groups, such as the *Sicherheitswehr* and the *Einwohnerwehr,* to surrender concealed arms, and to reduce the army to 100,000 men by the first of the following year. Negotiations regarding the coal deliveries were more difficult, especially after Hugo Stinnes, an industrial magnate, presented the German case. His tone and attitude were almost insolent, and his demand that his country must be treated on terms of equality, angered the Allies. The French delegate pressed for occupation of the Ruhr valley to stimulate the payments, but General Maglinse, Belgian chief of staff, presented such weighty arguments against it that the plan was rejected. The mere threat was enough to induce the Germans to surrender. On July 16 the Allied requirement of 2,000,000 tons of coal monthly was acceded to, and the protocol was signed at once.[10]

The next conference, held in Paris from January 24 to 30, 1921, was marked by serious divergences in the French and British points of view, which once more threatened Allied unity. The British contended that Germany could not pay more than 3,000,000,000 gold marks annually, while the French insisted on exacting four times that sum. Jaspar, Belgian foreign minister since the previous November, together with Theunis, premier and finance minister, worked hard to reconcile these differences, and it was in large measure their efforts which preserved the entente.[11]

[10] Chambre, *Annales,* July 20, 1920, II, 2091-2092; Great Britain, *Parl. Papers,* 1924, Cmd. 2258, p. 18.

[11] Karl Bergmann, *The History of Reparations* (London, 1927), p. 56. This statement seems to be borne out by the following evidence: D'Abernon, the British Ambassador at Berlin, said that Jaspar and Theunis concurred with the British delegates in condemning the unreasonableness of the French attitude; D'Abernon, *An Ambassador of Peace,* I, 118, entry of Jan. 26, 1921. But Lloyd George described Jaspar as being at Paris "an unequivocal supporter of France on all questions relating to the application of the Treaty," and said that his

It was Jaspar who proposed that the imposition of a tax on German exports could increase receipts, although at the same time he warned against any artificial stimulus to these exports which would harm Allied commerce.[12] This suggestion was included in the demands presented to the German government, the most important of which were that all German customs were to be pledged to the payment of reparations; and Germany was to pay two series of annuities for forty-two years. One series was to be a fixed sum, the other was to be equal to 12 per cent of the annual value of German exports. In case of default, the creditor countries could impose sanctions at their will.[13] After agreeing on these demands, the Allied statesmen separated, to give time for the German government to consider the proposals.

The fruit of the study was presented at the London Conference, which held its first session on March 1, 1921. The German government rejected the demands, and presented a counter proposal, offering to pay 50,000,000,000 gold marks. The German foreign minister, Dr. Simons, stated that 20,000,000,000 marks had already been surrendered in the form of payments in kind. The 30,000,000,000 marks outstanding would not be paid at once; 8,-000,000,000 would be raised by loan, but on the remainder only interest charges would be met. Although Simons made some concessions on March 5, when he offered to accept the Allied valuation of payments in kind, Briand, the French premier, refused to consider the proposals, since they were made contingent upon

"sympathy with France was intransigent"; Lloyd George, *The Truth about Reparations and War-debts* (Garden City, 1932), pp. 51 and 73. (However, as the British Prime Minister was writing ten years after the event, and in an attempt to justify his policies, his testimony is less valuable than that of D'Abernon and Bergmann, both of whom were also present at the conference.) The point is that the very fact that the Belgians could seem pro-British to one observer and in the same setting pro-French to another, would seem to indicate a conciliatory attitude toward both nations, and an effort to bring about mutual concessions for the sake of unity.

[12] Riddell, *Intimate Diary*, p. 274.
[13] Toynbee, *Survey*, 1920-1923, pp. 127-128.

German success in the Upper Silesia plebiscite. On March 8, therefore, French, British, and Belgian troops occupied the towns of
Dusseldorf, Ruhrort, and Duisberg in the Rhineland. On March
24 the Reparations Commission declared Germany in default;
consequently, on April 29, when another inter-Allied conference
met in London, the French favored the imposition of further sanctions, notably a military occupation of the Ruhr valley.

At this point the Belgian delegates experienced another change
of heart. At Paris in January they had worked to reconcile the French
and British points of view, and had been in close harmony with
the British delegates. In March, in spite of their successful effort
to dissuade the French from occupying the Ruhr,[14] their general
attitude at the meeting had been pro-French.[15] When on May 5,
the Allies decided to occupy the Ruhr if Germany remained ob-
stinate, Belgian policy veered once more toward the program of
moderation favored by the British. The influential socialist leader
Emile Vandervelde was strongly opposed to the use of force, and
if only a face-saving compromise could be found, Belgium would
be most happy to escape the odium and expense of further military
action.[16] Jaspar finally found an effective formula: let the Allies
vote to resort to sanctions, but move their troops slowly, giving

---

[14] Henri Jaspar, "Locarno et la Belgique," *Revue Belge,* III (1925), 162.

[15] D'Abernon, *An Ambassador of Peace,* I, 134-135, entry of March 14, 1921,
and I, 146, entry of March 28, 1921. The British Ambassador could not repress
his surprise at the momentary change in Belgian policy. He was evidently only
considering the affair from a diplomatic standpoint and failed to realize that
practical considerations might have motivated the Belgian shift in policy. Perhaps Carton de Wiart, Belgian premier, gave the key to it when he expressed
his indignation at German proposals because they would give Belgium only
2,400,000,000 gold marks. He evidently felt that if Franco-British unity was
to be of no assistance in the country's immediate and desperate financial need,
the wisest plan would be to back up the French who were more demanding in
their exactions on Germany, and then work for conciliation between the two great
powers after their own immediate needs had been provided for. Chambre, *Annales,* March 8, 1921, II, 776. *Cf.* also Sénat, *Annales,* Dec. 27, 1922, *pp.*
244-245.

[16] Whitlock's *Journal,* II, 656, April 9, 1921; II, 661, May 1, 1921.

the German government time to make concessions. This suggestion was adopted and the plan worked successfully, much to the
relief of the sponsor and his government.[17] Up to this time the
total amount due from Germany had not been specified, but, according to the terms of the peace treaty, the Reparations Committee had to name a figure by May 15, 1921. The sum decided upon
was 132,000,000,000 gold marks, payable in fixed quarterly in-
stallments of 500,000,000 gold marks; an annuity amounting to
26 per cent of the value of German exports was likewise to be met
by quarterly payments by the German government. These figures
were accepted and the first million marks of the fixed annuity
were duly remitted in a lump sum in June.

A meeting of Allied finance ministers was then held at Paris to
arrange the division of this sum among the creditors. The armies
of occupation were entitled to absolute priority. On this score
Great Britain received 450,000,000 francs. The balance was allo-
cated to Belgium which was henceforth to receive payments calculated to extinguish by August, 1922, the priority of 250,000,000
francs. This plan was not accepted by the French cabinet.

Meanwhile the German government stated that the sums due
under the London agreement of the previous May could not be
raised, and that no payments would be forthcoming in February.
At once French and British representatives met in London to discuss the situation resulting from this declaration. They worked
out a new plan, limiting the annuity for 1922 to 500,000,000 marks,
a concession made possible by reducing Belgium's share in the
quarterly payments.

This Franco-British scheme was the basis for the negotiations
at the inter-Allied conference which opened at Cannes on June 6,
1922, to discuss the request for a moratorium.

The Belgian delegates, premier Theunis and foreign minister

[17] Henri Jaspar, "La Belgique et la politique occidentale depuis le traité de
paix," loc. cit., 393 ; Whitlock's Journal, II, 661-662, entry of May 2, 1921.

Jaspar, had a difficult task. The premier, a financial expert, insisted that Germany could raise 900,000,000 marks, thus doing away with the plan for a reduction in his country's receipts. Finally, however, he compromised on the sum of 750,000,000 marks.

A more serious threat to Belgium's interests was that which jeopardized the right to priority of payment. After what Theunis called "some agitated and feverish days" the question was settled by the untimely end of the conference with the sudden overthrow of the Briand cabinet. The conference was indefinitely adjourned.[18] This turn of events was probably a great relief to Theunis and Jaspar, since it was the French finance minister, Loucheur, who had taken the initiative in suggesting a modification of the Spa percentages.[19] If France made such a proposal, where could Belgium look for support?

Once again that spring was the Belgian position threatened. A group of financial experts invited by the Reparations Commission to consider the possibility of a German loan suggested that the money might be raised if the sum total were lowered. This could be done if Belgium would waive all claim to further payment once the priority was extinguished. The Commission did not adopt the report.[20]

However, when circumstances required concessions, the Belgians were not too stubborn to make them. This was evident during the conference which met from August 7 to 14, 1922, in London. Poincaré, the French premier, strongly urged the seizure of German state mines and forests, and the collection of customs duties and taxes in the occupied zone by the occupant. Lloyd George would not hear of such action. The crisis had reached an acute stage when, on August 9, Theunis intervened with a plea for unity:

[18] Chambre, *Annales,* Jan. 24, 1922, I, 123-128.

[19] D'Abernon, *Diary,* I, 248, entry of Jan. 16, 1922.

[20] Sénat, *Annales,* June 13, 1922, pp. 622-623; U. S. Bureau of Foreign and Domestic Commerce, *The Reparation Problem, 1918-1924,* (Washington, 1924), p. 5.

For us Belgians the Entente is an article of the Creed. The Entente seems to us to have been made sacred by the sacrifices out of which it was born, and we are not willing to believe that, for a matter of detail, anyone would endanger the solidarity of the Entente. Belgium is resolved to subordinate its immediate interests to the general interests which are at stake, for these represent the interests of all the Allies.[21]

He and Jaspar also privately argued with Poincaré, but were unable to make him change his attitude. Failing in this they resolutely opposed him, when on August 14 he reiterated his demands.[22] That they were sincere in their convictions was shown on August 31, when they accepted German treasury notes, maturing in six months, in lieu of cash. As the remaining German payments for 1922 were earmarked for Belgium on account of priorities, this action was, to all intents and purposes, equivalent to granting Germany the desired moratorium.[23] Such temporary measures, however, could give only partial relief: the problem was as yet far from being solved.

To aid in bringing about a final solution, the Belgian government invited Germany and the Allies to a conference at Brussels in January, 1923. A preliminary meeting of the entente powers at London in December was designed to iron out any obstacles which might prejudice complete unity of action at Brussels. Such was the plan; such was not the event. At London Poincaré brought forward his proposal to take "productive guarantees" in the form of occupation of the Ruhr industrial area, insisting that no moratorium be granted without such action. This precipitated a storm of opposition on the part of the British delegation led by Bonar Law.

---

[21] Great Britain, *Parliamentary Papers,* 1924, Cmd. 2258, pp. 42-43.
[22] *Ibid.,* pp. 61-63.
[23] John Wheeler Wheeler-Bennett, *Information on the reparation settlement, being the background and history of the Young plan and the Hague agreements 1919-1930* (London, 1930), p. 48; Toynbee, *Survey,* 1920-1923, pp. 182-183, p. 199.

At this inter-Allied meeting the Belgian delegates remained discreetly silent, Theunis intervening but once, to ask that the question of Allied war debts be included in the discussion.[24] This was done, but Bonar Law's offer to cancel the debts to Great Britain was rejected by Poincaré, since he hoped to receive more from Germany than France owed Britain.

The London conference having thus failed to achieve its purpose, a second preliminary meeting met in Paris on January 2, 1923. The British and the French representatives each made proposals looking to a final settlement; the French insisting on full reparations and severe sanctions, the British suggesting an absolute moratorium for four years, and a reduction in the amount of German payments. This was to be made possible by a general cancellation of inter-Allied debts, and the abolition of the Belgian priority. At once Theunis objected strongly. His country would reap no benefit from the cancellation of inter-Allied debts, as liability for the Belgian debt was by the treaty transferred to Germany; therefore any threat to the right of priority was unthinkable. The Belgian government was willing to make some sacrifices for the sake of preserving peace, but was not prepared to offer a complete holocaust.[25] The following day, after the Italian delegate had followed the Belgian example and expressed his country's agreement with French policy, the conference adjourned. The fundamental differences between the British position on the one hand, and the French, Belgian, and Italian on the other were too great to admit of compromise.[26]

After that, events moved swiftly. On January 9 the Reparations Commission declared Germany in default on coal deliveries to France, and on January 11 the occupation of the Ruhr basin by

[24] Great Britain, *Parliamentary Papers,* 1923, Cmd. 1812, p. 3.

[25] Great Britain, *Parliamentary Papers,* 1923, Cmd. 1812, pp. 130-133.

[26] As early as Dec. 1, 1922, acute observers had known the probable stand that France would take, and the fact that Belgium would support French policy; Herrick to Hughes, Dec. 1, 1922, *U. S. For. Rel.* 1922, II, 186.

French and Belgian forces, assisted by Italian engineers, began. The Belgian government did not desire the occupation, but under the circumstances did not see how it was possible to take any other position, for it could ill afford to be isolated from its only ally.[27] Moreover, economic considerations played some part in determining Brussels to action. To the north Holland was somewhat unfriendly, refusing to permit improvements in the approach to Antwerp. Should France become master in the industrial area of western Germany, the Antwerp entrepôt trade was doomed. The only way to prevent economic encirclement was to go with France, and thus secure an untrammeled outlet to Germany.[28] Nor could any government remain in power in Brussels if it abandoned reparations.

Consequently on January 6 the cabinet had decided to participate in the occupation, the Belgian Chamber ratifying the decision three days later. Only the Socialists were hostile, Vandervelde resigning when the cabinet made its decision; yet they, too, insisted on the maintenance of Belgian priorities and the right to complete reparations. No one disagreed with Theunis when he said: *"Ces réparations il nous les faut, impérieusement, absolument."*[29] The difference of opinion was confined to the question of the appropriate means to be used.

The Belgian government was not long in discovering that the means it had chosen was not without serious drawbacks. The original plan of the French and Belgian governments had not been a military occupation in the strict sense of the word, but military pro-

[27] Hughes' memorandum of a conversation with Cattier (Belgian Ambassador), Jan. 11, 1923, *U. S. For. Rel.* 1923, II, 49.

[28] James A. Logan, comp., *Secret Dawes Report, The Reparation Question* (Paris, 1924). IA, XXII. (Hereafter cited as *Reparations*).

[29] Chambre, *Annales,* Jan 9, 1923, I, 360-363; Jan. 15, 1925, p. 358. The Socialists even sent a commission of inquiry to examine conditions in the Ruhr; the report, however, was favorable to the government; Chambre, *Annales,* June 13, 1923, III, 1935. In the budget debate the following June the government policy was again given strong support. Chambre, *Annales,* June 12-15, 1923, III, 1928-1937.

tection for an Allied commission of control.[30] The commission of control. *Mission interalliée des Contrôle des Usines et des Mines* (Micum), was indeed set up, but when it tried to carry out its appointed task, insuperable obstacles at once arose. Although German industrialists and workers signed an agreement with the *Micum,* promising to begin deliveries of coal and coke, the population of the Ruhr district, resentful of the situation, refused to cooperate, and were supported in this by their government, which forbade any collaboration with the occupants.[31] Belgium and France found themselves obliged to send additional troops, to occupy territory beyond the original limits set for the occupation, and not only to supervise, but actually to work the German mines and railways. The embittered population often passed from passive resistance to active sabotage, thus calling down upon their heads harsh retaliatory measures.[32] At the same time the German state was going into bankruptcy, having exhausted its resources by undertaking the financial support of the workers who refused to collaborate with the occupying powers. The effects were so disastrous to the country that on September 27, 1923, President Ebert of Germany announced that passive resistance was unconditionally abandoned by the German government.

This action on the part of the German government, while ending the trouble in the Ruhr, did not do away with all the disorders in the occupied territory. The movement to separate the Rhineland from the Reich was gaining added momentum. More than four years earlier, on May 31, 1919, an independent Rhineland Republic

---

[30] Belgium, Ministère des Affaires Etrangères, *Documents diplomatiques relatifs aux réparations (Du 26 décembre au 27 août 1923) (Brussels,* 1923, pp. 15-16, doc, no. 7. (Hereafter cited as *D.D. rep.)*

[31] Chambre, *Annales,* June 12, 1923, III, 1937.

[32] For an account of the actual workings of the occupation, by one of the French officials, see Paul Tirard, "Comment nous avons occupé la Ruhr," *Revue des Deux Mondes,* pt. 7, LX (1930), 122-148, 319-344.

had been proclaimed at Wiesbaden, and although the French attitude of neutrality caused the "Republic" to collapse in less than a week, the Separatists did not cease their agitation, which, however, made little headway until after the Ruhr occupation.[33] At the same time particularist tendencies made their appearance in the other German states, notably Bavaria and Saxony. The movement came to a head on October 21, 1923, when a second Rhineland Republic was proclaimed, this time at Aix-la-Chapelle in the Belgian zone. The occupying authorities there preserved a "neutral attitude," which, with the German police too few in numbers to preserve order, meant giving support to the Separatists. On October 24 an attempt of the population to destroy the "Republic" failed, and the Belgian gendarmerie promptly disarmed the German police.[34]

The British government at once notified Paris and Brussels that it considered an independent Rhineland as a violation of the treaty of Versailles. This probably caused the marked change in official Belgian policy manifested on November 2, when a group of Separatists captured the Hôtel de Ville at Aix, and Rolin-Jacquemyns, the High Commissioner, took effective measures to keep order and expel the invader. Before the day was over Belgian soldiers had routed the last Separatist. The movement made no further headway in the Belgian zone, and soon all traces disappeared there.[35]

As Stresemann himself admitted, the Belgians were more "European" in their judgment of the situation than were the French, who considered the movement from an imperialist point of view.[36]

[33] Cf. Henry T. Allen, *The Rhineland Occupation* (Indianapolis, 1927), pp. 194-202; Hans Dorten, "The Rhineland Movement," *Foreign Affairs,* III, (1925), 405-406.

[34] *Stresemann,* I, 180-189.

[35] Chambre, *Annales,* Nov. 20, 1923, I, 10-20. Jaspar denied that his policy was dictated by the British. It is quite possible that the attitude of the Socialists, who favored a parliamentary investigation of the action of the gendarmerie at Aix-la-Chapelle, was an important factor in motivating the change of policy.

[36] *Stresemann,* I, 258.

The French government continued to give the Separatists active support, even going so far as to desire that the Rhineland High Commission register the decrees of the "Autonomous Government of the Palatinate." As such registration would imply at least *de facto* recognition of the Rhineland Republic by all the states represented on the Commission, the British High Commissioner dissented, and was supported by Rolin-Jacquemyns. On January 24 Jaspar was able to announce that he had prevailed upon Poincaré to withdraw Frence support from the separatist movement, which within a month completely collapsed.

While these developments were going on within the occupied territory, the Belgian government had been working actively to reestablish the Anglo-French entente without at the same time compromising either the Franco-Belgian policy, or the claim to reparations. From the beginning of the occupation the Brussels cabinet had insisted that its sole purpose was to put pressure on the Germans to make full payment, and that, as soon as this end was achieved, Belgian troops would evacuate the Ruhr.[37] After the Franco-Belgian conference of March 12, 1933, a joint communique was issued, affirming the intention of the two governments not to relax their pressure on Germany until the latter fulfilled its obligations.[38] The Belgian government never permitted any other interpretation to be given its actions, emphatically denying the imperialistic motives with which it was occasionally taxed.[39] These denials were accepted by the governments of Germany and of Great Britain; consequently Belgian statesmen were in a good position to work for a rapprochement not only between France

[37] So Jaspar told the Foreign Affairs Committee of the Chamber, on Jan. 10; Chambre, *Annales,* June 14, 1923, III, 1976; see also Jaspar's speech, Sénat, *Annales,* Jan. 16, 1924, p. 255; Jaspar, "La Belgique et la Politique Occidentale," *loc. cit.,* 400.

[38] *D.D. rep.,* March 12, 1923, p. 20, doc. no. 16.

[39] *Ibid.,* Jaspar to Belgian Ambassadors, March 13, 1923, pp. 20-21, doc. no. 17; April 13-14, 1923, p. 21, doc. no. 18; Chambre, *Annales,* July 11, 1924, II, 1864.

and Great Britain, but also between the entente and Berlin. Late in April, 1923, when passive resistance was at its height, it was the Belgian government which the Germans sounded, to discover whether or not some understanding could be reached. Although at that time the Belgians did not feel able to approach the Quai d'Orsay on the matter, they did favor the opening of negotiations by the Germans, and suggested to the French government that whatever propositions might be made ought to receive careful consideration.[40]

When, however, the negotiations were opened by the German note of May 2, 1923, the proposals contained therein were not acceptable to any of the Allied powers. Jaspar objected especially to the suggestion that a neutral commission replace the Reparations Commission set up by the Versailles Treaty. He also felt that the guarantees offered were insufficient. Of course the whole idea of reducing the value of the payments to be made was not pleasing to him.[41] The official reply to the German note, however, stressed only one point: in agreement with France, Belgium refused to consider any plan until passive resistance in the Ruhr was ended.[42] In spite of this rejection, the Germans had opened the way for further discussions, which centered around a plan for raising reparations money which had been formulated by a group of Belgian economists. As early as the Franco-Belgian conference of April 14, Theunis had tried to secure the cooperation of French experts in outlining such a plan. After the rejection of the German note, he again brought up the idea of an allied commission of experts. The French apparently did not act on this suggestion, so the Belgians went ahead with the work alone.[43] On June 6 Poincaré gave

[40] Jaspar to Gaiffier, May 2, 1923, D.D. rep., p. 21, doc. no. 19; Bergmann, History of Reparations, pp. 189-190.

[41] Jaspar to the Belgian Ambassadors, May 3, 1923, D. D. rep., pp. 24-25, doc. no. 21.

[42] Jaspar to Roediger, May 6, 1923, D.D. rep., p. 25, doc. no. 22.

[43] Jaspar to Gaffier, May 17, 1923, ibid., p. 27, doc. no. 23, and May 24, 1923, ibid., p. 28, doc. 24.

his approval to the plan they drew up.[44] It provided for an annual German payment of approximately three billion gold marks, to be raised by setting aside for this purpose the revenue from the German state railway and certain taxes.[45] Between this plan and the second German note, presented to the Allies on June 7, there were certain points of similarity. Nevertheless the Belgians regarded the proposals embodied in the latter as unsatisfactory, although conceding that they were an improvement on the earlier offers. Accordingly, premier Jaspar suggested that all the powers concerned join in a collective reply, advising the Germans to abandon passive resistance as a necessary prelude to further discussion.[46]

Instead of acceding to this suggestion, on June 13 the British foreign office submitted to Poincaré and Jaspar a questionnaire asking for more detailed information. The particular items on which clarification was desired were: the means the German government was expected to use in order to end the passive resistance in the Ruhr, the meaning of the expression, "continued occupation of the Ruhr," the minimum payment demanded by France, and the guarantees desired.[47] The replies given by the French and Belgian governments were not identical, nor did they show the close union of purpose that for some months had characterized Franco-Belgian policy. On July 3, Baron Moncheur, the Belgian Ambassador at London, handed Curzon his government's answer. It stated that the ces-

---

[44] Jaspar to Belgian Ambassadors in London and Rome, June 7, 1923, *ibid.*, pp. 28-29, doc. no. 26.

[45] Jaspar to Moncheur, June 9, 1923, *ibid.*, pp. 31-41, doc. no. 30. According to this plan the revenues to be assigned were:

German state railway .... (gold marks)	1,000,000,000
Tax on tobacco, beer, sugar, salt, alcohol, etc.	1,530,000,000
Coal deliveries	340,000,000
25% profit tax on industry and commerce	250,000,000
	3,120,000,000

[46] Jaspar to Belgian Ambassadors, June 8, 1923, *D.D. rep.*, p. 31, doc. no. 29.

[47] Moncheur to Jaspar, June 13, 1923, *ibid.*, pp. 42-45, doc. no. 34.

sation of passive resistance was a necessary preliminary to any negotiations with Germany. This would have as its inevitable consequence a modification of the form of the occupation. Further concessions would depend on the attitude of the people. If the British
government wished to discuss the matter among allies, Jaspar affirmed his readiness to enter upon conversations.[48]

Poincaré's answer to the questionnaire was more definite, and
perhaps for that reason, offered less promise of a speedy settlement
of the problem. He expected the German cabinet to permit transfers of payment in kind, to stop paying wages to idle workmen
in the Ruhr, and to cease punishing Germans who worked for the
occupying authorities. When official passive resistance had thus
come to an end, the number of French troops in the Ruhr would
be reduced to the smallest figure required to protect the civil officials charged with supervising the collection of duties and of coal
deliveries. Poincaré insisted upon fixing French reparations at 26,-
000,000,000 gold marks to pay the cost of reconstruction, and an
additional sum sufficient to cover the debt to Great Britain and to
the United States. As guarantees he demanded that the Allies collect German customs duties and receive a quarter share in leading
German industries.[49]

In spite of the unpromising nature of these replies, particularly
of the second, on July 20 Curzon, the English Foreign Secretary,
suggested that the Allies send a concerted answer to the proposals
made on June 7 by Chancellor Cuno of Germany. The note planned
by Curzon stipulated that the German government must abandon
passive resistance as necessary prelude to evacuation of the Ruhr.
To deal with the main problem of reparations he advocated the
creation of a committee of experts with instructions to study Germany's capacity to pay. The report of this committee, which should
include an American citizen, would be submitted to the Allies,

---

[48] Jaspar to Moncheur, July 2, 1923, *ibid.*, pp. 46-47, doc. no. 37.
[49] Great Britain, *Parliamentary Papers*, 1923, Cmd. 1943, doc. no. 4.

who would then confer together in order to develop a comprehensive plan for a final settlement. The experts' report, he concluded, should include a description of the guarantees of future payment which the German government would be called upon to provide; once these guarantees had been put into operation, the Ruhr occupations would be brought to an end.[50]

On July 30 separate replies were made by the French and Belgian governments. The tone of the former, dictated by Poincaré, was unyielding. The proposal of a joint reply to the note of July 7 was passed over in silence, arguments were proffered to prove the legality of the Ruhr occupation, the statement was made that evacuation would take place only in proportion to the payments received, and the idea of a fresh investigation of Germany's capacity to pay was flatly rejected.[51]

The Belgian answer was only slightly more cooperative in tone. It accepted the joint reply advocated by Curzon, and was willing to admit an investigation of the capacity to pay. On the other hand, however, Jaspar maintained that not a committee of experts, but the Reparations Commission should be delegated to study the possibility of a revised scale of payments. He further insisted that if any change were adopted, special priority must be conceded to the devastated regions, and reiterated Poincaré's claim that the Ruhr occupation was legal. In closing, Jaspar gave a warm welcome to the offer of a discussion of the security problem, contained in the last paragraph of Curzon's note.[52] In spite of these slight differences, the two answers were in reality dictated by the same policy, as Belgium was now closely tied to France, which had recently advanced the sum necessary to support the Belgian franc.[53]

---

[50] Curzon to Jaspar, Great Britain, *ibid.*, doc. no. 5.
[51] St. Aulaire to Curzon, July 30, 1923, *Parliamentary Papers*, 1923, Cmd. 1943, doc. no. 6.
[52] Moncheur to Jaspar, July 30, 1923, *D. D. rep.*, pp. 56-57, doc. no. 44.
[53] Bergmann, *History of Reparations*, p. 200.

The British reply of August 11 expressed regret at the Franco-Belgian attitude, and refuted point by point, the arguments advanced in the July 30 notes. The conclusion of this long and elaborately reasoned note seemed to promise continuance of the split between the Allies:

They [the British government] cannot, having regard to the heavy material losses of this country both during and since the war, and to future tax burdens on its trade, admit that other countries are justified in claiming that agreed percentages of reparations payments should now be further modified or changed in order of priority. . . . They are reluctant to contemplate the possibility that separate action may be required in order to have a settlement which cannot be much longer delayed without the gravest consequences to the recovery of the trade and peace of the world.[54]

On August 27 Jaspar made a final futile effort to restore the entente by suggesting direct conversations of Allied statesmen, and at the same time admitting the possibility of a reduction in the sum total of German payments.[55]

The Belgian government made no secret of its wish to see the whole question speedily reach a satisfactory conclusion,[56] and two months later, after passive resistance was finally abandoned, made another attempt to reach a solution. Theunis persuaded Mussolini, and the new British prime minister, Stanley Baldwin, to instruct their delegates on the Reparations Commission to force that body to consider the plan drawn up the previous May by the Belgian experts.[57] Internal troubles within Germany caused the British and Italian governments to change their minds before this scheme could be carried into effect.[58] Nevertheless Theunis was undiscouraged.

[54] Great Britain, *Parliamentary Papers,* 1923, Cmd. 1943, doc. no. 10.
[55] Jaspar to Grahame (British Ambassador at Brussels), August 27, 1923, *D. D. rep.,* pp. 78-81, doc. no. 54.
[56] Hughes to Fletcher (Paris), August 17, 1923, *U. S. For. Rel.,* 1923, II, 66-68; D'Abernon, *Ambassador of Peace.* II, 249, entry of Sept. 7, 1923.
[57] Logan to Hughes, September 29, 1923, *Reparations,* IA, 28.
[58] Logan to Hughes, October 3, 1923, *ibid.,* IA, 29.

On October 6 the Belgian representatives in Paris, London and Rome invited the Allied governments to study the plan and recommend it to the Reparations Commission for expert criticism.[59] As this brought no results, on October 17 Léon Delacroix, the Belgian delegate to the Reparations Commission, formally submitted the plan to that body. Sir John Bradbury, the British delegate, refused his support as he believed that matters in Germany would have to become even more serious before France would see reason. Moreover, acceptance of the proposal might weaken the British case against the legality of the Ruhr occupation.[60] As Barthou, the French delegate, was also opposed, the plan was shelved.

Meanwhile the British government had revived the suggestion made in December, 1922, by Secretary of State Hughes, that the reparations tangle could be untied by a committee of experts free from governmental interference. When this proposal was communicated to Jaspar on October 12, he at once replied favorably, fearing that any delay would strengthen the opposition Poincaré would undoubtedly offer.[61]

Poincaré was incensed at this independent action by his satellite, for he had counted on Belgian support in his effort to restrict the scope of the inquiry to the immediate present.[62]

At this juncture an incident occurred which brought home to the French premier how greatly the Belgian attitude had changed. On November 19 Jules Cambon, president of the conference of Ambassadors, informed his colleagues that if the Allies did not apply further sanctions to Germany, his government would do so independently. Lord Crewe, the British Ambassador, replied that in

---

[59] Committee of Experts entrusted with the preparation of the Conference of Finance Ministers to be held on January 6, 1925, *Annexes to Report* (London, 1925), "Note verbale," Oct. 18, 1923, p. 37.

[60] Whitehouse (Paris) to Hughes, Oct. 23, 1923, *U.S. For. Rel.* 1923, II, 76-78; Logan to Hughes, Oct. 18, 1923, *Reparations,* IA, 32.

[61] Fletcher to Hughes, Oct. 22, 1923, *U. S. For. Rel.* 1923, II, 74-75.

[62] Fletcher to U. S. Embassy, Paris, Brussels, Nov. 2, 1923, *Reparations,* IA, 74.

this case, British representatives would be withdrawn from all inter-Allied bodies. When Crewe was supported by his Belgian and Italian colleagues, Cambon capitulated on the sanctions issue.[63] This surrender paved the way for a more important one, when Barthou voted for the creation of two expert committees, one with authority to study the means of balancing the German budget and stabilizing the currency, the other to estimate the amount of exported capital that had fled Germany and propose means of bringing it back to the country. No time limit was attached. This was a big concession on the part of Poincaré, who had tried to maintain that any inquiry must be concerned only with methods of raising money for immediate payments. Another French surrender was made on November 28 when, after much heated discussion with Delacroix, Barthou was persuaded to accept the presence of an American delegate on the commission.[64] This was of major importance, since the participation of the United States was essential to the success of the plan. Only after these protracted negotiations, was the famous Dawes committee called into being.

Pending the decisions of the experts, the German government asked Belgium to discuss a *modus vivendi* for the regulation of Belgo-German relations in the occupied territory. The regime thus agreed upon remained in force until November 15, 1924, when, four weeks before the date prescribed by the Dawes plan, the last vestiges of Allied occupation disappeared from the Ruhr.[65]

The year 1924 marked the opening of the second phase of reparations, the phase wherein payments were regularly made, and international tension decreased. This happy state was in large measure due to the Dawes plan, the result of the work of the committee of experts which had been the object of so much negotiation. It is not the purpose of this investigation to discuss either the economic

[63] D'Abernon, *Ambassador of Peace*, II, 277-278.
[64] Herrick to Hughes, Nov. 28, 1923, *U.S. For. Rel.* 1923, II, 98-100; Dec. 6, II, 102-104.
[65] Sénat, *Annales*, Jan. 16, 1924, p. 256; Toynbee, *Survey*, 1924, pp. 338-339.

implications of this plan, or the detail of the negotiations that preceded its adoption. Only the work of Belgian experts and the contributions of their country will be considered.

The Belgian representatives on this Dawes committee, Janssen, Houtart, and Francqui, rendered great service to the cause of peace by their suggestions and by their spirit of cooperation.[66] It was Francqui who proposed inviting the German expert Schacht to participate in the discussions, as it was he who the previous May had awakened the idea of a mortgage on German industry and a new Reichsbank.[67]

While Francqui and his colleagues were giving valuable technical cooperation within the committee, Theunis and Hymans, now Belgian premier and foreign minister respectively, were taking steps to pave the way for the adoption of the committee's report.[68] By February their government had made the decision to act on the report and to evacuate the Ruhr regardless of the action taken by France, although it would prefer to act in concert with its ally, and above all, to restore the Anglo-French entente.[69]

Hymans and Theunis were indefatigable in their efforts to carry out this policy, but their work would have come to naught had not new leaders been raised to power in both France and Great Britain.

---

[66] Charles G. Dawes, *A Journal of Reparations* (London, 1939), p. 50, entry of Jan. 20, 1924. This constructive attitude was part of a deliberate Belgian policy as well as Francqui's own wish; Fletcher to Hughes, *Reparations*, Jan. 7, 1924, IA, 185.

[67] Dawes, *Journal*, p. 32; Georges Janson, "Emile Francqui, l'homme d'état," *Flambeau*, XVIII, (1935), 678-680. Young's biographer gives a good picture of Francqui's personality: "Emile Francqui the Belgian, a man of big affairs, one of the richest in his country, a keen practical mind: 'one of the best minds I ever came in contact with' Mr. Young has said of him. . . . He had a talent for shattering over calculations, too finely spun arguments, bringing them down to earth in homely illustrations. . . ." Ida M. Tarbell, *Owen D. Young, a new type of industrial leader* (N.Y.1932), pp. 189-190.

[68] See Dawes, *Journal*, 78-82, entry of Feb. 8, 1924; and Rufus Dawes, *The Dawes Plan in the making* (Indianapolis, 1925), pp. 142-145.

[69] Dawes, *Journal*, pp. 120-121, entry of Feb. 24, 1924, report of a conversation between Dawes and Van de Vyvere, Belgian minister of reconstruction; and p. 223, entry of April 4, 1924, report of conversation with Theunis.

The first of these changes came in January when the Labour party, committed to a policy of international cooperation, formed a Cabinet headed by Ramsay MacDonald.

Meanwhile on April 7 the Dawes report was published, to be officially adopted by the Reparations Commission eight days later. The essence of the plan contained in this report can be briefly stated. During the first five years after the adoption of the plan Germany was to pay annuities which in the fifth year would reach the normal amount of 2,500,000,000 marks. This sum was to be raised partly from taxation, partly from railroad and industrial earnings. After the normal annuity was attained if there was a growth in prosperity in Germany the payments would show proportionate increase. In order to prevent the financial upset that might arise as a result of the large purchases of foreign exchange by the German government which the payments would entail, elaborate precautions were taken. The sum in marks raised by Germany was to be delivered to an Agent General for Reparations, who could only transform it into foreign exchange if no harm would result thereby to German currency. Important details of the plan included a new Bank of Issue and a new currency, an international loan of 800,000,000 marks to help the bank and to finance the first deliveries in kind, and foreign control of certain revenues, as the tax on tobacco, beer, and other luxuries.[70]

On April 24, Belgium, first of all the Allies, formally announced its adhesion in the following terms:

The Belgian government received the reports of the committees of experts with the greatest interest. The indisputable competence of their members, their anxiety to be objective, and the collaboration of America, give their unanimous conclusions a great moral authority which the Belgian government is quick to recognize. It has the honor to inform the Reparations Commission that it is prepared to adopt the conclusions of the experts in their entirety,

[70] *Reparations,* IB.

in view of a practicable and equable solution of the problem of reparations.

It expects the Reparations Commission to examine the laws and decrees which it has asked the German government to submit to it, which are necessary to insure the complete execution of the experts' plan.

The Belgian Government hopes that the Reparations Commission will prepare the measures whose details were left to its care by the report, so that, its task being ended, the plan can be promptly executed by common agreement among the Allied governments.

The Belgian government will at once make contact with its Allies.

HYMANS, THEUNIS[71]

The last sentence of the note showed that Hymans desired to discuss the matter directly with the heads of the Allied governments, a procedure which he considered preferable to the slower method of written negotiations.[72] MacDonald, who shared this sentiment, responded by inviting Hymans and Theunis to the prime ministers' country seat at Chequers, forestalling every objection by suggesting that they consult with Poincaré before leaving the Continent. On April 28 the two Belgians were in Paris, and four days later they met MacDonald, who took the lead in the ensuing negotiations. After talking the situation over with him, they recrossed the Channel for a second visit with Poincaré. All the details of these meetings, as well as of the other private discussions carried on during the spring and early summer of 1924, have never been made public; yet a certain amount of information has been released, enough, at least, to show the stand taken by each country. In his memoirs Stresemann wrote that the Belgians prevailed upon Poin-

[71] Chambre, *Annales,* July 10, 1924, II, 1826.
[72] Sometime during the week preceding April 26 Hymans had suggested to MacDonald and Poincaré the advisability of holding conferences at this time. The prime minister's invitation was the outcome of this. Dunn to Hughes, April 26, 1924, *Reparations,* II A, 11. Poincaré's invitation to Hymans sprang from a desire to secure Belgian support for an obstructionist policy; Logan to Hughes, April 24, *Reparations,* IB, 135-136.

caré to accept the plan "in a spirit of conciliation," and on the understanding that the German government would give its full cooperation.[73]

On May 2 Hymans and Theunis returned to England to report to MacDonald. Together they laid plans for a small Allied conference which would decide upon the arrangements necessary for putting the experts' suggestions into operation. At the same time they acquiesced in the Prime Minister's desire for the withdrawal of economic sanctions.[74]

After another visit to Poincaré, the two Belgian statesmen accepted Mussolini's invitation to confer with him in Milan. There on May 18 they secured Italian support for the proposed Allied conference.[75]

In France, meanwhile, there had been a general election, resulting in a victory for the Left, and the overthrow of Poincaré. His successor, Edouard Herriot, who assumed office on June 14, was much more favorable to the Dawes plan, but he had to be constantly on his guard not to alienate French opinion. As soon as he had obtained a vote of confidence he left Paris to confer with MacDonald. Together the two statesmen drafted a "moral pact" stipulating that the Dawes plan would be put into operation as soon as the Reparations Commission reported that Germany agreed to the necessary legislation; that France had suppressed the system of productive guarantees; and finally, that a conference was summoned to meet in London to discuss the plan, and it alone. After leaving England Herriot passed through Brussels to consult with Theunis.[76] On June 23 the invitations were sent out to the Allied nations for a conference scheduled to open on July 16, 1924, in London.[77]

[73] Stresemann, I, 333.
[74] MacDonald to Graham; June 23, 1924, Great Britain, Parliamentary Papers, 1924, Cmd. 2184, p. 3. doc. no. 1; Chambre, Annales, July 10, 1924, pp. 1825-1826.
[75] Toynbee, Survey, 1924, pp. 364-365.
[76] D'Abernon, An Ambassador of Peace, III, 70-71.

Then came a series of misunderstandings which threatened to destroy the precarious entente so recently established among the Allies. Reports circulated in Belgium and France that MacDonald had offered these countries a military guarantee in case Germany should evade the obligations imposed by the plan. On June 26 he publicly denied the truth of these statements to the House of Commons.[78] More serious was the difference that arose over the question of sanctions. The British felt that the new arrangements should be such as to preclude the possibility for independent action by France. They wished, moreover, that the question of default should not be decided by the Reparations Commission, where France had a preponderant voice, but by some other body in which an American should have not only a voice but a vote.[79] MacDonald's statement to this effect in the House on July 7, aroused a storm of protest across the Channel. To counteract this the Prime Minister hurried to Paris. His consultation with Herriot resulted in a compromise whereby the British agreed to allow the Reparations Commission, with the addition of an American, the power to declare Germany in default, and the French government agreed to forego discussion of inter-Allied debts in connection with the Dawes plan.[80] The French Senate then authorized the premier to participate in the London meeting.

On July 16, 1924, delegates from ten nations met in London to attend the long awaited conference. Three committees were set up, the first to deal with the difficult problem of German default, the second to consider the best way of restoring German economy, the third to plan ways and means of effecting the transfer of payments from Berlin to the creditors. During the next few weeks

---

[77] MacDonald to Graham, June 23, 1924, Great Britain, *Parliamentary Papers*, 1924, Cmd. 2184, pp. 3-7.
[78] Great Britain, *Parl. Debates*, 5 ser., CLXXIII, 2310.
[79] MacDonald to Graham, June 23, Great Britain, *Parliamentary Papers*, 1924, Cmd. 2184.
[80] Great Britain, *Parl. Debates*, 5 ser., CLXXIII, 2463-2466.

while these committees were engaged in their arduous technical tasks, some of the serious problems facing them were also under discussion by the representatives of the leading nations. This council of five, as it was called, included MacDonald, Herriot, Theunis, Stefani, and Kellogg. At times Hymans and James Logan, the American observer on the Reparations Commission, were also present. Unfortunately no records were kept of these meetings, at which the chief problems of the conference were settled.[81] From the fragmentary minutes of the committee meetings it is possible to glean some idea of their proceedings, particularly in the first committee, which was the most significant from the political point of view.

At its first meeting a serious disagreement arose between Snowden, Chancellor of the Exchequer, and Hymans. Snowden proposed that the committee should consider the whole problem of securing the German loan so as to safeguard the bondholders. Hymans disagreed, believing that the terms of reference limited the committee to the discussion of measures to be taken should Germany default. Although Hymans had the support of Pirelli, the Italian delegate, in the end Snowden's stubbornness won the day.[82]

At the next two meetings the debates centered around the opposing British and French conceptions of the use of sanctions. The British delegates submitted a draft report providing for the creation of an independent body of experts, including one American, to

<hr>

[81] James Logan, "Memorandum for Professor Adams, The London Conference, Paris September 5, 1924." From a manuscript in the James A. Logan papers, Hoover Library on War, Revolution, and Peace, Stanford University. A very much expurgated edition of the minutes of the conference with the more heated arguments nearly entirely omitted was published by the British government as a white paper; Great Britain, *Parliamentary Papers,* 1924, Cmd. 2270. The same documents, in French translation, were published by the Belgian government: Belgium, ministère des affaires étrangères, *Documents diplomatiques relatifs aux réparations* (*conférence de Londres du 16 juillet au 16 août 1924*) (Brussels, 1924).

[82] London Reparation Conference July-August, 1924, *Proceedings* (London, 1924, I, 289-292. (Hereafter cited as *L.R.C.*)

decide whether or not, in any disputed case, Germany was default-
ing on the obligations imposed by the Dawes plan. The French
draft left this important decision to the Reparations Commission,
which was largely under French control.[83] Although this draft did
concede that an American should be added to the membership of
the commission, it at the same time contained a clause guaranteeing
the rights of all the creditors under the Versailles treaty, which in
effect would give France the right to impose sanctions independently of the other powers. On July 19, the deadlock caused by these
stipulations was broken. Theunis submitted a suggestion that the
French draft be adopted with an additional clause providing that
the creditors would agree

that they will not have recourse to sanctions unless the Reparations
Commission shall have declared a default by a reasoned decision
embodying an equally reasoned report of the Agent General for
Reparations payments.[84]

Although Niemeyer, the British treasury representative, did not
think that this went far enough, Snowden accepted it, and it was
thereupon incorporated into the committee's report.[85]

Unfortunately this report was prematurely communicated to the
press. At once the bankers, represented by Montagu Norman, governor of the Bank of England, and T. L. Lamont, spokesman of
the Morgan interests, who were to underwrite the stabilization
loan which was the keystone of the Dawes plan, protested that
they could not find investors under such terms.[86] In spite of a conference between the French delegates and the bankers on July 21,
and a meeting of Herriot, Clémentel, French finance minister,
Secretary Hughes, and Secretary Mellon (the latter two "unoffi-
cially resting" in London), little progress was made for five days.

[83] *Ibid.,* I, 290-293.
[84] *Ibid.,* I, 294.
[85] *Ibid.,* I, 268-274.
[86] Logan to Hughes, July 29, 1924, *Reparations,* II A, 98.

Then on July 27 Herriot, who had been insistent that the Germans should have no voice in the negotiations, surrendered that point. This seemed to pave the way for further concessions, and the following day the first committee met again, hoping it would be possible to agree on a more satisfactory report.

The session was stormy. Theunis had prepared a new version of his draft of July 19, according to which the Reparations Commission would have to take counsel with a committee of experts composed of some of the framers of the Dawes plan. This formula was objectionable to both French and British representatives, the former insisting that it made recourse to sanctions too difficult; the latter taking the stand that the safeguard was too weak, since the Reparations Commission was placed under no obligation to follow the advice given by the experts. The debate became acrimonious. Snowden then added a requirement that the Agent General also be consulted. When Clémentel and Hymans agreed to this, he said would accept the Theunis draft, but only if a sentence of default were made contingent upon the unanimous vote of the Commission. Clémentel flatly refused. Snowden at once withdrew his proposal, saying that nothing further could be done to reach agreement. At this point Colonel Logan, the American observer, intervened with what proved to be a valuable suggestion, namely that the whole matter of default and sanctions should be dealt with only as part of the terms and conditions of the Dawes loan. To this end the German government and the Reparations Commission should appoint representatives empowered to negotiate the question with the bankers. Although Clémentel was not too favorable to this plan, Theunis supported it so strongly that the committee adjourned to give its members time to study the proposal.

Later the same day the experts met again, but the atmosphere was not yet calm enough for clear thinking. On Clémentel's suggestion, strongly supported by Theunis, the experts agreed to delay their decision until the bankers had negotiated the terms of the loan with the German government and the Reparations Commission.[87] The French experts spent the next two days elaborating a formula which they hoped would prove acceptable to their Allies. One of its most prominent features was the establishment of an arbitral committee to decide the question of default if the Reparations Commission could not reach a unanimous decision. This plan was acceptable in itself, but Clémentel desired to include a further clause providing that

only in the event of an agreement not being arrived at between the governments in this respect, shall each of the governments resume liberty of action.[88]

This was abruptly rejected by Snowden. As it received no support from Jung, the Italian expert, or from Hymans, Clémentel finally withdrew it.

At the eighth and last meeting of the committee, the final text of the committee report was finally agreed upon, but not without another serious disagreement between Snowden and Clémentel. The former insisted that America be represented on the arbitral committee; the latter seemed to consider this suggestion as a reflection on French fairness. Hymans intervened to settle the dispute by proposing the insertion of the words "impartial and independent persons"; this might apply to Frenchmen as well as Americans, and removed all cause for argument. With the adoption of this solution the labors of the first committee came to an end.[89]

The work of the second committee having been more purely technical, its proceedings aroused little controversy. But the trans-

[87] *L.R.C.*, I, 274-283.
[88] *L.R.C.*, I, 298.
[89] *Ibid.*, I, 288-289. It was probably during this stage of the negotiations that Snowden threatened to resign. To his colleague Arthur Henderson is given the credit for soothing his feelings, for his resignation might have raised serious difficulties for MacDonald and jeopardized the success of the conference; Mary Agnes Hamilton, *Arthur Henderson, a biography* (London, 1938), p. 243.

fer problem, though equally technical, had political aspects, and created such difficulties that the third committee confined its activities to drawing up two draft reports, embodying the British and the French proposals, respectively. On August 2 the latter were adopted by the conference, after they had been amended to provide for the creation of an arbitral commission similar to that which was to judge German default.[90]

The Allies having reached agreement on these important points, the next step was to issue an invitation to the German government to send delegates to London for the International Conference. Henceforth the Belgian delegates were less in evidence, their chief preoccupation having been to work for Allied unity, which by this time was an accomplished fact.

On August 5, at the first session, the leading German representatives, Chancellor Marx and foreign minister Stresemann, were informed of the work of the inter-Allied conference and the reports of the various committees. The following day Marx presented his counter proposals, the chief clauses of which can be briefly stated. In the matter of default he refused to admit a one sided verdict by the Allies, and claimed that the agreement of the German government should also be obtained. He insisted, moreover, that default should only be established in the event of proved bad will on the part of Germany. As to the reports of the second and third committees, he said that the time had been too short for him to prepare counter proposals on such complicated technical financial problems, and asked for a further delay.

The conference then adjourned until evening, to enable the members to study Marx' suggestions. On reassembling, the delegates soon realized that they were not yet ready to discuss the matter.[91] The following morning, however, some progress was made, when the decision was adopted that "flagrant default" should

---

[90] L.R.C., I, 32-44. The third committee kept no minutes of its meetings.
[91] L.R.C., II, 155-164.

be interpreted as meaning a serious failure to meet the obligations of the Dawes plan when that failure was the result of the complicity of the German government. Stresemann also secured recognition of his demand that the amnesty to be granted those who had been arrested as a result of the Ruhr occupation should be extended to all political offenders in the occupied territories.[92] In spite of differences of opinion between Herriot and Snowden on nearly every subject discussed in the Conference, the Germans felt that progress was being made.[93]

The following day, however, a serious problem arose during the discussion of the report of the third committee. In this report, which dealt with the Transfer Committee to be set up under the Dawes plan, provision had been made for an arbitral board to decide what investments were to be made with the resources at the disposal of the Agent General. Luther, the German finance minister, was opposed to any plan whereby any neutral could control the disposal of so large a sum, saying that this matter touched upon German economic sovereignty. He also insisted that the Dawes experts had not envisaged such an arbitral board, but had suggested that the matter should be arranged between the Transfer Committee and the German government. Herriot disagreed. He pointed out that members of the Dawes committee had attended the meeting of the inter-Allied conference at which arbitration had been decided upon, and that they had said such procedure was essential to the smooth working of the plan.

Thereupon Theunis intervened with a reminder of the nature of the sum involved. As no investments could be made until the sum at the Agent General's disposal reached a total of two billion marks, and as the maximum he could receive was five billion marks, he would only have three billion to invest, a sum hardly large enough to modify German economic life. This reasoning

[92] *Ibid.*, II, 165-169.
[93] *Stresemann*, I, 378, entry of August 7, 1924.

was rejected by Snowden, who said that as the lowest figure for investment was two billion, Germany must be doubly cautious in insisting on safeguards.

Eventually it was decided to ask the experts who had served on the Dawes committee what their plan had been. Herriot gave warning that, if arbitration were rejected in this instance, it must also be rejected in other eventualities, such as the decision on default.[94]

While these financial and political questions were absorbing the attention of the main conference, the French, Belgian and German delegates were discussing the military aspects of the situation. On August 7, Breitscheid, a socialist deputy in the Reichstag, held a long conference with Herriot during which the latter asked if the Germans were willing to negotiate on the basis of Ruhr evacuation after the conclusion of military control. This was not acceptable to Stresemann, as German public opinion would not wait so long for the evacuation.[95]

French nationalists were equally intransigent, so much so that on August 9 Herriot was forced to return to Paris to confer with his cabinet. General Nollet, minister of war, refused to allow the question of evacuation to be separated from that of military control, in spite of MacDonald's resistance. Happily, the other members of the cabinet supported the premier, who returned to London with Clémentel and Nollet.[96] Herriot's success in Paris made it possible for him to continue the Ruhr negotiations. He had come to London in July believing that the question would not be raised at the conference; such was the interpretation he had given to MacDonald's statements during the preliminary conversations in June. In reality, however, the British prime minister had meant only that the subject would not form part of the agenda of the official pro-

[94] *Stresemann,* II, 175-179.

[95] *Ibid.,* I, 381-385.

[96] The surrender of the French nationalists on this occasion was attributed by D'Abernon to the wise advice given Poincaré by Secretary Hughes; D'Abernon, *Diary,* III, 84-85, entry of Aug. 8, 1924.

ceedings.[97] Although Herriot was finally induced to allow the evacuation to be discussed, he insisted that the French armies must continue the occupation for another year, until the first receipts from the plan would reach Paris.

For four days, from August 11 to August 15, the debate continued, while Herriot held fast to a minimum delay of one year. He became even more stubborn after the arrival of Loucheur, a French nationalist, who threatened to withdraw his following of forty-two deputies if any surrender were made on the question of occupation. When it became obvious that Herriot could not yield to the German demand without seriously endangering his position, he won the support of the Americans, and finally of MacDonald as well. At a three-cornered conference on August 13, Theunis tried to bring Stresemann to a realization of the situation. He pointed out that the French premier had made one very important concession, for whereas Poincaré had repeatedly stated that the occupation would last until the last pfennig was paid, his successor was willing to end it as soon as the first had been handed over. The same day Herriot expressed his belief that once the Dawes plan was actually in operation, he would be in a position to reduce either the strength of the army of occupation in the Rhineland, or the size of the occupied area, or else to make some other concession.[98] Nevertheless, until the evening of August 14, Stresemann continued his insistence that evacuation be immediate. Finally, early on August 15, he agreed to withdraw this demand, provided that the French reduce the number of troops, reform the administration of the Rhineland, and give no moral support to the Separatists. With Herriot's acceptance of these conditions, the way was paved for a speedy conclusion to the conference.[99]

The protocal of the London Conference, with annexes, initialled

[97] Ibid., III, 99, entry of Sept. 14, 1924.

[98] Stresemann, I, 388-401.

[99] Ibid., I, 401-402. Logan believed that Snowden was encouraging Stresemann to resist; Logan to Hughes, Aug. 15, 1924, Reparations, II A, 126.

on August 16 and signed August 30, provided for the adoption of the experts' plan, the establishment of arbitral commissions to settle any disputes that might arise under it, and the full restoration of Germany's economic unity. The decision taken to evacuate the Ruhr within a year was embodied in an exchange of letters between Herriot, Theunis, and Marx.[100]

One important question raised by the Dawes plan was left unsolved at London, that of the allocation of German payments. This problem was referred to a conference of Allied finance ministers, which was set to open in January, 1925, at Paris. Before they met, the subject was carefully examined by a group of financial experts, who assembled at Paris late in October.

Much of their discussion dealt with the Belgian priority, which the British claimed had by now been exhausted. The Belgian delegation, led by Camille Gutt, naturally contested this statement, bringing figures to prove that their country had received only 1,-745,000,000 gold marks, out of their 2,000,000,000 priority. The experts' report stated that this was "perhaps the most complex question" that they had been called upon to consider. They were able to give no recommendation to their governments since the sums received were not yet in their hands.[101]

The question of the repayment of the priority added to the complexity of the situation. The British maintained that the reimbursement, as provided for by the Spa agreements, would reduce the Belgian percentage to about two and one-fourth percent of the Dawes payments. Gutt, on the other hand, claimed that his country was entitled to two and seven-tenths percent of each of the annuities. The French tried to take an intermediate position, the Italians agreed with the British, and only Colonel Logan, the American

---

[100] *L.R.C.*, II, 122-154.

[101] Committee of experts entrusted with the preparation of the Conference of Finance Ministers to be held on January 6, 1925, *Report*, p. 19.

expert, was in sympathy with the Belgians.[102] His stand was the result of an astute bargain. The State Department was most eager to have support for its claim to a percentage of the Dawes payments in order to cover the costs of the American army of occupation, which had long since returned to the United States. In return for strong backing when this topic was argued by the experts, Logan worked for the Belgian contentions, which he described as "well founded."[103]

Finally Gutt and his colleagues, while maintaining their principles and insisting that after the extinction of the priority the Belgian share should be fixed at six percent, made the following proposals: They offered to accept payment of the balance of the two billion marks over the first two years of the Dawes plan, to drop the claim to arrears, and to renounce the eight percent agreed on at Spa until the priority should have been repaid.[104]

This was the situation when on January 7, 1925, the Finance ministers opened their conference at Paris. Theunis made a gallant and successful fight for his country's rights. He first showed that although Belgium had received nearly fifty percent of all German payments to date, these sums had by no means covered the cost of restoration, so that he could not consider waiving the priority in order to assign a larger share to France and Great Britain. Having won this argument, he proceeded to show that even after the two billion had been exhausted, his country, which, he said, had gained very little territory from the war, should be given four and one-half percent, not two and one-half percent of the annuities. This reduction of the Spa percentage would cover the reimbursement of the priority. Again he was victorious, and both the stip-

---

[102] Committee of experts entrusted with the preparation of the Conference of Finance Ministers to be held on January 6, 1925, *Annexes to report.*

[103] Logan to Hughes, November 26, 1924, *Reparations,* III, 21; Phillips to Logan, Dec. 4, 1924, *ibid.,* III, 30; Logan to Hughes, Dec. 12, 1924, *ibid.,* III, 44.

[104] Committee of Experts, *Report,* pp. 19-20.

ulations he desired were contained in the agreement signed on January 14, 1925, by the thirteen allied creditors. Repayment of the Belgian war debt was also provided for at Paris; five percent of all German payments was allotted to this claim, 46 percent of this amount going to France, 42 percent to Great Britain, and twelve percent to Belgium, on account of its debt to the United States.[105] This last arrangement was necessary because the United States refused to accept the money directly from Germany, lest any connection between war debts and reparations be thereby acknowledged.

Thus was the Ruhr adventure liquidated. It had brought Belgium only slightly more than 300,000,000 marks in receipts,[106] but a much larger harvest of ill-will, and the loss of the special prestige that it had gained by the statesmanlike attitude of its representatives during the immediate post-war period. To quote the British members of the Reparations Commission:

Now that the Belgians have definitely lined up with the French [by joining the Ruhr occupation], they have surrendered their position of 'compromiser' which they held since the Armistice. In the past the Belgians have been in an especially strong position due to the absence of an American vote in the [Reparation] Commission. They held a position enabling them to intervene and suggest the compromise between the divergent French and British points of view which have arisen in the past, and incidentally to reap considerable national benefits from such position. . . . Belgium is a small Power and is now definitely relegated to the position of a small Power.[107]

[105] Chambre, *Annales,* Jan. 15, 1925, pp. 348-351; Allied Powers, Reparation Commission, *Agreement regarding the distribution of the Dawes Annuities* (14th January 1925) (Paris, 1925), pp. 8-9.

[106] The figure adopted by the commission of experts which met in Paris to decide the allocation of the Dawes annuities was 393,900,000 gold marks. The Belgians on this commission gave the figure 317,200,000 gold marks. Committee of experts, *Annexes to report,* pp. 23, 17. Most of this came during the first year, for by December 31, 1923, the Belgian government claimed to have received 262,074,413 gold marks, without deducting army costs. Chambre, *Documents,* May 15, 1924, p. 1288.

[107] Introduction, *Reparations,* IA, xxii xxiii.

Happily, during the next few years there was little need for any power to play the role of pacifier, since there were no serious problems dividing the Allies. The most successful as well as the most uneventful of the three phases through which the reparation problem passed was that inaugurated by the Dawes plan. Yet there were certain defects implicit in this plan, such as the need of foreign loans to balance the German budget, the danger inherent in a project which placed what was essentially an economic transaction on a political plane, the insecurity resulting from ignorance as to the total amount Germany would pay. The need for revision of the plan was pointed out by the Agent General in his annual reports,[108] but not until the summer of 1928 were any steps taken to bring about such revision. By that time the Dawes plan had been operating for nearly four years; two more were to elapse before the adoption of its successor, the Young Plan.

The first step in the series of conversations that led eventually to the Young Plan was taken early in 1928, when Stresemann raised the question of the evacuation of the Rhineland, which he hoped might take place before the time limit set by the Versailles treaty. The French Government replied to the overture by stating that the occupation had been planned as a means of guaranteeing German reparation payments, and that early evacuation could be considered only if some other guarantees were substituted. The Belgians not only supported this condition, but added a reservation of their own, insisting that any concessions regarding the Rhineland would also be dependent on a settlement of the troublesome question of the "occupation marks."[109]

It will be remembered that in 1919 the Belgian and French delegates to the Paris Peace Conference had tried to write into the treaty a clause forcing Germany to redeem the currency brought

[108] Allied Powers, Agent General for reparation payments, *Report of the agent general for reparation payments, annual report,* 1925, 1926, 1927 (Berlin, 1925-1927), p. 2; p. 106; p. 171.

[109] Chambre, *CRA,* Jan. 29, 1930, p. 137.

into the invaded portions of their respective countries. The two
Allies had agreed to act in concert in this respect, but when French
support proved unavailing, the Belgian government opened separate negotiations with Germany. Before the end of the year it
was rumored that Francqui, the eminent financier, had signed an
agreement with Erzberger. At once France protested, claiming that
by granting a special advantage to one Ally, Germany had diminished its power to pay reparations.[110]

Although Belgium's right to negotiate the question separately
was eventually admitted, the victory was rendered sterile by the
refusal of the German government to ratify the Erzberger agreement.[111] This action was due less to a desire to repudiate the obligation of making restitution, than to a well-founded belief that
the claim was unwarrantably large. In the first flush of victory the
Belgian government had redeemed the marks at the ratio of one
mark to one and a quarter francs. As the mark was then worth
about sixty-five or seventy centimes, there had naturally been a
considerable amount of smuggling, which had been facilitated by
the lax supervision exercised by the authorities. In all about 6,-
109,000,000 marks had been redeemed, about one billion of which
the Germans claimed had been fraudulently imported.[112]

By the summer of 1920 the Belgian government was willing
to make some concessions, and in July during the conference at
Spa reopened negotiations. The Allies, who at first were hesitant,
finally gave their approbation, and a second convention was signed.
Again the German government refused to ratify.[113]

An agreement reached in September, 1921, also failed of ratification, and six months elapsed before anything further could be
done. In April, 1922, after Belgium had made further concessions,
another convention was drawn up. According to premier Theunis

[110] Note from French Delegation Dec. 7, 1919, *HD* 109, Appendix 4.
[111] Chambre, *Annales,* Oct. 24, 1922, II, 1839.
[112] Franck, *La stabilisation monétaire en Belgique,* p. 10.
[113] Chambre, *Annales,* July 23, 1920, II, 2169.

he had agreed to hold Germany responsible for only 4,000,000,000 marks, with interest at two per cent, and had granted a moratorium for five years. Moreover he was willing to return all the property seized under the Versailles treaty which was not as yet liquidated.[114] This arrangement came to nothing, since the next month Germany was forced to request a moratorium, and the mark became almost valueless on the international exchange.

The events of the next three years caused the mark question to recede into the background, whence it only emerged in 1925, during the abortive negotiations for the return of Eupen and Malmédy to Germany.

In the reopening of the subject of reparations in September, 1928, Hymans saw his opportunity. During the Assembly meeting at Geneva, representatives of the interested powers discussed the German request for a settlement of the still unresolved problems of disarmament, evacuation of the Rhineland, and reparation. On September 16, after three secret conclaves, the delegates issued a statement of their agreement to the following measures:

The opening of official negotiations relating to the request put forward by the German Chancellor regarding the early evacuation of the Rhineland; 2. The necessity for a complete and definite settlement of the reparations problem, and for the constitution for this purpose of a committee of experts to be nominated by the six governments; 3. The acceptance of the principle of the constitution of a committee of verification and conciliation.[115]

When agreeing to this Hymans made one reservation; the marks question must be solved as part of the final settlement. Although unsuccessful in his effort to put this subject on the agenda of the discussions among the powers, he succeeded in obtaining their acquiescence to separate Belgo-German negotiations. This position was officially stated by the Belgian government in its note of No-

[114] Chambre, *Annales,* Oct. 24, 1922, II, 1839.
[115] *New York Times,* September 17, 1928.

vember 8, accepting the German request for a committee of experts. The second condition laid down in the note was that the Belgian share in reparations payments in the future should be no less than the receipts under the Dawes plan.[116]

Meanwhile the French government had announced that it would accept a change in the schedule of payments only if France's share in the revised allotments were large enough to cover both war damages to French property and the service on the debts of Great Britain and the United States. The British and Italian governments likewise maintained that their reparations receipts would have to be sufficient to enable them to meet their war debt obligations. Their demands in this respect were reinforced by the publication in January, 1929, of Parker Gilbert's report, wherein he clearly showed that there was no reasonable doubt that Germany was quite able to pay the Dawes annuities, which were, so the report said, not unreasonably high in comparison with the cost of liquidating the war in the Allied countries.[117]

Under these conditions there seemed little likelihood that Germany would be granted substantial reductions, as the experts, theoretically not bound by instructions, would hardly deviate from the known wishes of their respective governments. Such proved to be the case. When the experts met it was evident that they were not ready to make concessions, but, on the contrary, were prepared to insist upon increasing their countries' shares of German payments. For some time it proved difficult to persuade either the Allied or the German experts to propose a definite figure for the standard annuity. Early in April, when Young succeeded in getting the representatives of the creditors to state their demands, it was found that the sum total of the amounts asked was 2,900,000,000

[116] Chambre, CRA, Jan. 29, 1930, pp. 137-138 and 1928, p. 125; Sénat, Documents, Feb. 27, 1929, doc. no. 88.

[117] Allied Powers, Agent General for reparation payments, Annual Report 1929, pp. 130-143.

marks annually, a sum greater than that due under the Dawes plan. On the other hand the Germans refused to consider any payment larger than 1,650,000,000 marks, to be paid only if Germany had direct contact with East Prussia and access to raw materials.

As both groups refused to withdraw their demands, the conference nearly broke down. An adjournment caused by the death of one of the British delegates gave a much-needed breathing spell to the over-excited delegates. When the committee met again the Germans asked Young to assist them in preparing a set of figures which would meet both Germany's capacity to pay and the requirements of the Allies.

The annuities suggested by the Americans: 1,675,000,000 marks for the first year, increasing to 2,050,600,000 for the thirty-seven year period, were those finally adopted in the experts' report. The crisis was safely weathered, thanks in large measure to the tact of Owen D. Young.[118]

The conference seemed to be nearing the end of its labors with a workable scheme for settling the reparation problem, when Francqui and Gutt, the Belgian experts, again raised the mark claim. They had brought up the question in March, only to meet a categorical refusal of the German government to discuss the matter.[119] Now, in May, acting on instruction from Brussels, Francqui and Gutt insisted that if the new plan did not provide for direct German purchase of the marks, it must allot to Belgium a sum large enough to cover the cost of redemption, over and above the amount necessary to meet the service on the Belgian debt to the United States. Again Young saved the situation. He supported the Germans in their contention that the committee had no authority to discuss the question, while at the same time he persuaded them to promise to open separate negotiations with the Belgians. This solution was

[118] Thomas W. Lamont, "The Final Reparations Settlement," *Foreign Affairs*, VIII (1930), 346-348.
[119] *Stresemann*, III, 420-421, letter of March 31, 1929.

embodied in an exchange of notes. All parties understood, however, that, if these separate negotiations failed to reach a satisfactory conclusion, Francqui and Gutt would not sign the report of the Young committee.[120]

The German government at once took up the question with the Belgian embassy at Berlin, where the first exchanges of views were so promising that on June 4 Francqui consented to sign the report, provided it was understood that the plan embodied in it would not become operative until the Belgo-German negotiations had reached a successful conclusion. This understanding was contained in Annex VI of the report.[121] The negotiations officially opened in June, soon after the publication of the Young plan, and on July 13 an agreement was reached. By its terms Belgium, which had claimed reimbursement for 6,000,000,000 gold marks, was to receive 520,000,000 gold marks, and in return was to restore all German private property seized in Belgium during the war, and not yet liquidated. The question being satisfactorily settled, on July 24, 1929, the Belgian government officially accepted the Young Plan as outlined in the experts' report.[122]

Before the plan could be put into operation, it was necessary for the creditor nations to come to agreements among themselves on the modality of applying the plan, and on other kindred subjects. These matters were taken up at a conference which opened on August 6, 1929, at The Hague. It at once set up two committees, one to deal with political, the other with financial questions. In the discussions of the first committee the Belgian representatives expressed their government's intention to evacuate the Rhineland

[120] Wheeler-Bennett, *The Reparation Settlement*, pp. 91-92; Chambre, *CRA,* Jan. 29, 1930, p. 138.

[121] *Ibid.,* p. 139; United States, Committee of experts on reparations, nominated January 10, 1929, *Report of Committee of experts on reparations with annexes and concurrent memorandum; also settlement of Belgian mark claim* (Washington, 1929).

[122] Toynbee, *Survey,* 1930, p. 495.

as soon as possible, without waiting for the Young plan to come into effect. As this stand was in harmony with that taken by the British government, the Belgians fully supported Arthur Henderson, British foreign secretary, in his successful efforts to work out a compromise between the German demand for speedy evacuation and French reluctance to surrender a valuable pledge of future payments. When Stresemann wrote Briand that he would be forced to resign, Henderson redoubled his efforts and prevailed upon the French to sign a convention binding them to evacuate the occupied territory by June 30, 1930, five years before the date set by the Versailles treaty.[123]

The financial problems awaiting solution by the conference were even more difficult to settle. Philip Snowden, Chancellor of the Exchequer and spokesman of the British government on financial matters, maintained the policy first enunciated in the Balfour Note of 1923, of requiring the sum total of German reparations payments and of Allied payments to Great Britain to be equal to British payments to the United States under the debt funding agreement. The Young plan provided reparation payments large enough to cover current British remittances to the United States, but too small to cover those already made by Britain to the United States before the Allies had begun the repayment of their debt to Great Britain. Consequently Snowden refused to accept the new plan as it stood. The figures upon which he based his refusal were challenged by a French expert, M. Cheron. The resulting argument between the two men nearly caused an international incident. The intervention of Baron Houtart, Belgian delegate and president of the financial committee, prevented a disgraceful scene at the meeting itself, and gradually feeling cooled down, but Snowden stubbornly held to his point.

[123] Great Britain, *Parliamentary Papers*, 1929-1930, Cmd. 3417; Chambre, *CRA*, Dec. 12, 1929, p. 34; Toynbee, *Survey*, 1929, pp. 181-182; Hamilton, *Arthur Henderson*, p. 316.

The experts convened to work out a compromise which would be acceptable to all parties. Better than anyone else they realized that the Young plan was a series of delicately balanced reciprocal concessions, and that to vary its proposals to the advantage of any one state would immediately disrupt the equilibrium of the whole. The recommendations which they presented, while taking cognizance of this indisputable fact, pointed a way out of the impasse. They advised increasing the British share, not by an alteration of the schedule of payments, but by an agreement whereby the other creditors would transfer a portion of their receipts to Great Britain. To this Snowden assented, on condition that the total received be no less than 40,000,000 marks annually. Although willing to make some payments to Great Britain, the other Allies balked at this sum. Jaspar, president of the conference, then assumed the thankless and difficult role of mediator between the obdurate British Chancellor and the representatives of the other powers.

From August 17 to August 26 the situation remained unchanged. At least five proposals, each offering more than its predecessor, were made by the delegates of France, Belgium, and Italy; each of them was categorically rejected by the unyielding Briton.[124]

On August 27 the climax was reached. By this time sixty per cent of the British claim had been conceded by the Allies, who felt that they could not afford to grant more. Snowden held his ground in refusing to settle for less than the terms he had previously demanded. The situation seemed hopeless when, late that night, under pretext of airing the conference room, Henderson separated the British delegates from the others. He had realized that if any concessions were to be made, the other delegates would find it easier to make them in writing than to express them verbally.[125]

This proved to be the case. During the next few hours Jaspar

---

[124] Snowden, *Autobiography*, II, 804-817.
[125] Hamilton, *Henderson*, 318.

shuttled back and forth between the rooms of the two sets of delegates. By midnight the proposals he brought Snowden were within 240,000 marks of the British demands, but still the Chancellor held firm.[126]

Early in the morning of August 28 a solution was found, by which the fifth Dawes annuity would run for five months longer than had been planned, and the 200,000,000 marks thus raised would be transferred to Great Britain. A readjustment in the dates of paying the monthly instalments brought the amount transferred to the British treasury up to the necessary sum.[127]

Henderson had already persuaded the Germans to promise to accept any settlement on which the creditor powers reached agreement. Convinced that such settlement was impossible, they had given the desired promise, only to find themselves bound to terms they were reluctant to accept. With no way out of the predicament, they grudgingly acceded to the agreement.[128] Thus ended the most dangerous crisis; henceforth the sucess of the Young Plan was practically certain. However, as there were several technical questions requiring further expert study, the conference adjourned at the end of August, to meet again on January 3, 1930.

The final settlement arrived at by this second Hague Conference reduced the German annuity from 2,500,000,000 to an average annual payment of 2,050,000,000 gold marks. Of this sum 612,-000,000 marks were unconditional payments; the remainder was subject to postponement should the financial situation require it.

[126] When Snowden refused this offer Jaspar was in despair. "He said, 'What do you say when a horse will not run for your Derby?' 'You mean "scratched."' 'Yes,' he said, 'I am "scratched," I cannot do more. You have emptied our pockets.' 'Go through your pockets again,' I said, very kindly, 'I am sure you will find enough to cover what remains between us.' 'You told me you had a kind heart,' he said. 'You are a bit too hard. I have never met a man like you before. You are a new type.'" Snowden, *Autobiography*, II, 818-821.

[127] Harold G. Moulton and Leo Pasvolsky, *War Debts and World Prosperity* (New York, 1932), p. 205.

[128] Hamilton, *Henderson*, p. 317.

France received the lion's share, 500,000,000 marks, of the unconditional part of the annuity; the British Empire 55,000,000 marks;
Italy, 42,000,000; and Japan, Jugoslavia and Portugal shared the
remaining 15,000,000 marks. Belgium's part came entirely from
the conditional portion of the annuity, payments in kind, and receipts under the marks agreement; on the other hand the 8 per cent
allotted at Spa was restored.[129] This meant that after meeting its
obligations to the United States and Great Britain, Belgium would
have a balance of 782,000,000 francs to cover the cost of reconstruction, 89,000,000 francs more than the Dawes plan had provided.[130]

When these Hague agreements were presented to the Belgian
Parliament in April, 1930, they aroused little enthusiasm. By that
date the depression was making itself felt throughout Europe, and
it was obvious that the conditional payments could not be met. On
the other hand, there was no likelihood that the decisions made by
the Great Powers would be changed. The Catholic Senator Van
Overburgh expressed the opinion of many of his countrymen when
he said that he realized the necessity of ratification, but that he
could not dissimulate his disappointment at the agreements.[131] In

---

[129] Belgium did not participate in the "Young loan," and Jaspar feared that
in the event of German default on the conditional payments, his country would
receive only the small amounts due in kind or under the marks agreement. To
remedy this he negotiated with Tardieu, the French foreign minister, a convention whereby if Germany defaulted, France would transfer to Belgium 6 per
cent of the proceeds of the Young loan.

When Germany repudiated all reparations claims, Belgium invoked this Jas-
par-Tardieu agreement, but France was unwilling to honor it. For several years
no settlement was made, until finally in 1937 the two governments referred
the matter to a Dutch umpire. He pronounced in favor of France, on the ground
that since 1934 Germany had made no tranfers of any kind to the Bank of
International Settlements. As, however, some payments had been made on the
Young loan in 1932 and 1933, in December 1937 the French government
agreed to remit 73,000,000 francs to Belgium. Sénat, *Documents*, April 1, 1938,
doc. no. 137, Annex III, pp. 2-4.

[130] Chambre, *CRA*, Jan. 20, 1930, pp. 140-143.

[131] *Ibid.*, April 3, 1940, pp. 281-282.

the Chamber the only opposition was voiced by the Flemish
Nationalists, who abstained from voting, and by the Communist
Jaquemotte, who cast the one negative vote.[132]

The Young Plan was not destined to yield Belgium, or the other
creditors, more than a small fraction of what its clauses had promised. This third period of reparations turned out to be one of default, then repudiation, by Germany. The world depression, instead of abating, became more alarming; and, as the stream of international trade diminished, the sources whence the German treasury procured the gold needed for the payment of reparations dried
up with it. This state of affairs was soon obvious to all observers, but
the European governments insisted that they were powerless to
grant Germany any concessions, since they themselves had to meet
their obligations to the United States.

The action of President Hoover, on June 21, 1931, in suggesting
a one-year moratorium on all intergovernmental payments, was the
first practical step taken in the direction of international recovery.
However, the realization of the President's proposal required not
only the consent of Congress, but the cooperation of all the governments concerned. The idea of moratorium was not welcomed
in Belgium, where many had not forgotten the wartime promise
of full reparation.[133] As, however, many also feared that German
default was inevitable, and that unless the moratorium were accepted, Belgian payments to the United States would continue
while nothing was received from Germany, Hoover's proposal was
finally accepted, with the proviso that payments under the mark
agreement should be excluded from its working.[134] Other nations
also made difficulties, but on July 6, 1931, President Hoover was

---

[132] Chambre, CRA, April 10, 1930, pp. 499-501; 504.
[133] Sénat, CRA, June 23, 1931, p. 383.
[134] Sénat, CRA, July 16, 1931, p. 520; John Wheeler Wheeler-Bennet, The
Wreck of Reparations, being the political background of the Lausanne Agreements, 1932 (New York, 1933), p. 55; Chambre, CRA, June 24, 1931, p. 641,
July 3 1931, pp. 712-717.

able to announce that all the important creditor powers had subscribed. The British government then called a conference of experts to meet in London in July, for the purpose of discussing the technical details involved in the application of the moratorium. Several disastrous bank failures which intensified the crisis occurred before the meeting, causing the experts to feel that their discussions would be fruitless. They therefore adjourned in order to give a seven-power conference of statesmen the opportunity to deal with the situation. After four days of debate which eventually resulted in the drawing up of the standstill agreements to relieve the situation in Germany, the conference disbanded. The policy of Belgium, to accept the moratorium but insist on the marks agreement, was personally directed by King Albert, who left Switzerland in the midst of his vacation to take the helm. To keep the country united he asked the newspapers to remain silent on the issues involved until after a settlement was reached.[135]

The experts then reassembled, this time to work until August 11. The main lines of the agreement they reached can be summed up briefly. All European intergovernmental debts affected by the moratorium were to be repaid in ten annuities with interest at 3 percent (later raised to 4 per cent). German service on the Dawes and Young loans to continue; other payments were to be postponed. The experts recognized the justice of the claim of the Belgian government to a continuance of payments under the German mark agreement, yet the arrangements made at London meant for Belgium a further loss of £2,400,000 despite the concession.[136] All told, Belgium received under the Young Plan only 194,411,-909.60 gold marks, bringing the total of Belgian receipts from

---

[135] *Indépendance Belge,* August 8, 1931.

[136] Toynbee, *Survey,* 1932, pp. 97-116. This claim was also recognized by the German government, which on August 11, 1931, confirmed the oral promise given on July 31, that the payments would be continued; Great Britain, *Parliamentary Papers,* 1931, Cmd. 3947, pp. 28-29.

Germany to 721,911,179.01 gold marks,[137] a far cry from the astronomical sum, approximating 30,000,000,000 gold marks, once hoped for by the more optimistic, and nearly 18,000,000,000 gold marks less than the total amount spent by Belgium for reconstruction.

Before the end of the moratorium year the powers met again at Lausanne, Switzerland, on June 16, 1932, to discuss the resumption of payments. Renkin, Belgian premier and minister of finances, reiterated his country's claim to special consideration. He pointed out the juridical basis of this claim. Then he showed how particularly damaging to Belgium's interests would be the annulment of all intergovernmental debts, including reparations, for full cancellation would give Belgium no such advantage as it would give France, because the Belgian war debt to France and Great Britain had been assumed by Germany. Consequently, cancellation would mean for Belgium the end of much-needed reparations receipts scarcely compensated by the annulment of the debt to the United States. The premier then made an appeal for the end of "closed economies," and asked that the work of the conference be undertaken in a constructive spirit.

During the course of the negotiations the Belgian delegates, chief among whom was the veteran Francqui, succeeded in obtaining three concessions for their country: first, the reductions in German reparations were not to apply to the payments made under the Belgo-German marks agreement; second, the British government consented to consider the Belgian reconstruction loan and the 1916 loan to the Congo as war debts, to be given special consideration; and third, Belgium was alloted a cash annuity corresponding to the receipts

---

[137] United States, Office of the Commissioner of Accounts and Deposits, *Memorandum covering the indebtedness of foreign governments and showing the total payments made by Germany under the Dawes and Young Plans* (Washington, 1939), p. 36.

the other creditor nations would hold under the workings of the Young Plan loan.[138]

These concessions were important in view of the fact that the Lausanne Conference scaled down the total amount owed by Germany to 3,000,000 Reichsmarks, with the possibility of even further reductions, should economic necessity require them.[139] Although by the Gentlemen's Agreement of July 9 the operation of the Lausanne Protocol was made contingent upon a reduction of the inter-Allied debt to the United States,[140] the reparations question was in reality closed. In January, 1933, Hitler became Chancellor of Germany. No further reparations payments were made.[141]

---

[138] Chambre, CRA, July 13, 1932, pp. 893-895; Janson, "Emile Francqui," loc. cit., p. 694.

[139] Great Britain, Parliamentary Papres, 1932-1933, Cmd. 4126.

[140] Ibid., Cmd. 4129.

[141] Although after 1933 there were still receipts listed under the caption "Receipts of Reparation" in the Annuaire Statistique, an examination of the details given in the annual budget of Ways and Means shows that these figures relate to payments made by Belgians to the Office of Reparations, or to the liquidation of various reconstruction services. Cf. Annuaire Statistique, 1938, p. 137; Chambre, Documents, 1934, doc. no. 41, pp. 50-52. The question of German payments under the marks agreement was finally settled by a convention signed on July 27, 1935. It provided that part of the liquid assets constituting the exchange value of German exports to Belgium would be applied to the payment of the annuities due the Belgian government by the 1929 agreement. Sénat, Documents, Nov. 24, 1936, doc. no. 28, pp. 16-17.

CHAPTER SIX

War Debts

THE QUESTION of reparation was closely connected with another financial problem resulting from the war, that of inter-Allied debts. During the world war the Belgian government, cut off from its normal sources of revenue, and faced with increased expenditures, had been obliged to borrow heavily from France, Great Britain, and the United States. At Paris in 1919, Hymans and his colleagues had endeavored to have this war debt cancelled, but succeeded only in obtaining from Wilson, Clemenceau, and Lloyd George pledges to recommend to their respective parliaments that the Belgian liability be transferred to Germany. The promise was not ratified by the United States Senate, but it was kept by France and Great Britain.

The war debt properly so called, was not, however, the only obligation the Belgian government contracted toward its allies; during the years immediately following the armistice the need for funds to finance relief and reconstruction, and, a little later, exchange stabilization, necessitated heavy borrowing. By the end of 1921 Belgium had received £15,799,000 from Great Britain, $175,430,-000 from the United States, and 241,472,300 francs from France, making an approximate total of 2,372,272,000 gold francs.[1]

---

[1] Shepherd, *Monetary experience of Belgium,* p. 39. Of the sum borrowed from Great Britain after the armistice £6,799,000 were considered "war debt,"

The debt to the United States was the first of these debts to be funded, and was the subject of much discussion in both countries. The British debt-funding operation, which occurred four months later, was the object of practically no argument in the parliaments or press of either nation. The debt to France was handled so quietly that relatively little information has been published. Consequently it has seemed simpler to treat the French settlement first, then the British, and lastly to take up the agreement with the United States, which besides arousing the most discussion, had repercussions in later years.

The arrangements made for paying the post-armistice debt to France have not figured in any published documents. A study of the budgets of the two countries reveals the fact that there was a Belgian debt of approximately 240,000,000 French francs, which was liquidated by 1927. Apparently this was done by turning over to France the sums due to Belgium from the Ruhr occupation.[2]

The funding of the debt to Great Britain received more publicity. On January 13, 1923, at the Cannes conference, the Belgian government for the first time admitted that an agreement ought to be made.[3] The debt had been contracted on January 31, 1919, when the British treasury opened a reconstruction credit of £9,000,000 to enable the Belgian government to place orders for needed goods in Great Britain; an additional £3,500,000 was bor-

though not charged to Germany. This amount was repaid in cash at the beginning of 1925, and did not figure in the funding operation. Great Britain, *Parliamentary Papers,* 1925, "Financial statement of the Chancelor of the Exchequer," no. 84, p. 24.

[2] Gay and Fisher, *Public relations of the Commission for Relief in Belgium,* II, 224. According to one writer the balance was in favor of Belgium to the extent of 150,000,000 francs; by an agreement signed in August, 1926, this sum was to be repaid out of the French share in the Dawes annuities; Walter S. Batsell, *The War Debt Settlement and the Future* (Paris, 1927), p. 84.

[3] Chambre, *Documents,* March 4, 1926, doc. no. 205.

rowed on June 29, 1916, to cover the budget deficit of the Congo.[4] Negotiations moved slowly, as the British government realized the undesirability of any further disruption of European economy by premature insistence on debt payments, and, of course, Belgium was not anxious to meet the bill. By the end of 1924 agreement was reached as to the amount owed, a total of £109,856,078. 17s. 2d., but no understanding could be reached as to the rate of exchange.

The funding of the debt to the United States in August, 1925, hastened the Belgo-British agreement, which was signed on December 31, 1925, at London. By its terms Belgium was allowed a five-year moratorium on amortization, but payments of interest at 5 per cent were to commence at once. Thus during the first five years, from 1927 to 1931, the British treasury would receive £450,000 yearly from Belgium and £180,000 from the Congo. Beginning in 1931 the annual payments would rise to £640,000 and £245,000 respectively. As the principal was paid off and the interest consequently became smaller, the amount of principal included in each yearly payment was to increase, thus keeping the annuities of equal size. Payment was to be made in two equal annual instalments, due June 30 and December 31 respectively.[5] This arrangement received no criticism from the Belgian Parliament, where only the Flemish extremists voted against it, in accordance with their policy of obstruction.[6]

At the Lausanne Conference of 1932 the British negotiators agreed to consider the Belgian reconstruction loan as a war debt and to give it special consideration.[7] As, however, the government

---

[4] Committee of Experts entrusted with the preparation of the Conference of Finance Ministers to be held on January 6, 1925, "Memorandum of British experts on Belgian war debt. 31.10.24."

[5] Chambre, *Documents*, Feb. 9, 1926, doc. no. 165; Sénat, *Documents*, March 23, 1926, pp. 385-386, doc. no. 94.

[6] Chambre, *Annales*, Mar. 11, 1926, I, 1023.

[7] Sénat, *CRA*, July 19, 1932, p. 553.

of the United States made no concession to the Allies in the matter of war debts, the Gentlemen's Agreement became operative. Consequently the British government was not bound by the agreement with Belgium, and the debt, therefore, was carried on the books of the British Treasury as a postwar debt; but no further Belgian payments were recorded.[8]

The settlement with the United States was, as had been said, the most widely publicized and the most thoroughly discussed of the three. The history of the loan dated back to the first years of the war, when in November 1915, unsuccessful negotiations with the government of the United States for an eventual postwar loan were carried on.[9] Only after the entrance of the United States into the war were direct intergovernmental credits opened for Belgium by the government at Washington. Twenty per cent of the pre-armistice, and 60 per cent of the post-armistice advances were turned over by the government at Sainte-Adresse to the Commission for Relief in Belgium, so that only $14,100,000 out of a total of $358,500,000 were used for munitions. The remainder was spent on food, probably destined for the Belgian army.[10]

The agreement contained in the exchange of letters between Wilson, Clemenceau, and Lloyd George, in June, 1919, by which each promised to recommend to his respective parliament the transfer of the Belgian debt to Germany, was not acted upon by the Congress of the United States, to which Wilson referred the matter after the rejection of the Versailles treaty by the Senate.[11] The result of this inaction was that Belgium owed the United States

[8] Great Britain, *Report of the Chancellor of the Exchequer*, 1932, p. 86; 1934, p. 86; etc.; Sénat, *CRA*, July 19, 1932, pp. 552-553.

[9] Sénat, *Annales*, Feb. 23, 1926, pp. 532-533.

[10] Gay and Fisher, *Public Relations of the Commission for Relief in Belgium*, II, 216; United States, Commissioner of accounts and deposits, *Memorandum*, p. 12.

[11] United States World War Foreign Debt Commission, *Combined Annual Reports*, 1922-1926, "Report for the fiscal year 1925" (Washington, 1927), p. 4.

not only the post-armistice relief debt, but the war debt properly so-called, as well.

No move looking to a payment of any part of this debt was made until 1922, although on August 18, 1921, Secretary of State Hughes reminded Cartier de Marchienne, the Belgian ambassador at Washington, of the condition attached to the 1919 relief loan: i. e., that the Belgian government give the United States a first lien on German reparation payments. This reminder received no answer. It was twice repeated, but not until January 7, 1922, did Cartier reply that he had notified his government. In April, after the creation of the World War Foreign Debt Commission, Cartier informed Hughes that he had been appointed to carry on the negotiations. Later he notified the commission that Belgium would pay the interest on the notes maturing in August, but would be unable to pay anything on the principal. He added that he would soon be in a position to make definite proposals for the settlement of all outstanding debts.[12] These proposals were never made. On June 9 Cartier informed the Commission that notes falling due on August 5 and August 22 could not be redeemed, although the interest on them would be met.[13] There the matter rested. The question of reparations came to the fore during the next few months, and the occupation of the Ruhr in January, 1923, created a situation which practically ended any possibility of inter-Allied payments.

After the adoption of the Dawes Plan in August, 1924, the way seemed open for a settlement of the debt question. In November, 1924, when the allied representatives met in Paris to discuss allocation of the Dawes annuities, the Americans were particularly eager to have the American Army occupation costs given priority right. In order to gain their support for this claim, Logan, the representative of the United States on the expert committee, intimated to the

[12] Cartier to Hughes, April 27, 1922, *U. S. For. Rel.,* 1922, I, 100.
[13] United States, World War Foreign Debt Commission, *Minutes,* 1922-1926 (Washington, 1927), p. 3.

Belgians that Washington would not press for payment for the time being. As Brussels was equally anxious that Washington make no public statement of its refusal to accept Germany as a debtor for the Belgian debt, agreement was easily reached at Paris on these points.[14] In the final settlement of the Dawes annuities, made at Paris by the Finance Ministers, in January, 1925, certain German reparations were payable to Belgium "by reason of her debt to the United States." Mr. Logan later made an arrangement with Gutt, by which Belgium accepted these payments in kind, and make the equivalent available to the United States. These payments were applied by the Treasury to the interest on the debt.[15]

Meanwhile the British government had been pressing for some advances on the reconstruction loan of 1919, and early in 1925 £8,-096,680.12s.7d. was turned over to the British Treasury. This, however, violated an agreement made in February, 1919, by which the Belgian government engaged to give American loans for food and relief the same treatment accorded French and British reconstruction loans. Secretary Kellogg thereupon consulted with the debt commission and with Secretary of Commerce Hoover, and on their advice decided to insist that the debt be funded.[16] Accordingly on April 22, Ambassador Phillips delivered to Hymans a strongly worded note asking that negotiations be opened, and laying down the conditions which would be acceptable to the United States. These were: first, that "Germany may not be substituted directly or indirectly for Belgium in respect of the pre-armistice debt"; second, that the funding agreement would be made along the lines of the British-American agreement; third, that some modifications might be made, "as may be required by the fiscal and economic condition of Belgium.[17]

---

[14] Whitehouse (U. S. chargé at Paris) to Hughes, Oct. 21, 1924, *U. S. For. Rel.*, 1924, II, 66-67; and Logan to Hughes, Nov. 21, 1924, *ibid.*, II, 82-83.

[15] Winston (U. S. Treasury) to Hoover, June 17, 1925, and Logan to Hughes, Jan. 11, 1925, *Reparations*. III, 310.

[16] WWFDC, *Minutes*, August 6, 1925.

[17] Kellogg to Phillips (Brussels) March 26, 1925, *U. S. For. Rel.*, 1925, I, 107-114.

Even this brought no result, and Secretary Kellogg finally re-
sorted to pressure. Early in 1925 the Belgian government negotiated a $100,000,000 stabilization loan with J. P. Morgan and the
Guaranty Trust Company. When the bankers applied to Kellogg
for authorization to float this loan on the American market, he
refused until a specific promise to fund was received. As this promise was not followed by any definite action, authorization for the
second installment of the loan was withheld.[18] Although the
money was badly needed to stabilize the franc, Brussels did not
surrender immediately. The situation was complicated by the state
of Belgian politics, because since the general elections of April
no one had been able to form a cabinet. There were, nevertheless,
certain essentials which the *ad interim* government felt in a position to require: that a distinction must be made between pre- and
post-armistice debts, and that the claims to special consideration on
account of the character and circumstances of the German invasion
must be taken into account. Moreover the figure of $480,000,000
specified by the United States was questioned.[19] In spite of these
conditions Kellogg was relentless; he insisted that if Belgium did
not give an unequivocal statement accepting the position taken
by the government of the United States and did not open negotiations in July, the Morgan loan would not be authorized.[20] This
ultimatum caused an immediate and unconditional surrender.[21] In
return, on June 11 the embargo on the loan was raised.[22]

This action of the temporary cabinet was ratified when on June
17 premier Poullet assumed office.[23] The debate on the ministerial

[18] Kellogg to Phillips, May 29, 1925, *ibid.*, I, 114-115; Janson, "Emile Francqui, l'homme d'état," *loc cit.*, p. 680. This was the fourth loan made by American bankers to the Belgian government since the armistice. A total of $1,100,-
000,000 had been borrowed since 1920. *Annuaire Statistique de la Belgique*, 1924-
1925, p. 141.
[19] Phillips to Kellogg, May 31 and June 2, 1925, *U. S. For. Rel.*, 1925, I,
116-118.
[20] Kellogg to Phillips, June 3, 1925, *U. S. For. Rel.*, 1925, I, 118-119.
[21] Phillips to Kellogg, June 5 and June 7, *ibid.*, I, 120-122.
[22] Victor de Laveleye, "La dette belge envers les Etats-Unis," *Revue Belge*,
XII (1925), 5-6.
[23] Chambre, *Annales*, June 23, 1925, p. 69; June 30, 1925, p. 117.

declaration, however, was so extended that it was some days before the government received a vote of confidence, and not until August 10 could negotiations open.

Prominent members of the American debt-funding commission were Secretary of the Treasury Mellon, the chairman, Secretary of State Kellogg, and Secretary of Commerce Hoover, who certainly knew both sides of the question. The Belgian representatives were the Ambassador, Cartier de Marchienne, former premier Theunis, Francqui, and Cattier.

After the customary exchange of polite compliments, and references to Belgium's gallant stand in 1914, Theunis stated that it seemed to him that there were four points to be decided in attempting to determine his country's capacity to pay. These were:

1. The rate of interest on arrears to date.
2. The possibility of a moratorium.
3. The extension of the funding period beyond the 62 years provided in the British agreement.
4. The rate of interest to be paid on the funded debt.[24]

The following day Cattier, after dilating at length on the difficulties under which his countrymen were laboring, and the high tax rate required to meet reconstruction problems, submitted the following proposal. He suggested that the debt be divided into two classes: the first would include money loaned during the war, which would be repaid within 75 years, on a progressive scale, with no interest; the second would include all sums loaned since the armistice. Arrears of interest since December 15, 1922, would be granted until 1931, after which interest would be due, first at one per cent, then gradually rising to three per cent.[25]

That afternoon the Americans met alone to discuss an alternative to this plan. They admitted that a distinction ought to be made between the pre-armistice and the post-armistice debt, and that

---

[24] WWFDC, *Minutes,* 32nd Meeting, August 10, 1925.
[25] WWFDC, *Minutes,* 33rd Meeting, August 11, 1925.

the former ought to be settled on a lower basis. Then came an interesting bit of casuistry. While refusing to agree that Belgium's payments might depend on German reparations, the Americans were willing to consider "Belgium's expectancy regarding such payments as affecting its capacity to make payments to the United States." The annuities were to be exactly equal to the receipts under the Dawes plan and were to run for sixty-two years.

The post-armistice debt, the Americans felt, should be repaid on the same conditions that governed the settlement of the Belgian post-armistice debt to Great Britian.

When Theunis arrived and was informed of these proposals he expressed his appreciation for the concessions made on the pre-armistice loan. He vigorously opposed the suggestion that the other debt be handled in the same manner as the British loan. By accepting German payments directly, Great Britain lost over thirty per cent of its pre-armistice advance, and this fact had been taken into consideration in funding the post-armistice debt.[26]

Mellon coldly replied that if Theunis examined the proposals carefully, he would see that they were within Belgium's capacity to pay. The meeting then adjourned.[27]

The Belgians were grateful that a distinction had been made between the pre-armistice and the post-armistice debt, but they firmly refused to accept the American proposals. One of their strongest arguments against them was that they called for the addition to the principal of the funded interest payments on which a fifteen year moratorium was offered. This would make the principal greater after fifteen years than it was at the time payments began. In advancing this and other points, Cattier also asked that all interest on the pre-armistice debt be cancelled. He suggested

[26] Theunis failed to remind the commission that the British loan had been primarily commercial, whereas 90 per cent of the American loan had been applied to relief.

[27] WWFDC, *Minutes,* 34th meeting, August 11, 1925.

that a committee be appointed to discuss these proposals. In accordance with this suggestion, Francqui, Theunis, Mellon and Smoot, with Terlinden and Winston as Treasury representatives from the two governments, withdrew to consider the situation.[28]

The following day, Friday, August 13, the Debt Commission agreed to accept the Belgian proposal regarding the pre-armistice debt. They still insisted on their own terms for the other debt.[29]

At length on Saturday, August 14, both sides were able to reach an agreement. The principal of the post-armistice debt was to be determined as of June 15, 1922, and the unpaid interest to that date was to be calculated at the rate of four and one-half per cent. From December 15, 1922, to June 15, 1925, interest at the rate of three per cent would be charged, but amounts already paid by Belgium on account of war supply obligations during that period would be credited against the interest.

The principal as of June 15, 1925 would be the basis of subsequent payments. Cattier's request for the inclusion of a clause stipulating that if any nation were granted more favorable terms, Belgium would receive them also, was rejected.[30]

The settlement thus decided upon was referred to President Coolidge for approval. When this had been obtained, the final agreement was signed.

For the first six years the payments on the post-armistice debt were to be deferred, but after 1931 the total Belgian payments on both debts was fixed at $12,700,000 yearly. This represented a reduction of nearly $291,000,000 in interest charges, and was possible because the American commissioners recognized the existence of a weighty moral obligation and conceded everything possible, given the restrictions imposed by Congress.[31] In Belgium, however, there were some misapprehensions as to the nature of the debt.

[28] *Ibid.*, 36th meeting, August 12, 1925.
[29] *Ibid.*, 37th meeting, August 13, 1925.
[30] *Ibid.*, 38th meeting, August 14, 1925, pp. 83-85.
[31] WWFDC, *Report*, 1925, pp. 178-180.

Many did not fully realize that the United States had not been one of the guarantor states, and had never subscribed to the Declaration of Sainte Adresse which had promised full economic recovery to Belgium. In fact, there were those even in Parliament who apparently did not know that their government had borrowed large sums from the United States Treasury, quite distinct from the gifts made by individual Americans.[32]

When the matter was brought up in the Chambre during the discussion of the ministerial declaration of the Poullet-Vandervelde Cabinet, the idea of repayment was vigorously opposed. Carlier, one of the Socialist deputies, reminded his auditors how in that very Chamber, President Wilson had said "Our wish, our desire, is to make Belgium arise from her ruins."[33] Another deputy, M. Franck, a Fleming, expressed his astonishment that the United States claimed repayment after the debt had been settled by the allottment of the Dawes annuities.[34]

In a masterly exposition Vandervelde, the newly appointed Socialist foreign minister, clarified the situation, rectifying the mistaken ideas, and pointing out that in the debt settlement the United States had taken Belgium's special position into consideration, and had waived any claim to interest on the money borrowed before the armistice. He also showed that the payments to be made under the Belgo-American agreement were smaller than receipts under the Dawes plan, so that the country had something to apply to reconstruction.

This explanation was well received by the Socialists and the Catholics, whose spokesmen, Barnich and de Broqueville, expressed their satisfaction.[35]

[32] Sénat, *Annales*, Feb. 23, 1926, pp. 518-519.
[33] Chambre, *Annales*, July 15, 1925, p. 304.
[34] *Ibid.*, July 17, 1925, pp. 384-385.
[35] Sénat, *Annales*, Feb. 23, 1926, pp. 528-530. One of the dissenting senators remarked, *à propos* of the settlement, "On nous a couverts de fleurs, mais on nous envoie la facture du fleuriste." He well expressed the feelings of the average Belgian on the subject.

From June 15, 1926, until June 15, 1931, the Belgian government made regular payments, remitting to the United States $31,-590,000 during the five years. The Hoover Moratorium of June 20, 1931, interrupted the payments, making a supplementary agreement necessary. By the terms of this Belgo-American convention of June 10, 1932, the Belgian government arranged to pay the delayed annuity of the moratorium in yearly instalments, so that at the rate of six per cent the whole would be liquidated in ten years.[36] Before the December instalment for 1932 fell due, however, a note from Brussels brought a request for a suspension of payments until the question could be re-examined in the light of existing circumstances. There followed an exchange of notes between the two governments wherein each defined its position: Belgium considering payment impossible in view of the economic crisis and of the Lausanne agreement; the United States insisting that payment of the war debts should not be made contingent on the German payments, and that what had been borrowed must be repaid. On December 14 the Belgian government gave formal notice that it was unable to pay.[37] Regularly every six months thereafter the State Department informed the Belgian Embassy of the amount due, and, just as regularly, the reply followed that conditions made payment out of the question. These exchanges continued even after the invasion of Belgium.[38] Of a total indebtedness of $449,080,212.01, the United States Treasury estimated that it had received from Belgium $52,191,273.23 in principal and interest.[39]

[36] De Laveleye, "La dette Belge," loc. cit., p. 9.

[37] May (Belgian Ambassador) to Stimson (Secretary of State), Nov. 15, 1932, United States, Department of the Treasury, Financial Report, 1933 (Washington, 1933), pp. 211-215; answer to Nov. 23; Belgian note of Dec. 6, answer of Dec. 13; Belgian note of Dec. 14, 1932.

[38] Department of State, Press Releases, June 16, 1934, p. 397; Dec. 15, 1934, p. 357, and every six months thereafter. December 1, 1940 is the date of the last published note from the State Department.

[39] United States, Office of Commissioner of Accounts, Memorandum, pp. 22-23.

The lend-lease agreement between the United States and Belgium, signed on June 16, 1942, attempted to forestall a repetition of the debt problem of the "postwar" period by providing that the final determination of the terms of payment and of credit should be deferred until the best interests of both nations can be determined.[40] Such an arrangement seems to promise a greater degree of understanding and mutual cooperation, and a more realistic outlook, than was evident in the 1925 debt settlement.

[40] Department of State, *Bulletin*, June 20, 1942, p. 551.

CHAPTER SEVEN

Security

ONE OF THE major aims of Belgian policy after 1919 was that of securing a guarantee of military aid from France and Great Britain in case of a possible German attack. At the peace conference of Paris Clemenceau had insisted that the governments of the United States and Great Britain guarantee the frontiers of France in return for that country's renunciation of the long-desired Rhine boundary. This was done by two treaties; one between France and the United States, the other between France and Great Britain.[1] Neither of these treaties was to go into effect until the other had been ratified. When, therefore, the Senate of the United States refused to ratify the treaty in which it was concerned, France was left without an ally on which to count for immediate support against the greatly feared German aggression. It was natural, then, that France and Belgium, each of which desired promises of support against hostile Germany, which Great Britain and the United States had refused to give, should be drawn together. Nevertheless the independent Belgian people, particularly the Flemish section of the population, were not too eager to be drawn into what

[1] Great Britain, *Parliamentary Papers,* 1919, Cmd. 221. The draft treaty between the United States and France was approved by Wilson and Clemenceau on April 20, 1919; two days later Lloyd George accepted a similar treaty for Great Britain, subject to Balfour's approval. Great Britain, *Parliamentary Papers*, 1924, Cmd. 2169, pp. 95, 97.

the press termed "vassalage."[2] Consequently French diplomats found that they would have to offer a substantial *quid pro quo* before they could reach an agreement with their northern neighbor. The material for this bargaining was the grand duchy of Luxemburg.

Many Belgians had expected the acquisition of the grand duchy to be one of their country's gains from the war, forgetting that in the eighty years that had passed since Belgium and Luxemburg were separated, the latter had acquired a national spirit of its own. The Belgian government, which had unsuccessfully tried to enlist the support of the United States in its attempt to annex Luxemburg,[3] was equally unsuccessful in its efforts to have Belgian, not French, troops named to occupy the grand duchy until after the negotiations at Paris were completed.[4]

The little grand duchy was too small to exist without an economic union with one of its larger neighbors. In the nineteenth century it had turned eastward, and in 1842 it had joined the Zollverein. And though never a member of the German Empire, after 1872 its railways were under the direction of the Imperial Alsace Lorraine Railway Company. The neutrality of the territory had been guaranteed by a treaty of May 11, 1867, signed by Austria, Great Britain, France, Italy, Prussia and Russia. At the outbreak of the war this treaty was violated by the German armies, and the country was occupied until the armistice. As many of the Allies believed that the Grand Duchess Adelaide had been too compliant to the will of the invader, her abdication was taken for granted, but the whole problem of Luxemberg's future remained in doubt for some months. The people themselves solved it by the

---

[2] However, there was a strong sympathy with France, fostered by effective French propaganda. Cf. Whitlock's *Journal,* I, chapter XIII, *passim,* also Whitlock to Lansing, Dec. 7, 1918, *U. S. For. Rel.,* 1919, *The Peace Conference,* II, 442.

[3] Cartier to Lansing, Nov. 13, 1918, *ibid.,* II, 436-440.

[4] Whitlock's *Journal,* II, 538, entry of Dec. 13, 1918; Haskins and Lord, *Problems of the Peace Conference,* pp. 59-60.

exercise of self determination. In a plebiscite held on September 28, 1919, a vast majority of the voters, 66,811, expressed their wish to have Charlotte, Adelaide's sister, as their ruler. At the same time 60,735 votes were registered for an economic union with France, as against 22,241 for union with Belgium.[5] This referendum decided the recall of the Belgian mission which, at the request of the grand ducal government, had been sent to Luxemburg to examine the possibilities of an understanding.

Nevertheless desire for a union was still strong in Belgium since the Luxemburg railway commanded the communication of Antwerp with its hinterland. In order to secure control of these lines, negotiations were opened in December 1919 with France.[6] While they were under way, the French government quietly made a contract with the grand duchy effecting a settlement. Brussels had no inkling of this arrangement until formal notice was given by Luxemburg, and even then the terms were not divulged.[7] The French cabinet was now in a position to induce Belgium to enter into a military alliance by offering in exchange to repudiate the Luxemburg treaty.[8]

On May 12, 1920, premier Reuter announced to the Luxemburg parliament that Paris had rejected the proposed customs union, and that his negotiations with Belgium, interrupted by a "deplorable misunderstanding," would be reopened.[9]

More than a year elapsed, however, before a settlement was reached. The representatives of the agricultural interests in Luxemburg feared that they would suffer if tariff barriers with Belgium were removed; and in the latter country the metallurgists entertained similar anxieties. In June, agreement seemed near, and sub-committees were appointed to study minor details. When they reported in December, however, it was discovered that the problem of control of the railways was still not solved, each country

[5] Current History, XI, (1919) 465.

[6] Chambre, Annales, Dec. 23, 1919, p. 86.

[7] Whitlock's Journal, II, 590, entry of March 14, 1920.

[8] Ibid., II, 595-596, entry of April 25, 1920.

[9] BPB, no. 31, May 29, 1920, p. 1.

claiming the right to a majority on the board of directors. The following May this obstacle was temporarily disposed of when both parties agreed to reserve the whole question for future negotiations.[10] Finally, on July 25, 1921, the treaty of economic union was signed. By its terms the customs frontier between the two states was abolished, the railway system of the grand duchy was unified and placed under the control of a company whose composition was to be the subject of future discussion, the currency of Luxemburg was to be withdrawn from circulation and replaced by that of Belgium, and the agrarian and metallurgical interests of the grand duchy were to be safeguarded from competition by a complicated system of subsidies and tax debates, subject to the decisions of a mixed commission.[11]

Ratification of this treaty was not a foregone conclusion. The foreign affairs committee of the Belgian Chamber to which it was referred for study, could not agree on it findings, and published two long reports, the majority favoring and the minority emphatically opposing the union. Hymans claimed that the second report was drawn up at the request of leading industrialists, and that it was therefore manifestly biased in its outlook. The chief arguments it adduced against the treaty were three: it gave to foreigners the right to interfere in Belgian affairs; in exchange for an insignificant market already closely connected with Alsace-Lorraine, it opened the home market to strong competition in metallurgical products; it did not provide adequate safeguards against this threatened loss of both internal and external markets. The report concluded with the criticism:

The affair is not only mediocre; it is disastrous, it is bad, it is a trick.[12]

[10] Jacques Crokaert, L'accord belgo-luxembourgeois, (Brussels, 1921), pp. 11-12; Sénat, Annales, March 1, 1922, p. 275.

[11] Chambre, Documents, 1920-1921, pp. 1597-1605, doc. no. 522.

[12] Chambre, Documents, 1920-1921, doc. no. 23, p. 100.

The majority of the committee viewed the matter in a different light. Frankly admitting that Luxemburg had become a strong rival in the world market, it insisted that union would be a protection for Belgian goods and that its rejection would inevitably drive the grand duchy into the big German and French cartels. In conclusion the report stressed the point that the mixed commission set up by the treaty would be an adequate safeguard of the interests of both contracting parties.[13]

In January, 1922, when the treaty was discussed in the Belgian Chamber, the opposition was based around two arguments: the metallurgical interests of the country would suffer, and the treaty would injure Franco-Belgian relations.[14] These arguments were ably refuted by foreign minister Jaspar, who took the stand that in the long run too much protection for the steel manufacturers would eventually do more harm than good, since not higher economic barriers but union among producers, would cause an improvement in business. In answer to the second charge he showed that when the French government relinquished the prospect of economic union with Luxemburg, it had done so on condition that its relations with the grand duchy would suffer no prejudice. Even so, Belgian representatives had been invited to participate in the Franco-Luxemburg negotiations which had regulated business relations between the two states. In conclusion he demonstrated that the very ardor of the attack on the treaty in the Luxemburg Chamber proved that it was not weighted in the grand duchy's favor.[15] The Belgian Chamber voted for ratification on February 2, 1922, by a vote of 136-14, with three members not voting.[16] Henceforth treaties and agreements involving Belgium were always negotiated in the name of the Belgo-Luxemburg Economic Union.

[13] *Ibid.*, July 25, 1921, doc. no. 23, pp. 97-99.
[14] Chambre, *Annales,* Jan. 25, 1922, I, 147, 150-160.
[15] *Ibid.*, Jan. 25, 1922, I, 137-146.
[16] *Ibid.*, Feb. 2, 1922, I, 211.

From a military point of view the importance of the union lay in the control of the strategic railways of the smaller country, which Belgium hoped to exercise. It was fourteen years before the details of the railway administration were finally worked out to the satisfaction of the two governments, the chief difficulty being that the grand ducal government was averse to allowing too many Belgians on the board of directors of the railroads. The treaty settling this point was finally signed on June 1, 1934.[17]

By making the Belgo-Luxemburg union possible, the French government had paid the price for a military alliance with Belgian. Statesmen in Brussels would have preferred a joint Franco-British promise, but failing this, a French guarantee was better than nothing.

In April, 1920, as soon as the French government signified its intention of relinquishing the Luxemburg customs union and control of the railways in the grand duchy, military conversations between the general staffs of the two countries began. They were furthered by the action of the Belgian government in supporting the French occupation of Frankfurt, a decision made at the instance of Hymans.[18] The staff discussions were carried on during the summer of 1920, and resulted in an agreement signed on September 7 of that year. Although the convention was registered with the League of Nations and communicated to the Great Powers, the clauses were not made public. This silence gave rise to suspicions that a political alliance had been formed, or that in some way Belgium had been made dependent on France. The two governments claimed that the reason for secrecy was simply that a military plan

---

[17] Sénat, CRA, March 8, 1934, pp. 245-246. A provisional convention had been signed on October 14, 1924, but was rejected by Luxemburg. Then a commission of experts was named to study the matter. The railways having become involved in a lawsuit, further delay ensued. Meanwhile their administration was provisionally granted to the French Alsace-Lorraine Railway.

[18] BPB, no. 30, Apr. 23, 1920, pp. 1-4.

would lose its effectiveness if the provisions were known to the enemy.[19]

More than once Belgian statesmen were called upon to explain the nature of the treaty. Its defensive and non-political character was stressed in the letter of September 10, 1920, in which premier Delacroix informed the French government of the assent of the Belgian cabinet; on October 29 this letter was communicated to the Senate. It stated explicitly that:

. . . the purpose of this agreement is to reinforce the guarantees of peace and security resulting from the covenant of the League of Nations. It is recognized as a matter of course that the two states retain intact their sovereign right to impose military burdens on their respective peoples, and to determine in each case, whether or not the eventuality provided for by the present understanding has arisen.[20]

Nevertheless, there was an alarmed flurry among the Flemings, who feared French influence. They were loud in their denunciations of an understanding with their neighbor to the south, which they branded as "militarist, imperialist, and an enemy to Flemish culture." Frans van Cauwelaert, an influential deputy from Antwerp, stressed the danger of the agreement in his editorials in the well known paper, the *Standaard*.[21] In answer to these criticisms, the new premier, Henry Carton de Wiart, twice repeated the assurance that the pact was a purely defensive agreement, intended only to aid peace.[22]

In 1927 the Flemish deputy Declerq claimed that General Maglinse, Belgian chief of staff who helped draw up the military clauses

---

[19] *ESH*-1181, Nov. 10, 1920; Chambre, *Annales*, Nov. 23, 1920, I, 10; Dec. 1, 1920, I, 65.

[20] "Il va de soi que la souveraineté des deux états demeure intacte quant aux charges militaires qu'ils imposeront à leurs pays respectifs et quant à l'apprècia-tion . . . . de la réalisation de l'éventualité en vue de laquelle le present accord est conclu." Sénat, *Annales*, Oct. 27, 1920, p. III7.

[21] *BPB*, no. 23, Nov. 7, 1920, p. 3.

[22] Chambre, *Annales*, Nov. 23, 1920, I, I0; Dec. I, 1920, I, 79.

of the agreement, had informed the commission for national defense that the country had to have a large army because of the terms of the Franco-Belgian treaty. This statement was not taken seriously; only the Frontists and Communists supported Declerq.[23] A much more serious attack on the agreement came in February, 1929, when the Dutch newspaper *Het Dagblad* published what purported to be the text of the agreement, including among other startling clauses, provision for an immediate invasion by Belgium of Dutch Limburg, in case a Franco-German or Belgo-German war should break out.[24] It was eventually disclosed that the pseudo "treaty" had been fabricated by a certain Albert Franck, an *agent provocateur* in the service of the intelligence branch of the Belgian army, and sold by him to a gullible Frontist, who published it in order to further the Flemish policy of "Los van Frankrijk."[25] The extremists wanted a parliamentary investigation of the affair, but the only supporters they could muster were one Communist and two Socialist deputies, who wished to learn the exact contents of the treaty.[26] From this time on, the attack on the treaty grew in violence. One absurd accusation, among others, stated that the agreement required the use of French instead of Flemish as the "word of command" in the army.[27] In March, 1931, Hymans was again forced to explain the agreement. He insisted that it left both parties free to determine whether or not the conditions which should bring military action into play had arisen; and for Belgium, he said, the obligation to fight had been clearly defined by the Locarno pact.[28] This assurance, however, was not enough to satisfy those who feared France; or even to reassure the moderates who merely wanted to avoid being entangled in another war. Fi-

[23] Chambre, *CRA*, Nov. 15, 1927, pp. 5-8.
[24] *Ibid.*, Feb. 26, 1929, p. 259.
[25] *Ibid.*, March 7, 1929, pp. 302-303 ; March 19, 1929, p. 349.
[26] *Ibid.*, June 6, 1930, p. 703.
[27] *Ibid.*, May 6, 1930, p. 575.

nally in March, 1936, premier van Zeeland, when explaining his attitude with regard to German remilitarization of the Rhineland, revealed that just the day before, the French and Belgian governments, by an exchange of letters, had agreed that the only clauses of the treaty that would still bind both governments were those providing for periodic meetings between representatives of the two general staffs. The other clauses, providing for cooperation in case of a sudden German attack, had been drawn up under the assumption of a continued Allied occupation of the Rhineland. The agreement had never implied any obligation concerning the measures to be taken to provide for the national defense of either nation.[29]

Belgian statesmen had never felt that French military aid would be sufficient to protect their country should Germany embark upon a war of revenge, and they never lost sight of the advantages that their country would reap from a British guarantee of support. In November, 1920, premier Delacroix announced that he had received the desired promise, but this was at once denied by Lloyd George.[30] In July 1921, King Albert's visit to London reopened the subject, but nothing came of the incident.[31] Downing Street would give only a five-year guarantee, which was to be contingent upon Belgian return to neutrality—conditions which were entirely unacceptable.[32]

At last, however, it seemed that an Anglo-Belgian treaty was about to become an accomplished fact. At the conference of Cannes, in January, there was a distinct improvement in the relations between the French and British premiers, with the result that they

[28] *Ibid.*, March 4, 1931, pp. 309-310.

[29] Chambre, *Annales,* March 11, 1936, pp. 789-790; Emile Cammaerts, "The Belgian Problem," *Contemporary Review,* CLI (1937), p. 659.

[30] Chambre, *Annales,* Dec, 2, 1920, I, 87.

[31] André Roussel le Roy, *L'abrogation de la neutralité de la Belgique, ses causes et ses effets. Etude d'histoire diplomatique et de droit public international* (Paris, 1923), p. 180; Chambre, *Annales,* June 2, 1921, II, 1442.

[32] "La déclaration allemande et la politique extérieure de la Belgique," *Revue Générale,* CXXXVIII (1937), p. 525.

drew up a tentative treaty of alliance. As rumors of this spread among the delegates, on January 9 Jaspar asked Lord Curzon, the British foreign secretary, to discuss a Belgian treaty. Lloyd George consenting, the negotiations opened the following day. To Jaspar's surprise, he discovered, on being shown the draft Anglo-French treaty, that both nations regarded Belgium as a neutral. He labored to dissipate this illusion, with the result that in the provisional understanding that was worked out by Curzon and Baron Moncheur, no mention was made of the objectionable term, neutrality, and Belgium expressly undertook the defense of its frontiers in case of attack or of violation of its territory by any third power; while in return Great Britain guaranteed immediate support by land, sea, and air.[33] This treaty was criticized at Paris because it was directed not specifically against Germany, but against any possible violation of Belgian territory. Of course the only other power which was geographically in a position to attack Belgium was France, and its government resented being classed with Germany as a possible aggressor.[34] The wording was, however, acceptable to Jaspar because it would allay any fears of French domination that might have been raised in the minds of the Flemings, and might even reconcile them to the military convention.

The friendly atmosphere at Cannes had been due in large part to the fact that at the negotiations the French government had been represented by the premier, the moderate Briand; with his fall from power, all hope for an immediate Franco-British understanding began to fade although the Anglo-Belgian negotiations continued until January of the following year.[35] But the British cabinet became increasingly colder, insisting first on the addition

[33] Henri Jaspar, "Les directives de la politique extérieure de la Belgique," *Esprit International,* VII (1933), p. 14; "La conférence de Cannes de 1922," *Revue Générale,* CXXXVIII (1937), 129. The terms of the draft were only made public in 1925; Chambre, *Annales,* Nov. 17, 1925, I, 15.

[34] D'Abernon, *An Ambassador of Peace,* I, 248, entry of Jan. 17, 1922.

[35] Henri Jaspar, "Cannes et Locarno," *Revue Générale,* LIX (1926), 15.

of a clause freeing the Dominions from responsibility, then delaying the final signature until relations with France had improved.[36] With the occupation of the Ruhr, however, the chances of a British guarantee became negligible, and the "Curzon note" of August 11, 1923, definitely ended all prospects.[37]

The adoption of the Dawes plan in 1924, and the resulting improvement in international relations gave impetus to a movement for strengthening collective security by additional guarantees. At Geneva a very inclusive "Protocol for the Pacific Settlement in International Disputes" was drawn up, and on October 2, 1924 submitted to the members of the League. The success of this plan depended largely on the attitude of the Great Powers, and there was much opposition in the British Empire. The Dominions were definitely opposed to such a guarantee as this agreement called for; moreover, in England itself those who supported the League of Nations feared that the protocol would dilute the general guarantee of the League, and the more insular minded feared that their country was being given the thankless task of policing the world. Eventually the protocol was dropped.[38]

In Belgium there was at first rather strong support for the Geneva plan. The *Indépendance Belge,* an influential liberal paper, approved it as reinforcing and making more definite the obligations of the League covenant.[39] *Le Vingtième Siècle,* organ of the Catholic party, also approved, saying that every intelligent Belgian would rejoice at an agreement that included compulsory arbitration and a definition of aggression. Other important papers, such as *Le Soir* and *La Flandre Libérale,* were of the same opinion.[40] The approval of the Socialist party was voiced in the Chamber by Vander-

---

[36] Jaspar, "La conférence de Cannes," *loc. cit.,* CXXXVIII (1937), 133.

[37] Great Britain, *Parliamentary Papers,* 1924, Cmd. 2169, p. 172.

[38] Frederick Maurice, *Haldane, the life of Viscount Haldane of Cloan, K.-T., O. M.* (London, 1939), II, 183-184.

[39] *Indépendance Belge,* October 4, 1924.

[40] *BPB,* no. 68, Nov. 8, 1924, p. 2.

velde, who stated that the protocol marked an immense progress by emphasizing arbitration, proposing strong economic and military sanctions, and providing for a disarmament conference. He recognized, of course, that it was not perfect; some of its chief weaknesses, he said, were its maintenance of the *status quo* based on the Versailles treaty, and its close dependence on the proposed disarmament conference.[41] At the very session where the Socialist leader gave such high praise to the protocol, Hymans, the minister of foreign affairs, opened the door for a more limited guarantee in case, as was beginning to appear probable, the Geneva plan should fail. While approving of the protocol, he stressed the idea of regional pacts, which had more appeal to the great powers.

The first important step in this direction, however, was taken by Stresemann, when in February 9, 1925, he proposed to the French government that the two nations guarantee their common boundary. As there was no mention of Belgium in this note, some anxiety was felt in that country as to the implications of such an omission. Representations were at once made in Paris and London, and assurances were received that Belgium would be treated as an equal in the coming negotiations, and that its boundaries would be included in the guarantee.[42]

Both these promises were kept. The note handed Stresemann on June 16, 1924, by the French ambassador at Berlin contained this sentence:

Among the latter [the contracting states] must certainly appear Belgium, which was not expressly named in the German memorandum, and which should be a party to the pact as a state directly interested.[43]

The British government had endorsed this statement with the

---

[41] Chambre, *Annales,* Nov. 12, 1924, pp. 14-15.
[42] *Indépendance Belge,* July 3, 1925.
[43] Crewe to A. Chamberlain, May 13, 1924, Great Britain, *Parliamentary Papers,* 1925, Cmd. 2423, p. 7.

remark that unless Belgium were included "the pact would obviously be incomplete."[44]

When de Margerie, the French ambassador at Berlin, presented the note to Stresemann, the latter explained that he had not mentioned Belgium in the first note because none of the neutrals had been included. De Margerie then hinted that the recovery of Eupen and Malmédy had some bearing on the omission. Stresemann replied, "The German government would only conclude a security agreement which did not exclude an understanding by peaceful means regarding Eupen and Malmédy."[45] There is no record of the Belgian government's reaction to these statements; certainly the allusion to "the neutrals" would not have been relished. It is quite possible that the other Allied powers refused to make further representations.

On August 26, 1924, after a conference between Austen Chamberlain, British foreign secretary, and foreign minister Briand, the world was informed that Germany had been invited to participate in a conference to open on October 5 in the Swiss city of Locarno, on Lake Maggiore. The German reply of September 26, after accepting the invitation, took up the subject of war guilt, and asked to be freed from the imputation of the Versailles Treaty. Both London and Paris refused to discuss the matter. Brussels went further, drawing Stresemann's attention to the admission made on August 4, 1914, by Chancellor von Bethmann-Hollweg. As far as Belgium was concerned, this settled the war guilt issue.[46] The subject was dropped for the moment but was taken up again during the conference, when Stresemann firmly rejected the Allied thesis that his country had been responsible for the outbreak of the war.[47]

[44] A. Chamberlain to Fleuriau, May 19, 1924, Great Britain, *Parliamentary Papers,* 1925, Cmd. 2435, p. 21.

[45] *Stresemann,* II, 113.

[46] Ernest Melot, "La conférence de Locarno," *Revue Générale,* LVIII (1925), 511.

[47] *Stresemann,* II, 215-216.

SECURITY style 189

The meetings at Locarno were conducted in the greatest privacy, one of the most important taking place during a yachting trip on Lake Maggiore to celebrate Mrs. Chamberlain's birthday.[48] It was on this occasion that Chamberlain, Briand, Vandervelde and Stresemann had their long and heated argument about war guilt.[49]

On at least two occasions Belgian interests formed the main topic of discussion. At the very opening of the conference one of the great problems was the relation between the existing Franco-Belgian military convention and the proposed pact of guarantee. Vandervelde settled this by saying that the two pacts complemented each other, by specifying the amount and kind of aid the two countries would give if either was attacked. Since the alliance was purely defensive, it could not be in opposition to the proposed guarantees, which were also essentially defensive in nature.[50]

On the second occasion Stresemann tried to have the boundaries of Belgium omitted from the guarantee, hoping by this to facilitate the restoration of Eupen and Malmédy to the Reich. Briand supported Vandervelde's successful resistance.[51] The treaty as it was signed included the entire eastern boundary of Belgium as it had been drawn after the peace conference; nevertheless Stresemann received assurances that the possibility of a peaceful change still existed.[52]

The conference closed on October 16 with the initialling of five conventions. Of these the most important from the Belgian point of view was the Rhenish pact, by which the governments of Germany, Belgium, France, Great Britain, and Italy mutually undertook to guarantee the maintenance of the frontiers between Germany

[48] Charles Petrie, *The Life and Letters of the Right Honorable Sir Austen Chamberlain, K.G., P.C., M.P.* (Toronto, 1939-1940), II, 215.
[49] *Stresemann*, II, 215-216.
[50] Chambre, *Annales*, Jan, 20, 1926, I, 650.
[51] Detry, "La Belgique et les papiers de Stresemann," *loc. cit.*, 499.
[52] *Cf. Stresemann* II, 217, and his remarks to the French chargé in August, 1926, *ibid.*, II, 426.

and Belgium, and Germany and France, as fixed by the treaty of Versailles; and to maintain the demilitarization of the zone established by articles 42 and 43 of that treaty. Germany and Belgium and Germany and France agreed that in no case would they resort to war against each other except in self-defense or to fulfill their obligations as members of the League of Nations. Arrangements were made for the peaceful settlement of disputes by conciliation and arbitration, and machinery was set up to enforce the treaty. In the preamble the abrogation of Belgian neutrality was expressly stipulated. This pact was supplemented by arbitration conventions between Germany and Belgium, Germany and France, Germany and Poland, and Germany and Czechoslovakia.[53]

In Belgium there was at first little enthusiasm for the idea of mutual guarantees, particularly as the plan was of German origin. "Timeo Danaos et dona ferentes" was apparently the underlying psychological reason for this attitude, since the reasons alleged in its support were feeble. In March, 1925, *La Flandre Libérale* suspected in print that the secret hope of the German government was to divide the Allies; *La Nation Belge* considered Stresemann's suggestion an attempt to conceal Germany's failure to disarm.[54] By May some of this suspicion had died away, even the nationalistic *Vingtième Siècle* giving a grudging approval.[55] At this point the publication by the French semi-official Havas agency of a telegram purporting to describe a Franco-British guarantee created great excitement in Belgium. According to the report, an agreement had been reached by the representatives of Great Britain, France and Belgium whereby Great Britain promised

to guarantee the frontier of the Rhine as it is left by the treaty of Versailles. It may be said that Great Britain makes her own, the frontiers of France and Belgium adjoining Germany, and that she

---

[53] Chambre, *Documents*, Dec. 8, 1925, doc. no. 51.
[54] *BPB*, no. 71, April 4, 1925, p. 2.
[55] *Ibid.*, no. 72, June 9, 1925, p. 1.

considers any violation by Germany of the territorial and military clauses relating to the Rhine a *casus belli*. . . . Finally, it is formally stipulated in the Franco-British agreement that, should the eastern allies of France be the object of manifest aggression, France shall be authorized to make use of the demilitarized Rhine zone as a field of operations in order to come to the aid of her attacked Allies.[56]

This product of "wishful thinking" was received with enthusiasm in Belgium, where a promise of British support had long been desired. Downing Street's vigorous denial of the existence of an agreement such as Havas described, awakened the Belgians to the realization that a pact including Germany would be the only means of securing a British pledge. The situation was improved after a statement of the foreign minister, Emile Vandervelde, that he was closely associated with the negotiations and had been informed of every move made by the Great Powers.[57] The press and parliament accepted this and allowed the government to continue the negotiations without having to answer carping critics.

Once the pacts were signed there was almost universal approval. Typical of the sentiments expressed was the statement of the Catholic *Libre Belgique* that the Rhenish pact was the most important international act since Versailles. Only two important papers were out of harmony with the paean of praise. The *Nation Belge* and the *Vingtième Siècle,* both nationalist in tone, considered that Germany had won a great victory and that Locarno meant the end of Versailles.[58]

Those who shared these fears were reassured by the explanation of the treaty given on November 17 by Vandervelde. He opened his speech by reminding his auditors that by the Locarno agreements Germany for the first time fully accepted the territorial changes in the west which had been imposed by the war. Another point he

[56] D'Abernon, *Diary,* III, 167, entry of June 11, 1925.
[57] Chambre, *Annales,* July 17, 1925, p. 383.
[58] *BPB,* no. 75, Nov, 19, 1925, p. 2.

stressed was the advantage of the arbitral machinery now set up. The only weak point in this arrangement, he said, was the fact that arbitration of political questions had not been made compulsory. The Belgian delegates had tried to change this, but they received no support and had to be content with a clause forbidding any of the signatories to resort to war to settle their differences. The adhesion of Italy was welcomed since it not only added to the number of guarantors, but seemed to be an important step in the direction of a closer union of the European nations.[59]

Hymans spoke in the same strain and showed further that Belgian security now was safeguarded not only by the defensive alliance with France, but by the promises of Italy and of Great Britain. He added that in the last analysis security depended on peace, which was assured by the arbitration pacts which were an integral part of Locarno.[60]

Jaspar, also a former foreign minister, and spokesman of the Catholic party as Hymans was of the Liberals, then expressed his support of Vandervelde and the Locarno pacts. He spoke, however, in a less enthusiastic vein than the other two men; where they dwelt on the possibility of peace that the agreements had created, he emphasized the danger of counting on a German promise, and recalled the broken treaty of neutrality.[61]

The comments in the Belgian press after the final signature of the pacts in London on December 1, 1925, showed that the speakers represented the trend of thought of their parties. The Liberal *Indépendance Belge* claimed that the treaties opened a new chapter in history;[62] while the nationalist Catholic paper, *Vingtième Siècle*, advised the government to be prudent in basing its policy on a

---

[59] Chambre, *Annales*, Nov. 17, 1925, I, 15-18.
[60] *Ibid.*, Nov. 17, 1925, I, 19-21.
[61] *Ibid.*, Nov. 17, 1925. I, 21.
[62] *Indépendance Belge*, Dec, 2, 1925.

German pledge. In general, however, the press showed itself satisfied with the treaty.[63]

This attitude marked the debate on ratification which on January 19, 1926, opened in the Chamber. The report of the foreign affairs committee, presented by the Flemish Catholic Frans van Cauwelaert, highly approved of the pacts. Although mentioning the fact that only one of Belgium's frontiers—that with Germany—was now guaranteed, it acclaimed the treaties as showing the country's independent status; now Belgium was guarantor as well as guaranteed. The almost unanimous vote of the committee was echoed in the welcome the Locarno pacts received in Parliament.[64]

Brunfaut and Van Overstraeten, Communist deputies, adopting the orthodox "party line," denounced Locarno as a plot against Soviet Russia. The next speaker, the Socialist Louis Piérard, said he was much less skeptical. His only objection to the treaties was that they obliged Belgium to go to the aid of France, in the event of unprovoked aggression against that country.

The following day the discussion was concluded, after a series of speeches praising the pacts. Van Cauwelaert gave as the chief reason for his attitude the security Belgium received from the system now set up. Jaspar claimed that Locarno was the culmination of the policy that he, in common with all the foreign ministers of the country since the war, had consistently pursued. He reiterated the expression of his fear of an eventual repudiation of the treaty by Germany, however, while agreeing that ratification was necessary. Vandervelde and Hymans repeated the substance of the statements they had made the previous November. In winding up the discussion, Carton de Wiart expressed his wish to see the signature of a representative of the Netherlands grace the treaty. Next day the Chamber voted 124 to 5 for ratification.[65]

[63] BPB, no. 76, Jan. 23, 1926, p. 3.
[64] Chambre, Documents, 1925, doc. no. 120.
[65] Chambre, Annales, Jan. 19-20, 1926, I, 630-655; Jan. 21, I, 569.

The debate in the Senate followed somewhat the same pattern. The only opposition was voiced by Lafontaine, a Socialist who had worked long years in the cause of international cooperation. He objected to the treaty not because he disapproved of the guarantees it provided, but because he believed that regional pacts tended weaken the League of Nations. He voted for the treaties, nevertheless, because he realized that under the circumstances they were a step toward peace, and because, unlike the treaty of Versailles, they had been freely negotiated, not imposed.

De Broqueville rejected the idea that the Locarno pacts would weaken the prestige of the League; on the contrary, he said, by aiding the cause of peace they would inevitaby strengthen the basic ideal underlying the system of collective security. He concluded his remarks by a fervid eulogy of Locarno, which had been "a work of life and of peace."[66] The next day the Senate unanimously voted to ratify the treaties.[67]

For nearly eleven years Belgians relied on the guarantees of the Rhineland pact, which came to be regarded as one of the three great documents establishing the position of Belgium in international affairs, the other two being the Covenant of the League and the Kellogg Pact.[68]

With the signature of the Locarno treaties the Belgian government had achieved one of the great aims of its immediate postwar policy, namely, an Anglo-French guarantee of military aid in case of aggression. After operating for eleven years, during which it was the cornerstone of the foreign policy of the nation, the treaty went into abeyance when circumstances forced a reappraisal of the situation, and the adoption of a new and radically different policy. It will be the work of the following chapter to study the chain of events leading to this important change.

[66] Sénat, *Annales,* March 2, 1926, pp. 579-578.

[67] *Ibid.,* March 3, 1926, p. 596.

[68] *Cf.* Paul Hymans, "Belgium's Position in Europe," *Foreign Affairs,* IX, (1930), 34-64.

CHAPTER EIGHT

Causes of the Reorientation
of Belgian Policy

SELF-PRESERVATION is the fundamental principle guiding the action of states, as it is of individuals. In times of peace there may be no conscious advertence to this fundamental goal, instead, governments may stress reform, expansion, or some other aim, but in periods of international crisis the dominant preoccupation of statesmen is security. If it can be assured by diplomacy without resort to force, the government has scored a success. During the years from 1919 to 1925, Belgian diplomats strove, as has been stated, to preserve their country from the real or fancied German menace. Because the era between 1925 and 1933 was one of decreasing international tension, they turned their energies to secondary aims. With the rise of Hitler and the ever more threatening danger of war, however, the maintenance of peace, essential to the existence of the nation, again became the guiding principle of their action. In the interval between the accession of Leopold III and his surrender, the growth of the German menace and the breakdown of the collective security system based on the Locarno pacts and the League of Nations, caused Belgian leaders to seek a new means of preserving their country from war. To study their reaction to the international crises that occurred during these years is the plan of this chapter.

The line of conduct finally decided upon by Belgium's statesmen was one of complete independence, to prevent the country's being dragged into war as a result of entangling alliances. This course had long been advocated by the Flemish section of the population, especially the Nationalists, with their traditional cry of "Los van Frankrijk." They were joined in 1923 by the Socialists, who had been alienated from the Republic by Poincaré's high-handed Ruhr policy. In 1924 these two groups acting together, forced the rejection of a tariff treaty whereby France lowered duties on iron and steel finished products in return for Belgian reductions on luxury goods.[1]

Although finally regulated by treaty in April, 1928, commercial relations with France, which was committed to a high protective tariff, remained unsatisfactory, and furnished the enemies of that country with an additional argument to justify their antagonism. This was especially true after the depression began, and all governments inaugurated an era of import quotas, exchange controls, and similiar barriers to international trade. Belgium suffered particularly from those imposed by its neighbor to the south. Several agreements were made, but until late in 1936 no satisfactory means of adapting commercial relations between the two states to the changing economic situation was discovered.[2] The method then established consisted in holding biannual meetings of the officials of the interested departments of both governments to settle outstanding problems.[3]

This arrangement came too late, however, to have much effect on the attitude of anti-French elements within Belgium. Meanwhile the government, which had perforce adopted a policy of bilateral trade pacts to replace the general free trade it would have preferred,

[1] Chambre, *Annales*, Feb. 20, 1924, I, 599; Feb. 27, 1924, I, 656.

[2] See Chambre *CRA*, Jan. 19, 1932, pp. 175-177, for agreement of January, 1932; another was signed July 29, 1933; *ibid.*, Nov. 30, 1933, p. 68. It was revised the following January; *BPB*, no. 114, Apr. 7, 1934, p. 9. By the agreement of February 21, 1935, French import quotas were enlarged; *ibid.*, no. 117, Apr. 8, 1935, pp. 8-9.

[3] *Indépendance Belge*, May 27, 1936.

turned its attention to the northern nations.[4] On Demember 22, 1930, a trade convention was signed at Oslo, Norway, by representatives of the Netherlands, Belgium, Denmark, and Sweden. The terms were not revolutionary; they merely bound the signatories not to raise their tariffs without giving one another due notice, and to support any efforts which might be made in the future to stimulate world trade.[5] The agreement, while of little immediate value, showed a tendency among the smaller nations to unite in protection of their mutual interests. In particular, it marked the first move of Belgium away from the Franco-British orbit.

This new direction was apparent in the Ouchy convention signed two years later. On June 20, 1932, during the Lausanne reparations conference, King Albert addressed to premier Renkin one of his well-known public letters. In it, after pointing out the harmful effects of such trade barriers as quotas, high tariffs, surtaxes, and exchange controls, he suggested a remedy:

... no country is able, by itself, to alter in its favor the course of economic evolution. A concerted action of the States towards international solidarity can alone cure the grave evils from which the world is suffering. It is time that this solidarity should assert itself otherwise than by speeches. It seems to me that Belgium should not hesitate to take the initiative which circumstances require and to secure to this end the help of the states which, like our country, feel keenly the necessity of a change in economic policy.[6]

The only government to adopt these ideas was that of the Netherlands, which on July 20 signed with the Belgo-Luxemburg eco-

---

[4] The best discussion of Belgian economic policy in the early postwar period is given by the commercial director at the foreign ministry, Fernand van Langenhove, "La politique commerciale de la Belgique," *Flambeau*, IX (1926), 55-70. The later policy is well described in the report on the budget of the ministry of foreign affairs, made by Carton de Wiart, Chambre, *Documents*, 1934-1935, doc. no. 116, p. 15.

[5] Chambre, *CRA*, July 16, 1931, pp. 813-815.

[6] Cammaerts, *Albert*, pp. 330-331.

nomic union an agreement having for its object the reciprocal and gradual lowering of economic barriers. The three countries bound themselves not to impose new duties, and to lower those already existing by an annual reduction of ten per cent. Other states were invited to adhere.[7] Because of Great Britian's commerical import- ance that nation's adhesion was essential to the success of the new plan. The terms of the recent Ottawa treaty, however, pre- cluded such action without special arrangements with all the Domin- ions, and there was little likelihood that the latter would agree to any changes in the Ottawa convention. Under these conditions, the Ouchy agreement was by mutual consent allowed to lapse.[8]

This setback, and the failure of the gold bloc conference of Oc- tober, 1934, did not, in themselves, provide motives sufficiently powerful to bring about a major shift in policy. The outstanding event causing the change was the advent of Hitler.

Although every change of government in Germany was care- fully watched and its result thoughtfully studied by Belgians, there was at first little official reaction to the new regime. Members of Parliament were guarded in their speeches.[9]

The journalists, however, were more outspoken. Le Peuple was indignant at Hitler's disregard of treaties, and clamored for allied action. The Liberal Etoile Belge was less extreme in its attitude; it merely advised all citizens to keep their self-control, while never forgetting that Germany had but one religion: that of Might. The

[7] Complete text in BPB, no. 110, Aug. 27, 1932, pp. 2-3.

[8] By the terms of the Anglo-Dutch treaty of commerce of 1837, Great Britain could claim equality of treatment in Dutch trade with all other nations. Belgium was opposed to granting Great Britain the benefits of Ouchy without receiving anything in return. Chambre, CRA, Nov. 30, 1933, pp. 67-68.

[9] Nevertheless the reader of the Annales can easily see where the deputies' sympathies lay. An early instance occurred on Feb. 1, 1933, in a debate in the Chamber. Piérard, a Socialist, in interpellating defense minister Devèze on his action in forbidding Le Peuple to be sold to soldiers, said: "A measure like that which you have just taken, fairly reeks of Hitler" ("Une mesure comme celle que vous venez de prendre, sent son Hitler à plein nez"), Chamber, Annales, Feb. 1, 1933, p. 254.

Indépendance Belge, also a Liberal paper, gave warning that Germany would seek to revise the treaty of Versailles; the Allies must be very vigilant, watching the political, military and financial plans of the Reich. And later, after pointing out the threat to peace, it begged for an increase in armament, for "it is not by going out to meet the invaders and waving the palm of peace that we will persuade them to retire."[10]

Even the Flemings became conscious of the threatening danger. Frans van Cauwelaert, leader of the Catholic Flemings, in April 1933, presented to the Chamber the report of the foreign affairs committee. The section describing Belgo-German relations, while apparently passing unnoticed abroad, attracted much attention in Belgium. It pointed out the dangers to peace inherent in the National Socialist regime, and the consequent necessity for a prudent reserve in Belgo-German relations. It also advocated participation in any collective action which might be taken if Germany violated the Versailles or the Locarno treaties. As the considered report of the head of a large group which had long advocated Belgo-German friendship, it deserves full quotation:

We do not desire to interfere in the internal politics of our neighbors, but the observations made by members of the Committee have been inspired by the known intentions of the leaders of the Third Reich on the subject of the treaty of Versailles, of disarmament, of the problems of eastern and central Europe, and of their systematic effort to carry the spiritual exaltation of Germany to a degree which rouses the apprehension of neighboring countries.

The violent language, the barely veiled threats against the status of Europe to which we had been accustomed during electoral campaigns carry more weight since they have spread beyond political rallies, and are brought to the knowledge of the public by the responsible heads of the government; and in the same way youth organizations and party militia acquire a more disquieting character when they leave a sporting or political framework to be incorporated into the armed forces of the State.

[10] *BPB,* no. 112, May 17, 1933, pp. 6-9.

In calling the government's attention to these facts, some members of the committee wondered if Germany were not wilfully transgressing certain stipulations of the Versailles and Locarno treaties regarding disarmament, the demilitarized zone, etc., and if the Belgian government were not authorized to protest to the League of Nations demanding that these be respected.

Belgium wishes to live at peace with Germany. It desires by constant effort, and in a spirit of reciprocity, to develop those economic relations which it knows are important to its general prosperity and that of its ports; it wishes that the tragic memories of the war may be obliterated, that intercourse between the two countries may become more and more active; and it has not hesitated to uphold with its best efforts the policy of reconciliation and of mutual understanding which made possible the settlement, before the date fixed, of certain measures and certain conflicts of interest which were the result of the war. Certain members of the committee believe that the Belgians have been too prompt in making friendly agreements, and exceeded the measure of legitimate trust, but this feeling is not shared by the majority of the committee. It has always encouraged the Government in the policy of pacification, and does not regret it.

But even those who were most attached to this policy when across the frontier there were governments more disposed to welcome it in a spirit of conciliation, now wonder if, under present circumstances, this good will should not give way to a prudent reserve. Public opinion will not understand that the governments which signed the treaty of Versailles with Germany, should show more trust in those who do not pretend to recognize the juridical value of the treaty than they did toward those who contented themselves with simply asking for revision by common consent; that they should be more yielding towards those who threaten to impose their claims by violence than towards representatives from whom loyal collaboration in the political reorganization of Europe could be expected. We do not wish to forget, however, that Belgium, which is exposed in the highest degree to the risks created by the new situation, can only exercise a very limited influence on the policy required by the situation. Our position imposes on us both vigilance and circumspection. It prohibits us from taking any isolated action, and our policy must consist in carefully noting the failures of which Germany may be guilty with regard to existing treaties; and, should the matter require it, in participating in the collective action to which the wrongs committed by the German government may give rise.[11]

The conclusion of the report, with its recommendation of vigilance and circumspection, and its reliance on collective action, did not point to any innovation in policy, a fact which may account for the silence with which it was received abroad.

As the months passed, and there were no signs either of a change in Germany or of any concerted action to oppose Nazi claims, Belgians began to reconsider their policy. In a significant debate on the foreign affairs budget in November, 1933, the opinions of various groups were made clear. The Catholic deputies of the right, the Liberals of the left, and the Socialists and Communists of the extreme left all expressed the same fear of Hitler. Vandervelde went so far as to say that the advent of the Nazis had caused a change in the policy of the POB. Since only France seemed really opposed to German rearmament, the party would now support a pro-French policy.[12] Only one group, the Flemish Nationalists, still kept to their own ideas. To them France was the great enemy, and they believed that the real reason for the forebodings expressed by the Socialist leader was his knowledge of the secret terms of the Franco-Belgian military alliance of 1920, which would, they thought, involve their country in any "preventive" war that France might decide to wage against Germany.[13]

Disregarding these criticisms of the Flemish Nationalists, foreign minister Hymans replied to the other speeches with a straightforward statement of his position. The tone of his discourse was given in its opening paragraph:

As everyone sees and feels, at this moment Europe is passing through a difficult and dangerous crisis. After long efforts to reestablish between the nations who fought one another during the

---

[11] *BPB*, no. 112, p. 8, May 17, 1933.
[12] Chambre, CRA, Nov. 29, 1933, pp. 54-55.
[13] *Ibid.*, Nov. 29, 1933, pp. 51-54.

war normal relations and the cooperation necessary for the restoration of trust and of international life, we see open before us deep and inflammatory disagreements from which sparks may fly. People are unnerved. Nevertheless it is a time to keep cool, to rule our thoughts and to measure our words.

He went on to recall, in a detailed description, the disarmament plans worked out, with much difficulty, at the Geneva Conference. But these had scarcely been completed when the Nazis came into power. The Powers were afraid to allow Germany to rearm under those circumstances. When this became obvious, Hitler left the conference and the League.

"The future is dark" Hymans continued. "Chancellor Hitler has, indeed, in solemn and repeated declarations constantly affirmed his will to peace, and his desire for an understanding with France. But the sudden withdrawal of Germany from the disarmament conference and the League of Nations, the precipitation and brusqueness of this rupture were disturbing symptoms. The German people are living in fever. The exalted mood, the military enthusiasm of the young men formed in the camps may lead to adventures.

He concluded on a slightly less pessimistic note, citing the various nonaggression pacts and treaties of friendship recently signed, particularly the closer union between France and Great Britain, whose "understanding is necessary for the maintenance of European order."[14]

The forebodings expressed in this speech were reechoed by premier de Broqueville in an important declaration of policy made the following March. In order to understand fully the motives for his action, it will be helpful to summarize briefly the attitude of Belgium toward disarmament. Like others of the Allies, the country as a whole was rather skeptical of the reality of German disarmament.

In February, 1927, Carton de Wiart interpellated Vandervelde,

---

[14]   Chambre, *Annales,* Nov. 29, 1933, pp. 150-151.

then minister of foreign affairs, on his actions in agreeing to the suppression of the Allied Military Commission, entrusted with the supervision of the clauses of Versailles which were intended to prevent the rearmament of Germany. Vandervelde explained that the decision had been taken in accord with the treaty, after the Council of Ambassadors decided that Germany's obligations were discharged. Defense minister de Broqueville came to Vandervelde's support with the unanswerable argument:

> We are reproached with having adhered [to the Council's decision]. Should we Belgians have played the lone cavalier, acting in opposition to an entente? It would have been . . . a truly ridiculous attitude.[15]

The subject was then dropped, to be brought up once more in the Senate debate on the Young plan in January, 1930, and again nearly four years later in the discussion of the budget. On these two occasions it was Hymans who had to defend the government's action; he did so in practically the same terms as those used by his Socialist predecessor.[16]

These suspicions as to the reality of Germany's disarmament motivated the Belgian attitude towards disarmament by the Allies. As early as 1926, Vandervelde explained that he could not give his delegates to the preparatory commission any more explicit instructions than they should work for a practical system of supervision, and always keep in mind "the particularly threatened position" of their country.[17] Likewise Louis de Brouckère, one of the delegates, declared at Geneva that he viewed the disarmament issue "as a function of the problem of security; that is only good sense."[18]

When at length the Geneva Disarmament Conference opened

[15] Chambre, *Annales,* Nov. 29, 1933, p. 151.
[16] *Cf. ibid.,* Nov. 29, 1933, p. 152.
[17] Sénat, *Annales,* Apr. 28, 1926, p. 774.
[18] Sénat, *Documents,* Feb. 27, 1929, p. 3, doc. no. 88.

on February 2, 1932, the Belgian views on the question had in no way changed. In a speech to the Senate, foreign minister Hymans made his attitude clear. First, all cruel offensive arms, such as bombers, heavy artillery, poisonous gas, and biological warfare must be prohibited. An international supervisory commission must be established, and given the power to enforce its decisions with adequate sanctions. Only then could armaments be reduced by progressive stages, and "of course Belgium must be allowed to keep what is indispensable for the defense of the territory.[19]

At the same time, the government did not forget that two important groups, the Flemings and the Socialists, were strongly in favor of total disarmament, and in particular, of a reduction in the time of military training. With the exception of the extremists of the Front Party, however, there was general agreement in the country with the statement that "Belgium must be the first to desire disarmament; the last to be able to disarm *before the others.*"[20]

With such unanimity of opinion at home the Belgian representatives did everything in their power to bring about the success of the conference. In March 1933, they presented a plan which, they hoped, would reconcile the divergent views of the Great Powers on the subject. Although this plan was adopted as a basis for discussion by the Conference on June 8, no headway was made, as the National Socialist revolution in Germany caused a feeling of alarm, and all attention was diverted from disarmament to the rising menace.[21] On October 14, 1933, Germany withdrew from the Conference and gave notice of withdrawal from the League of Nations. A month later the Conference adjourned until an understanding with the German government could be reached. The

---

[19] Sénat, *CRA,* Feb. 18, 1932, p. 218.

[20] Sénat, *Documents,* Feb. 27, 1929, p. 6, doc. no. 88. Italics in the original. Practically the same thing was said by General Denis, minister of defense, before his departure for the Geneva conference; Sénat, *CRA,* Jan. 21, 1932, p. 137.

[21] Sénat, *CRA,* March 7, 1934, p. 236.

French government was insistent that the German demand for the abrogation of the unilateral disarmament clauses of the Versailles treaty should not be granted.

Hymans considered this attitude a defiance of good sense, and, on the advice of King Albert, he visited the Quai d'Orsay to remonstrate with his French colleagues. When this action failed to change their point of view, premier de Broqueville decided to make an open statement of his opinion on the matter.[22] The death of King Albert delayed the statement, and so it happened that de Broqueville's speech came as the first important declaration of Belgian foreign policy in Leopold's reign. In answering an interpellation in the Senate on the government's attitude regarding German rearmament, the premier found the opportunity he sought. He pointed out that there were only two means of preventing German rearmament, either an appeal to the League Council, or a preventive war. If the first means were tried, the British and Italian governments would side with the German government, which would then refuse to accept a League summons to disarm; the other alternative, a preventive war, was worse than the evil it sought to remedy. The best that could be hoped for, he concluded, was an international agreement which "to attain security as its supreme goal, would involve the minimum of sacrifice and the maximum of safeguards."[23]

This statement which was at once recognized as a declaration of general policy, and not limited to the disarmament question, was received in many circles with surprised disapproval. Hymans. who had taken the floor after his chief to give some supplementary information regarding the Geneva Conference, found it necessary to give a long speech two days later in support of the premier's leading thesis. In it he strove to show that de Broqueville was not trying to adopt an isolationist policy. The guiding thread of his

[22] Charles de Broqueville, "Pourquoi j'ai parlé en mars, 1934," *Revue Générale,* CXLI (1939), 289-298.
[23] Sénat, *CRA,* March 6, 1934, pp. 221-222.

action was security against a future war. "There is only one means of conjuring away this peril, whether or not a disarmament treaty is concluded, that is, an understanding binding England, France, and Italy. This entente is our chief safeguard. The government is devoting every effort to encourage and to consolidate it, and to obtain compensatory measures of security."[24]

Outside of parliament there was a division of opinion. The Liberals, the Nationalists, and the Socialists were united for once in their denunciation. The *Nation Belge,* organ of the Nationalists, was most violent in its diatribes against the repudiation of alliances.[25] *Le Peuple* considered that it was "a betrayal of the most sacred interests of the nation."[26]

On second thought, and after private explanations, there were some changed opinions. On March 15, the Senate adopted the following resolution:

The Senate, acknowledging the declaration in which the prime minister has established the danger Belgium incurs as a result of Germany's rearmament,

Expresses the desire that an armament race may be prevented,

Invites the government not to be associated with any policy which would have for effect a German rearmament,

Insists that Belgium obtain at once the compensatory guarantees to which the increased dangers she runs give her a right,

Believes that, if the Powers should accept a solution of a nature to aggravate the danger, Belgium would have an even greater right to obtain measures of security,

Trusts that the government will assure the execution of this policy.[27]

Only one vote was registered against this resolution and, although the Socialists abstained from voting, they expressly stated

[24] Sénat, *CRA,* March 8, 1934, p. 244.
[25] *BPB,* no. 114, Apr. 7, 1934, p. 6.
[26] *Le Peuple,* March 9, 1934.
[27] Sénat, *CRA,* March 15, 1934, p. 276.

that they agreed fully with everything but the expression of confidence in the existing cabinet.[28]

The premier's outspoken statement of a policy toward Germany which was markedly different from that advocated by France and indicated a lack of faith in the League system of collective security, was the first important step taken by the Belgian government toward an independent foreign policy. There had, it is true, been some previous statements of a desire on the part of Belgian statesmen to keep their country out of its neighbors' quarrels. As early as 1930 and 1931, the Catholic leader, Poullet, in reporting on the foreign affairs budgets, had advocated a policy of voluntary neutrality, which had received the unqualified approval even of so constitutional an objector as Vandervelde, the head of the Socialist party.[29] But this was the first public and official statement, and the circumstances were such as to underline its significance.

The events of the next years confirmed the people and government of Belgium in their desire for an independent foreign policy, unhampered by the obligations of the Covenant of the League. The breakdown of the collective security system based upon the League of Nations was a tragedy to the small states which had placed their confidence in its power to safeguard them from war. The series of events following upon Hitler's rise to power forced them finally to reconsider their attitude and obligations toward the Covenant. In order to understand the position of Belgium with regard to the League at this time, it will be necessary to summarize the relations between the two since the treaty of Versailles.

At Paris in 1919 Belgium was one of the states represented on the commission for the League of Nations, and Hymans, the Bel-

[28] *Ibid.*, March 15, 1934, p. 277.
[29] Sénat, *Documents*, June 22, 1939, doc. no. 87, pp. 2-3. *Cf.* also the conclusion of an article written by Vandervelde in 1933: "Since 1914 Belgium has not been under any obligation to be neutral. But she aspires with increasing energy to be neutral of her own accord." Emile Vandervelde, "Belgian Foreign Policy and the Nationalities Question," *Foreign Affairs*, XI (1933), 670.

gian delegate, who had a command of both French and English, took an active part in the debates on the Covenant. On three points particularly did he intervene in the discussions. One of these, the location of the seat of the proposed League, though of relatively minor importance, loomed large in Belgian eyes. Internal politics forced the government to make every effort to secure the location of the League at Brussels, but in spite of French backing, the attempt failed.[30] The Belgian delegation took a strong stand on two more significant questions: the representation of the small nations on the commission for the League, and eventually on the Council; and the strengthening of the League by giving more weight to decisions of the Council and by enlarging the scope of the sanctions to be imposed on recalcitrant states.

Hymans was successful in his fight to include more of the smaller nations on the League commission, in spite of the disapproval of Wilson and Cecil. His avowed purpose in insisting on the inclusion of more states was the increase of the prestige of the League by eradicating from it any taint of resemblance to the Holy Alliance of a century earlier.[31] In acting thus he was motivated by a desire to increase the security of his country, for, since Germany's violation of the treaties of 1839, Belgium looked forward to the establishment of an international organization as protection against another invasion.

[30] David Hunter Miller, *The Drafting of the Covenant* (New York, 1928), II, 260, 339, 365, 704-706. Typical of the Belgian attitude toward the question were the remarks made by Jules Destrée, a prominent Socialist. The eloquence is untranslatable.: "Le siège de la Ligue [*sic*] des Nations à Bruxelles, c'est la croix d'honneur qu'on apporte à l'hôpital à un grand blessé. La Belgique est le grand blessé de cette guerre et avait droit à cette marque solennelle de reconnaissance. Si elle nous était refusée, nous nous inclinerions sans colère, mais non sans amertume et sans tristesse, non seulement parce que l'on nous aura fait tort, mais parce que cette Ligue des Nations, sur laquelle nous avions fondé tant d'espoirs, aura débuté par manquer aux idéalités qui justifient sa constitution. Où en espérer si elle n'est faite pour consacrer le droit? (Applaudissements émus, unanimes et prolongés.) Chambre, *Annales,* April 19, 1919, I, 801.

[31] Miller, *Drafting of Covenant,* I, 125 and II, 256-257, 259-260; Miller, *Diary,* V, 49, doc. no. 317; V, 51, doc. no. 318; V, 104, doc. no. 327.

It was with the same end in view that Hymans proposed to reinforce the coercive powers of the League. To achieve this he suggested that a majority vote should be sufficient to establish a violation of the pact; that acceptance of the League's decision should be made obligatory in a great number of cases; and that sanctions should be imposed for failure to submit disputes to arbitration, as well as for nonacceptance of an arbitral decision.[32] These proposals were rejected, but the Belgian government did not abandon its struggle to strengthen the Covenant.

In 1921, when amendments were presented to the Assembly giving the Council the right to decide whether a breach of the Covenant had occurred, and empowering the Council to regulate the imposition of sanctions, the Belgian delegates voted in their favor.[33]

Even more illustrative of Belgium's desire to strengthen the League was Hyman's active and intelligent participation in the work of the Council. Having collaborated in drawing up the pact, he was conversant with its meaning and procedures, and his action, notably in the Polish-Lithuanian dispute and in the Aaland Islands case, received high praise.[34] His government left him relatively free, binding him only in one respect: If any of the countries with which Belgium had been at war were to seek admission to the League, he was to ask that before taking up that question, the League should first examine the fidelity of the petitioners to treaty engagements,

---

[32] Miller, *Drafting of the Covenant,* I, 170-180.

[33] League, *Assembly Records,* II session, 30 meeting, Oct. 4, 1921, pp. 806-808.

[34] League, *Council Minutes,* II session, 7 meeting, Feb. 11, 1920, p. 5; IX session, 2 meeting, Paris, Sept. 1920, p. 7; *Assembly Records,* II session, 6 meeting, Sept. 1921, p. 63. Hymans wrote of his work on the Council: "I participated in the efforts of the Council to build up a positive foundation for the new institution. The role of Belgium never varied throughout; it was always inspired by the wish to create a state of mind which would permit of loyal cooperation without any mental reservation, among the states represented at Geneva and to set up a coordinated system of arbitration and of security." Paul Hymans, "Belgium's position in Europe," *Foreign Affairs,* IX (1930), 56.

particularlly in the matter of reparations. Until a satisfactory answer could be given, the Belgian government could not consent to their admission.[35]

As time went on, the people and government of Belgium became more and more satisfied that the League would benefit the cause of peace.[36] The *"aventure á deux"* with France, which led to the Ruhr occupation, the consequent lowering of Belgian prestige, and the deterioration in prosperity naturally increased confidence in measures strengthening the ideal of collective security.[37]

On September 26, 1925, Hymans solemnly assured the foreign affairs commission that Belgium would adhere to the optional clause of the Permanent Court of International Justice, whereby states bound themselves to submit all disputes to the Court. The statement was unanimously approved by the commission.[38] The law ratifying this action of the government was voted in the Belgian Senate without opposition, after passing the Chamber with only two negative votes.[39]

At the same time the government adopted the suggestions re garding education in internationalism made by the Committee of Intellectual Cooperation, itself a Belgian concept.[40] A course of

[35] Sénat, *Annales,* Nov. 30, 1920, p. 30; Chambre, *Annales,* March 3, 1926, I, 949.
[36] As early as 1920 Carton de Wiart said: "More and more this League of Nations appears as a living and acting institution." Chambre, *Annales,* Nov. 23, 1920, I, 11.
[37] *Cf.* Chambre, *Documents,* May 8, 1924, doc. no. 236, pp. 1226-1228; *Annales,* July 10, 1924; II, 1837.
[38] Chambre, *Documents,* 1925-1926, doc. no. 121, pp. 1-2.
[39] Sénat, *Annales,* March 2, 1926, p. 588; Chambre, *Annales,* Jan. 27, 1926, I, 684.
[40] The Belgians had suggested on March 26, 1919, that the following clause be inserted in the League Covenant:

Les états associés assureront, dans la plus large mesure possible, le développement des relations internationales, morales, scientifiques et artistiques

lessons was introduced into Belgian primary and secondary schools to explain to the pupils the aim and achievements of the League; and Henri Pirenne, the famous Belgian historian, was commissioned to write a history textbook that would stress internationalism as opposed to nationalism.[41]

This beginning of active Belgian interest in the League coincided with an incident regarding the organization of the Council. At Paris in 1919, Hymans had proposed that there be five permanent and four non-permanent places on the Council.[42] Although this plan was not adopted, the smaller powers were assigned four instead of the two seats originally allotted them. The refusal of the United States to join the League resulted in an equal division of seats between the permanent members, all of which were great powers, and the non-permanent members, chosen from the smaller nations. In 1922 an amendment increased the number of non-permanent members of the Council by two, without arousing much protest from the Great Powers, who were thereby outnumbered. When in 1926 Germany applied for membership in the league, in accordance with the Locarno program, a stipulation that it be given a permanent seat on the Council formed part of the application. This precipitated a storm that had been brewing for some time as several states, notably Brazil, Spain, and Poland, were eager for permanent seats. The Belgian government took the position that the Council should not be unduly enlarged, lest it become too cum-

---

entre les divers peuples et prouveront, par tous les moyens, la formation d'une mentalité internationale.

Il est créé, à cette effet, une Commission internationale de relations intellectuelles.

Although the idea was rejected then, it bore fruit later, when the Committee of intellectual Cooperation was founded. Miller, *Drafting of the Covenant*, I, 350.

[41] Chambre, *Annales*, Feb. 3, 1925, p. 452; Chambre, *Documents*, June 22, 1926, doc. no. 360, p. 17; June 8, 1927, doc. no. 230, p. 33; Chambre, *CRA*, Feb. 7, 1928, p. 162.

[42] Miller, *Drafting of the Covenant*, II, 259.

bersome for effective work. On the other hand an increase in the number of Great Powers with permanent membership should necessitate an increase in the number of non-permanent small states, in order to safeguard the rights of the latter.[43] The compromise by which the number of non-permanent members was increased, but with limited reeligibility, meant for Belgium the loss of the seat on the Council held since the foundation of the League.[44]

In spite of this disappointment, attachment to the League had by this time become recognized as one of the bases of Belgian foreign policy.[45] Unfortunately, a series of crises which were soon to appear, demonstrated the impotence of the League to settle disputes involving great powers, and Belgium's leaders were forced to adapt their program to changed circumstances.

The first of these crises was the Sino-Japanese conflict. It attracted little attention in Belgium, however, merely providing the opposition with an occasion for heckling the government.[46]

The second crisis, that caused by the Ethiopian war, aroused much more anxiety in the little kingdom. The significance for Belgium of any break between Italy and the League may be surmised from the fact that in the discussion in the Senate following de Broqueville's statement, foreign minister Hymans had said that the nation's "principal safeguard from invasion" lay "in the entente between England, France, and Italy."[47] The Abyssinian incident

[43] Chambre, *Annales,* March 3, 1926, I, 942-943; Sénat, *Annales,* April 28, 1926, p. 773. It is of interest that only during Vandervelde's term as foreign minister were reports on the sessions of the League included among the Parliamentary documents.

[44] Belgium's exclusion was not pleasing to Germany. Stresemann was particularly desirous to have Vandervelde on the Council because of his compliance with German wishes; *Stresemann,* III, 222, entry of Oct., 1927.

[45] *Cf.* Hymans speech, Chambre, *CRA,* Nov. 29, 1933, p. 53; Prosper Poullet, "Belgique," *Dictionnaire Diplomatique,* (Paris, 1933), I, 311.

[46] Vandervelde and Jaquemotte raised the question in Parliament in March 1932; Chambre, *CRA,* March 1, 1932, pp. 363-367. The following year Senator Rolin did likewise, but neither time was much interest aroused; Sénat, *CRA,* March 22, 193, pp. 75-77.

[47] Sénat, *CRA,* March 8, 1934, p. 244.

threatened this understanding, which for several years had seemed to be strong enough to serve as a solid basis for European peace. In February 1935, the Belgian government sent Hymans to London to discuss means of reinforcing the pact. As a result of his conversations there, the idea of an air agreement among the Locarno powers made headway.[48] The ensuing negotiations brought representatives of France, Great Britain, and Italy to the city of Stresa to discuss the action to be taken in reply to the German conscription law of March 16, which was in violation of the treaty of Versailles. The "Stresa front," as the union of the three powers was called, was popular in Belgium, where much reliance was still placed in the Locarno guarantees.[49]

This was, however, to be the last instance of a common action of the three powers; while Mussolini was conferring with Flandin, Laval, MacDonald, and Sir John Simon, Italian armies were concentrating on the frontier of Ethiopia, and Haile Selassie's government had twice requested the League Council to take immediate action. During the spring and summer of 1935, it became obvious that the Italian government was determined to force an African war and that the governments of Great Britain and France were unwilling to take drastic action against Italy.

From the beginning Belgium was indirectly affected by the conflict, because two Belgian officers had been authorized to serve as instructors in the Ethiopian army, and the Abyssinian government had placed large armaments orders with Belgian firms. Following the example of other states, the Brussels government, by a decree of August 19, 1935, refused to permit delivery of the armaments until the League's investigation of the matter should be completed. The instructors were allowed to stay until actual hostilities broke out, but Belgian volunteers in the Abyssinian army were urged to return at once, and those still subject to military

[48] Sénat, *Annales*, May 28, 1935, pp. 660-662.
[49] Chambre, *Annales*, April 15, 1935, pp. 1005-1006.

service were immediately recalled by the authorities.[50] As Belgium was not at that time a member of the League Council, its government was not involved in the negotiations between the League and the Italian government prior to the September 1935 meeting of the Assembly. On September 12, during the debate on the attitude to be taken in the dispute, premier van Zeeland stated the intention of his government to remain faithful to the Covenant and to fulfil its obligations; at the same time he expressed the hope that conciliatory measures would avert war.[51] The speech was warmly applauded in Belgium.

As Wauters wrote in the great Socialist daily, *Le Peuple,* "M. van Zeeland expressed in terms of pliant and measured firmness the opinion of the immense majority of a country which has not forgotten the memory of the humiliating destiny which the law of might imposed upon her in 1914."[52] These sentiments were echoed in the Liberal *Soir* and the Catholic *Libre Belgique.*[53]

Nevertheless on all sides there was opposition to the idea of applying military sanctions. On October 10 the foreign affairs committee discussed the matter thoroughly, and even Senator Wauters, who had supported the premier's speech, stated that he approved only of economic sanctions. The committee adopted a resolution inviting the government to "avoid military sanctions, but to follow the great powers in what concerns economic sanctions."[54]

When hostilities actually broke out in October and Italy was named as the aggressor, the Belgian government collaborated with the League in adopting the sanctions proposed by a special Coordination Committee on which it was represented. In reply to an inter-

---

[50] *Ibid.,* Nov. 19, 1935, p. 30; Jean de Failon, "La guerre d'Afrique et la paix de l'Europe," *Revue Générale,* CXXXIV (1935), 554.

[51] League, *Assembly Records,* 16 session, 6 meeting, Sept 12, 1935, p. 64.

[52] *Le Peuple,* September 14, 1935.

[53] *BPB,* no. 120, Nov. 16, 1935, p. 8.

[54] *Ibid.,* pp. 9-10.

pellation in the Chamber, van Zeeland explained this action, saying that he had supported sanctions not only because Belgium was bound to the League, but chiefly because on this occasion for the first time Great Britain had taken a decided stand in favor of collective security as it was understood on the continent. This policy was approved by all except the Flemish Nationalists.[55]

Nevertheless the Belgian cabinet was still eager to restore the entente uniting Italy with Great Britain and France. To this end on November 2, during a session of the Coordination Committee, van Zeeland suggested that the British and French representatives be given a mandate by the League to find a solution within the Covenant.[56] The outcome of this suggestion was that the Hoare-Laval plan, which resulted from it, received League backing, at least until it was rejected by Mussolini and repudiated by the British government.

When, on November 19, 1935, the three chief parties in the Belgian parliament pronounced in favor of sanctions, they were motivated by the consideration that their country's security rested in large measure on fidelity to the League.[57] But when the following months showed that the sanctions were insufficient to handicap Italy, and that for Abyssinia, at least, reliance on collective security had brought only disaster, there was a change of opinion in some circles which was not, however, openly manifested. Instead, excuses were made to cover up the failure of the League. It was this purpose which motivated Segers, one of the leaders of the

---

[55] Chambre, *Annales*, Nov. 19, 1935, pp. 30-32, and 37. For text of the sanctions, see Great Britain, *Parliamentary Papers*, 1935-1936, Cmd. 5071, pp. 42-50.

[56] Toynbee, *Survey*, 1935, II, 285-286, believes that van Zeeland was acting in agreement with Hoare and Laval in order to give some kind of legality to the Franco-British plans already being worked out.

[57] Chambre, *Annales*, Nov. 19, 1935, p. 37; Sénat, *Documents*, Dec. 12, 1935, doc. no. 27, p. 38. Certain sections of the Liberal press, however, denounced sanctions as bringing economic ruin to the country. *BPB*, no. 121, Feb. 12, 1936, p. 2.

Catholic party, when he reminded his colleagues in the Senate that, after all, Abyssinia was not civilized and that there was some justice to the Italian claims.[58]

The remilitarization of the Rhineland, which will be discussed later, intensified the desire of the Belgian government to see the end of the Italo-Ethiopian war, and if possible to placate Italy, one of the Locarno guarantors. This desire was strikingly evident in the speech with which van Zeeland, as president of the Assembly, closed the session of July 1936, which had taken the momentous decision to terminate sanctions against Italy. He declared that by the imposition of sanctions the League had done its duty, and that the Abyssinian government could ask no more.[59] It was not, however, until March 22, 1938, that Belgium resumed normal diplomatic relations with Italy by appointing Count de Kerchove de Denterghem as Ambassador to "the King of Italy and Emperor of Ethiopia," and even then the reservation was made that this action did not imply *de jure* recognition of the Italian conquest.[60]

While on the one hand expressing dislike for Fascism and its methods, many Belgians were as strongly opposed to Communism. This attitude was to a great extent conditioned by two important factors, one, the strong Catholic sentiments of a large portion of the population, and the other, the seizure—or nationalization—by the Soviet government of Belgian property.[61]

---

[58] Sénat, *Annales,* Feb. 5, 1935, pp. 218-222.

[59] League, *Assembly Records,* 16 session, 26 meeting, July 4, 1936, pp. 69-71. See Toynbee, *Survey,* 1935, II, 510-512 for a scathing criticism of this speech.

[60] Sénat, *Annales,* April 5, 1938, p. 1130.

[61] The Belgian losses, though in themselves not as large as those suffered by the nationals of other states, were proportionally quite heavy.

Segers' report on budget,
> Belgian claims.

13 mining, coal, and metallurgic companies	965,000,000
13 coal enterprises	100,000,000
3 coking furnaces	57,000,000
8 diverse mining enterprises	39,000,000
(gold francs)	1,161,000,000

At the Genoa conference of April and May 1922, foreign minister Jaspar caused a serious crisis by rejecting a British suggestion that the states claiming restitution of nationalized property would forego this claim, and be satisfied with long-term leases instead, as Russia refused to allow any private ownership of large industries. Thereupon the French delegates, who had previously accepted the British proposal, revoked their decision. As it turned out, the Russians would not grant even the leases; but had the opposite been the case, Jaspar's action might have had serious results. He held firmly to his claims, and before the end of the conference secured his colleagues' adhesion to an agreement binding them not to make individual settlements, nor to permit their nationals to make private arrangements with Russia until a general understanding was reached.[62]

In 1925 Russia approached Belgium through Ambassador Moncheur in London, to ascertain whether the demands had been

16 construction companies and foundries	142,000,000
4 glass factories	68,000,000
11 factories of glass products & construction materials	38,000,000
	106,000,000
3 oil and petroleum derivative companies	113,000,000
4 chemical products companies	107,000,000
7 textile societies	73,000,000
36 Miscellaneous enterprises	67,000,000
	360,000,000
43 Public utilities: RR., lighting, gas, water electricity, telephone	582,000,000
Total industrial enterprises (161)	2,350,000,000
Liquid assets and deposits in Russian banks	
Specie and current accounts 193,000,000	
Bonds 87,000,000	
	280,000,000
Belgian commercial credits	125,000,000
Russian public debts in Belgian hands	640,000,000
Capital goods, merchandise, etc. in Russia	105,000,000
Grand total, gold francs	3,358,000,000

$649,094,000

Sénat, *Documents,* Feb. 27, 1929, doc. no. 88, pp. 37-38.

[62] Chambre, *Annales,* May 23, 1922, I, 879.

reconsidered. As both parties maintained their positions—the Belgians insisting on full payment, the Russians offering only limited compensation—the negotiations were dropped.[63] As foreign minister, Vandervelde followed the same policy, refusing to open diplomatic relations until substantial guarantees were forthcoming that restitution would be made. He did, however, try to work out a temporary arrangement, whereby in return for a *de facto* recognition, a measure of economic intercourse would be restored.[64] Some Belgian firms had already tried to do business with the Soviets, but until 1928 such an undertaking was extremely hazardous, as it received no protection from either government. In that year, however, a semi-official Russian agency was established at Antwerp to regularize commercial intercourse. The business thus encouraged received a severe set-back two years later, when in October 1930, a decree was issued in Brussels imposing rigid restrictions on trade with nations not having a commercial treaty with Belgium; the importation of Russian wheat was thereby greatly diminished. Three years later the Soviet authorities tried to reopen the Belgian market by the foundation of another semiofficial organization, "La Société des Bois du Nord."[65] This time the project was mutually beneficial, for whereas in 1933, Belgian exports to Russia amunted to a mere 52,000,000 francs, the following year the total had risen to 113,000,000 francs.[66]

Official recognition, however, still seemed distant. At Geneva, in September 1934, during the deliberations on the admission of the USSR to the League, Jaspar again brought forward his country's claims, citing them as the reason why Brussels still refused to recognize the Soviet government. As, however, France and Great Britain favored Russian entry into the League, and it seemed highly

[63] Sénat, *Documents,* Feb. 24, 1927, doc. no. 52, pp. 7-8 ; Feb. 27, 1929, doc. no. 88, p. 37.

[64] Sénat, *Annales,* Apr. 28, 1926, pp. 771-772.

[65] Chambre, *Documents,* Mar. 31, 1936, doc. no. 191, p. 1.

[66] Chambre, *Annales,* Apr. 15, 1935, p. 1008.

desirable to increase its membership, Belgium abstained, rather than cast a negative vote.[67]

The political crisis that occurred in Belgium three months later abruptly changed the situation. In order to secure Socialist collaboration in his reforms, van Zeeland was forced to recognize Soviet Russia, as this condition was the *sine qua non* of the party's support.[68] Such a step implied abandonment of the claims, but it also meant that business relations could be placed on a treaty basis.

This was done on September 5, 1935, by the signing of a pact which bound the Soviet government to import a minimum of 190,-000,000 francs worth of Belgian merchandise during the year beginning with October 1, 1935, to be increased by 10,000,000 francs the following year. The agreement was to hold for three years.[69] In 1938 the treaty was prolonged for another year, during which the purchase of at least 200,000,000 francs worth of Belgian goods was guaranteed.[70]

In spite of the commercial advantages to be reaped from Russian trade, many Belgians remained profoundly distrustful of the Communist regime. Consequently when the terms of the Franco-Soviet pact were published early in 1935, there was strong disapproval in Belgium. The Liberal *Etoile Belge* prophesied that if ever Stalin thought it advantageous, he would break the pact and join Hitler. The Catholic *Libre Belgique* echoed this belief; while the Flemish *Standaard* headed its editorial comments "The Franco-Russ Military Pact, or, the Triumphal March of Bolshevism."[71]

The last criticism seems mild, when the fact that it emanated from a Flemish organ is taken into consideration. Many Flemings firmly believed the agitators who told them that because their country was bound to France by the military agreement of 1920,

---

[67] Chambre, *Annales,* Jan. 29, 1935, p. 210.
[68] *Indépendance Belge,* Jan. 14, 1936.
[69] Sénat, *Documents,* Oct. 12, 1935, doc. no. 27, p. 14.
[70] Chambre, *Documents,* Mar. 3, 1938, doc. no. 132, p. 18.
[71] *BPB,* no. 122, May 23, 1936, pp. 10-11.

they might one day be forced to join that country in a war to protect Soviet Russia.[72] The government did not accept so extreme
a view, nor did it admit Hitler's argument that the pact was in-
compatible with the Locarno treaties. In replying to a German note
to this effect, van Zeeland said that under no circumstances could
his country be involved in war against its will merely by the automatic play of alliances since "The Belgian Government retains
the right and duty to decide if and when they are to respond to
an appeal for assistance."[73]

The Belgian public was not fully reassured by this statement,
particularly as the French elections of 1936 had been a victory for
the Left. To some excitable persons it seemed as if Communism
were around the corner, above all when an epidemic of sit-down
strikes spread from France to the mines of the Borinage. Many
Walloons, hitherto friendly to the Republic, now began to believe that these social troubles were the result of the ties binding their country to a nation so closely allied to Soviet Russia,
and under a left wing government.[74] And that nation was apparently powerless to check the expanding power of Germany. Perhaps the most important single external factor in motivating a
reorientation of Belgian policy was the inability or unwillingness of France and Great Britain to force Germany to respect the
treaties of Versailles and Locarno. This state of affairs was clearly
evident after the remilitarization of the Rhineland by Germany
which violated both treaties.

On February 14, 1936, premier van Zeeland visited Flandin,
the French foreign minister, to discuss with him the situation in-

[72] Cf. Richard Whittier, "Belgium emphasizes security," Contemporary Review, CLI (1937), 29. A French commentator hit off the situation cleverly:
"Les flamands catholiques n'aiment ni la caserne, ni la Russie, ni la France. Il
y avait là une combinaison bien faite pour les exaspérer." Bertrand de Jouvenal,
"La nouvelle orientation de la politique étrangère belge; les raisons intérieures,"
Europe Nouvelle, XIX (1936), 1062.
[73] Great Britian, Parliamentary Papers, 1935-1936 Cmd. 5143, doc. no. 30.
[74] Whittier, loc. cit., 29-37; Indépendance Belge, July 15, 1936.

volved in the accelerated tempo of German rearmament. In the course of their conversations both men agreed that there was no immediate likelihood that Germany would violate the Rhineland clauses of the Locarno agreements.[75] The fallacy of this judgment was very soon made evident, for three weeks later German troops entered the demilitarized zone. On the same day, March 8, 1936, the German government presented to the Allied powers a memorandum attempting to justify the violation on the ground that the recently concluded Franco-Soviet treaty of mutual assistance, in that it was directed against Germany, was in effect a nullification of the Locarno agreement, and that the Reich would therefore no longer consider itself bound by its provisions. At the same time Hitler proposed that a non-aggression pact be concluded between Germany, Belgium, and France, with Great Britain and Italy as guarantors. He also expressed his willingness to sign similar pacts with the states bordering on the east of Germany, to enter upon an air pact, and to reenter the League.[76] The Belgian government at once recalled all troops on leave and followed the example of the French foreign office by asking for a special session of the League Council.[77] Before this could take place, there was a meeting of the Locarno powers at Paris on March 10, at which there was a serious divergence between the French and British as to the attitude to be assumed toward Germany. A transfer of the discussions to London and a simultaneous convocation of the Council was decided upon.

Van Zeeland went to London via Brussels, where he made a brief statement of policy in the Senate.

The Locarno Treaty has been repeatedly said to be the foundation and an essential part of Belgium's international status. Germany's actions in tearing it up strikes Belgium more gravely and severely than any other country. Yet Belgium has firmly adhered to her

---

[75] *Indépendance Belge,* Feb. 15, 1936.
[76] New York *Times,* March 8, 1936.
[77] *Indépendance Belge,* March 9, 1936; F. J. Berber, *Locarno, a collection of documents* (London, 1936), p. 233, doc. no. 44.

part in this pact. The German memorandum takes as a pretext a pretended violation in the Franco-Soviet pact, but Belgium had no part in nor connection with the Franco-Soviet negotiation. For us it has no consequences, for we are neither directly nor indirectly concerned. We can say without fear of contradiction that we have kept the Locarno treaty not only in letter but in spirit.

He went on to reveal that the Franco-Belgian military agreement of 1920 had just been abrogated by the two governments, so that Belgium was in an unassailable position, since it was not bound to France by any political or military ties of a bilateral nature, which might force it into a war should the Franco-Soviet pact become operative. The premier then formulated the policy he intended to follow in the London negotiations: to maintain the Locarno formula of mutual guarantees, to condemn treaty violations, and to work for a close union among the Locarno powers.[78]

In London two parallel sets of discussions were carried on: one by the Locarno powers, to decide on a common line of action in view of the remilitarization; the other by the members of the League Council, to decide whether or not Germany had violated the Versailles treaty. As France, Great Britain, and Italy were members of the League Council, and Belgium was invited to send a representative to the Council meetings, the two sets of deliberations were conducted by the same men, and tended to overlap somewhat. At both van Zeeland appeared in the role familiar to Belgian statesmen since 1918—that of mediator between conflicting British and French policies. At the first meeting of the Council on March 14, he put forward his country's case, showing that Belgium was not involved in the Franco-Soviet pact, as Germany averred, but that, on the other hand, Belgium was the greatest victim of the German action. He claimed that this was so because the remilitarization meant the practical abrogation of the Locarno treaties, which were the very foundation of Belgium's international status,

[78] Sénat, *Annales,* March 11, 1936, pp. 437-439.

as well as of its security.[79] Van Zeeland's brief and moderate speech made a good impression on the British representatives, who realized the force of his arguments.[80] His support of the British government in its refusal to apply sanctions to Germany, in spite of the demand of the French government, gained for him in return, assurances of military support in case of further aggression. These assurances, incorporated in the Anglo-Belgo-French agreement of March 19, 1936, specified that in case hostilities should break out, the three governments would at once consult as to the measures to be taken, and would act upon them immediately; to facilitate such prompt action, staff conversations were to begin if an agreement with Germany and Italy was not speedily reached. These military guarantees were only to be effective until the signature of a new Locarno pact which would restore to France and Belgium the security that had been lost with the remilitarization of the Rhineland.[81]

While the Locarno powers had succeeded in reaching this agreement, the League Council had been impotent. A resolution that Germany's action "was a clear violation of Articles 42 and 43 of the Treaty of Versailles and the Locarno Pact" was adopted March 19, but there the matter rested as far as the League was concerned, for when it appeared on the agenda of the Council in future sessions, discussion was invariably postponed.[82]

The French, British, and Belgian governments, on the other hand, went ahead with their attempt to negotiate a "new Locarno,"

[79] League, *Official Journal*, XVII, 314-315, minutes of 91st extraordinary session of the Council, I meeting, March 14, 1936.

[80] Great Britain, *Parliamentary Debates*, fifth ser., CCCX, 1437, J. Wullus Rudiger. *La défense de la Belgique en 1940* (Villeneuve, France, 1940), pp. 127-128.

[81] Great Britain, *Parliamentary Papers*, 1932-1936, Cmd. 5134; Chambre, *Annales*, Nov. 3, 1938, p. 38; Paul van Zeeland, "Aims of recent Belgian Foreign Policy," *Foreign Affairs*, XVIII (1939), 140.

[82] League, *Official Journal*, XVII, 340, minutes of 91 extraordinary session of the Council, 4 meeting, March 19, 1936; XVII, 543, minutes of 92 session, 3rd meeting, May 13, 1936; XVII, 751, 4th meeting, June 26, 1936.

in spite of the unfriendly attitude of Italy and Germany. These negotiations began inauspiciously when Mussolini refused to send delegates to a meeting unless the German government were represented.[83] On July 24, 1936, this condition was accepted and in addition the field of discussion was enlarged so as to include other
problems whose solution would forward the cause of peace.[84] The
complications which the Spanish war brought into international
affairs inevitably caused the new Locarno negotiations to assume
a secondary position. Notes were exchanged on the subject of the
proposed pact, however,[85] and by November 7, things had so far
progressed that Great Britain sent a note to the other powers
with a series of questions bearing on the procedure to be adopted
in the course of the proposed conference.[86]

The answers to this questionnaire were never published; it is
known, however, that France rejected the German and Italian
replies as "unacceptable." Although some further discussions were
carried on that spring during the regular meetings of the League
Council at Geneva, the tension caused by the Spanish war made
successful negotiations between France and Great Britain on the
one side and Germany and Italy on the other virtually impossible.
This was tacitly admitted when in July, Great Britain suggested
that an expert committee be appointed to study the technical aspects
of negotiations in the field. This was a convenient method of shelv-
ing the subject; in fact, the other states did not even go to the
trouble of naming the committees. The project of a new Locarno
quietly lapsed into oblivion.[87]

The failure to reach an agreement did not come as a surprise

[83] *Independance Belge*, July 15, 1936.

[84] *Ibid.*, July 24, 1936; "*Le problème locarnien*," *Europe Nouvelle documen-
taire*, XX (Dec. 18, 1937), pp. 4-5.

[85] Spaak to the Senate foreign affairs commission, *Indépendance Belge*, Oct.
22, 1936.

[86] Spaak to the Senate foreign affairs commission, *Indépendance Belge*, Nov.
8, 1936.

[87] Toynbee, *Survey*, 1937, I, 324, 361-362.

to the interested parties, for as early as April 15, 1936, the staff conversations which were to protect France and Belgium in such an event had been inaugurated, after an exchange of letters stipulating that the military conversations did not imply political commitments.[88] Moreover, as the Spanish civil war threatened to develop into a general European conflagration, and as Germany and Italy became more closely united, a general treaty implying concerted action of the great powers became more and more unlikely. Instead there appeared an ever widening breach between France and Great Britain on the one hand, and Germany and Italy on the other. The Belgian people did not see clearly on which side of this division their interests lay, as they feared both Communism and Fascism. With some misgivings they decided to follow the lead of France and Great Britain. On July 31, not two weeks after the outbreak of the Spanish revolt, the Belgian cabinet created a ministerial committee to study the situation and keep abreast of new developments.[89] And on August 15, Belgium formally adopted non-intervention, and accepted a seat on the supervisory committee set up to map out a unified line of action for all the interested states.[90] At the same time the embargo decree was revised to bring it into harmony with the suggestions of the committee.[91]

The increasing tension resulting from the actions of Germany, Italy, and Russia presaged a great ideological war. With a dangerous neighbor to the east, collective security an illusion, Locarno disavowed, and France bound to a distrusted ally, the Belgian people felt that the bases of their foreign policy needed drastic change. On October 14, 1936, their young King gave them the direction they sought.

[88] Chambre, *Documents,* Dec. 22, 1936, doc. no. 93, p. 2; *Indépendance Belge,* April 17, 1936. Not only were there no political commitments, but, according to Eden, the discussions were confined to an exchange of information, and no military agreements were made. *Parl. Debates,* 5 ser., CCCXVIII, 1229-1230.

[89] *Le Peuple,* August 2, 1936.

[90] Chambre, *Annales,* Nov. 24, 1936, p. 188.

[91] Great Britain, *Parliamentary Papers,* 1936-1937, Cmd. 5300, Appendix I, p. 10.

CHAPTER NINE

An Independent Policy

ON OCTOBER 14, 1936, the Belgian Cabinet met to deliberate on a new defense bill. So important was the occasion that, for the first time since his accession, King Leopold himself presided. He opened the proceeding with a speech which so well expressed the desires, fears and hopes of his subjects that it became the official statement of Belgian foreign policy, accepted as such both at home and abroad. For this reason it deserves full quotation.

"In taking the constitutional oath," his Majesty began, "the Belgian sovereigns bind themselves to maintain the integrity and independence of their country. Like my predecessors, I intend to keep this solemn promise. That is why I was anxious to preside over this council which is to draw up measures to be submitted to Parliament for the purpose of endowing Belgium with a military establishment adapted to present circumstances. More than a year ago the government took up the question of improving our military position. There were several reasons for this:
  1. The rearmament of Germany following upon the complete militarization of Italy and Russia, gave rise to extraordinary measures of precaution in most of the other states, even those which are deliberately pacifist, such as Switzerland and the Low Countries.
  2. The transformation of the methods of war, as a result of technical progress, notably in the fields of aviation and of mechanization, will make it possible in the future for the initial operations of an armed conflict to be of such power,

speed and magnitude as to be particularly alarming to so small a country as Belgium.

3. The lightning-like reoccupation of the Rhineland and the transfer to our very borders of the bases of a future German invasion, have increased our anxiety.

4. At the same time we have watched the foundations of international security being weakened by infractions of treaties, even those freely entered into, and by the virtual impossibility, under present circumstances, of adapting the provisions of the Covenant of the League of Nations so as to provide for the punishment of these infractions.

5. Finally, the internal dissensions of certain states threaten to become enmeshed in the rivalries between the political and social systems of other states, and to unleash a conflict even more desperate and more destructive than that from whose repercussions we are still suffering.

I think it will not be useless to recall here the successive stages of the military bill during the last few months. This summary will, at the same time, show that the series of studies has now been completed.

The need for adjusting our military strength to the risks of the foreign peril became evident in the spring of 1935. Several plans were submitted to me by the army general staff, and finally, in November, 1935, I signed my approval of a program of which the essential bases then constituted in my eyes a minimum.[1] This program was submitted to the members of the government, and the latter chose from among its members a committee charged with making a thorough examination of the problem of our security. On February 7, 1936, the cabinet agreed on the text of a military bill, which, however, did not secure enough votes in the sections of the Chamber; and the government accepted an amendment providing for the immediate application of article 53 of

[1] It is to be noted that Leopold took an active part in organizing the defense system. The plans were submitted to him first, and only after he approved were they referred to the cabinet. Thus Leopold's position, at least as commander-in-chief, bore a closer resemblance to that of the President of the United States than to that of either the King of England or the President of France. This point has some bearing on his action in May 1940.

the conscription law. Thus amended, the law was voted on April 6 by the Chamber.[2]

Meanwhile, as early as January 10, the idea was advanced that the problem should be fully discussed by a mixed commission. This idea received a favorable welcome in political and parliamentary circles. The mixed commission was created on March 25, 1936, by royal decree. After 37 meetings, the commission, having examined every aspect of the problem, ended its work and formulated a series of conclusions. These latter did not agree as to the exact measures to be taken, but they showed unanimity of opinion on general principles, particularly as to the need of permanent covering troops on the frontier.

The principal suggestions dealing with the purchase of material, anti-aircraft defense, preparation of fortifications, and improvements in mobilization require immediate action. In any event a new conscription law must be voted before the first of next December, the date on which the class of 1936 is called up. Moreover, confronted with the dangers of the international situation, the country would not understand any delay on the part of the government in submitting the necessary proposals to Parliament. It is fitting, then, that the problem be clearly stated to the public.

Our military policy, like our foreign policy, on which it is based, must aim, not at preparing for a more or less successful war, with the aid of a coalition, but at keeping war away from our territory.

The reoccupation of the Rhineland by breaking the Locarno treaties both in letter and in spirit has almost put us back in the same international position we occupied before the war. Our geographical situation requires us to maintain an army large enough to dissuade any of our neighbors from making use of our territory to attack another state. In fulfilling this mission Belgium greatly assists in preserving peace in Western Europe, and *ipso facto* acquires a right to respect and eventual assistance from all states interested in peace.

---

[2] This "amendment" was in reality a temporary expedient to man the frontier by empowering the government to retain the class of 1935 under arms after their period of service had expired. Robert Leurquin, "La nouvelle orientation de la politique étrangère belge; les conséquences pour la défense nationale de la Belgique," *Europe Nouvelle,* XIX (1936), 1060.

On these basic points I believe that Belgian opinion is unanimous. But our engagements must go no further. A unilateral policy will weaken our position abroad, and—rightly or wrongly—cause dissension at home. An alliance, even if purely defensive, does not lead to the goal; for, no matter how prompt the help of an ally would be, it would not come until after the invader's attack, which will be overwhelming. To meet this attack we would be alone in any case. Unless Belgium possesses a defense system capable of resistance, the enemy would penetrate deeply at the beginning, and the country would be devastated. After this stage is over, friendly intervention will certainly assure final victory; but the struggle will cover the country with destruction of which that of the 1914-1918 war would be but a feeble image.

For this reason, as the minister for foreign affairs said recently, we must pursue 'an exclusively and wholly Belgian policy.' This policy must aim resolutely at keeping us outside the quarrels of our neighbors; such an aim is in keeping with our national ideals. It can be maintained by a reasonable military and financial effort, and it will gain the support of the Belgians, all animated by an intense and basic desire for peace.

Let those who doubt the feasibility of such a foreign policy consider the proud and resolute example of Holland and Switzerland. Let them recall how decisively Belgium's scrupulous observation of neutrality weighed in our favor and in favor of the Allies during the war and the settlement which followed. Our moral position would have been incomparably weaker at home, and the world would never have given us the same sympathy, if the invader had been able to advance as an argument an alliance on our part with one of his adversaries.

It is then, I repeat, solely to preserve us from war, from whatever quarter it may come, that our military system must be planned, and the public must receive incontrovertible assurance of this.

Our military organization, based on the conscription law of 1929, though excellent in many respects, no longer corresponds to the new danger of a sudden invasion. It assures neither the permanent defense of our frontiers, nor the security of our mobilization, nor that of the concentration of the army. A more or less unexpected attack could in a few hours conquer valuable pledges, and paralyze irreparably the greater part of our troops.

This defective organization must be remedied at once. It was to decide on the means of accomplishing this that I called you together. Representing three great traditional parties which include the vast majority of Belgians, you will adopt as your own, I sincerely hope, the plan of the minister of national defense.

By solving the military problem in a union of patriotic understanding, you will give to the country, together with the necessary calmness of mind in the face of outward events, the conditions necessary for public prosperity.

Thus you will have shown the country once again that the chief preoccupation of the government of national union is to place the higher interests of Belgium before everything.[3]

The king's remarks were enthusiastically received by his ministers. Emile Vandervelde, who was particularly impressed, announced that his party would accept the policy outlined by the king, and would support the defense bill, to which it had formerly been strongly opposed. To explain this change to the country, and to rally all Belgians around the Government, he asked that the royal speech be made public. Premier van Zeeland agreed, and the king consented.[4]

From the preceding chapters it will be seen that there was little in this speech that was new. The reaction of the Belgian public to the rise of Hitler, to the breaking of the treaties of Versailles and Locarno, and to the collapse of collective security has already been described. Statesmen had begun to forcast a shift in policy, motivated not only by external events, but also by internal developments, particularly the growing strength of the Flemish Nationalists, and the appearance of a local variant of fascism in the form of Rexism. In a few well chosen words, the king had shown the relationship binding together these factors, his country's defense system, and its foreign policy. This statement from the head of the nation, publicly adopted by the cabinet, had the important

[3] *Indépendance Belge,* Oct. 15, 1936.
[4] Wullus-Rudiger, *La défense de la Belgique,* p. 135.

effect of bringing home to Belgians and foreigners alike, the extent and implications of the new policy. For this reason it deserves careful analysis.

On examination it is seen to have consisted of five parts. In the first he gave reasons why the nation's military policy should change. This section is skilfully worded, so as to give no offense, yet the statements are clear and direct. The rearmament of Germany, first on the list, was the specific action of the National Socialists which gave the greatest anxiety to Germany's neighbors. A dictatorship which contented itself with mere words would not have caused much alarm to hardheaded Belgians.[5]

Two years earlier, in March 1934, Premier de Broqueville had said that Germany's rearmament made a change in foreign policy inevitable. The following June, during Hitler's "purge", Parliament had taken some of the "extraordinary measures" referred to by the king, by providing for the administration of the country in time of invasion, and giving civil authorities the right to requisition property and to demand certain kinds of service.[6] The reintroduction of conscription in Germany and the rebuilding of the *Luftwaffe* seemed to call for further defensive measures by those states most liable to attack. Leopold was definitely thinking of the Flemings when he gave Holland and Switzerland as examples of peace-loving states which found themselves forced to rearm, for the Flemish Nationalists constantly referred to them—especially the Netherlands—in their arguments against armaments.[7]

---

[5] *Cf.*, the statements in the report of the Senate Foreign Affairs Committee for 1935: "Nous avons le désir de vivre en paix avec l'Allemagne. . . . La forme du régime qu'elle s'est donnée ne doit pas nous empêcher de nous entendre avec elle. . . . Mais il ne dépend pas de nous que l'esprit militaire de l'Allemagne, sa répudiation des traités, son réarmement à l'outrance, n'aient produit des réactions très vives, surtout chez ses voisins les plus exposés et obligent spécialement la Belgique à lui enlever la tentation de faire un jour du pays la route de l'invasion . . . " Sénat, *Documents*, Dec. 12, 1935, doc. no. 27, p. 5.

[6] Chambre, *CRA*, June 27, 1934, pp. 597-598, pp. 600-602.

[7] *Cf.* Sénat, *CRA*, April 16, 1930, p. 352: *Indépendance Belge*, Dec. 3, 1936.

The second reason given by the king for an increase in military preparedness was the transformation in strategy and tactics due to technical progress. Air attack, particularly, worried little Belgium, and to counteract the danger, in February 1935, the government readily agreed to the Franco-British suggestion for a "western air Locarno."[8] The failure of this suggestion to bear fruit was followed by the Ethiopian and Spanish wars, in both of which the terrible possibilities inherent in air bombardment were only too evident.

The third of Leopold's reasons for rearmament was the militarization of the Rhineland. None of the other causes was more important than this, for it not only deprived Belgium of the physical safeguard of the disarmed zone, but—and this was much more significant—although a deliberate violation of clearly defined treaty obligations it had aroused only notes of protest, instead of decisive action.[9] After March 7, 1936, few Belgians were desirous of obtaining the defensive alliances so eagerly sought in the early twenties and again in the first years of the Hitler menace.[10] Emphasis was laid, instead, on the idea of voluntary neutrality proposed as early as 1930 by Vicomte Poullet of the Catholic party.[11]

As the king expressed the situation in giving the fourth reason for rearming, "infractions of agreements had weakened the bases of collective security." Belgium bore some of the responsibility in this matter, for, as has been shown, premier van Zeeland had been a leading figure in the discussion of the Ethiopian question at Geneva, and apparently had some part in the formulation of the Hoare-Laval plan.

After the end of the unfortunate sanctions policy, the smaller

---

[8] Chambre, *Documents,* April 9, 1935, doc. no. 116.

[9] See Chapter VIII.

[10] *Cf.* Hymans' speech on German rearmament in which after saying "The Belgian Government can do nothing alone," he expressed his desire for closer union with France and Great Britain; Chambre, *Annales,* Nov. 29, 1933, p. 152.

[11] Sénat, *Documents,* June 22, 1939, doc. no. 87, pp. 2-3.

states were no longer able to count on League support in case of attack by a greedy dictator. That "international anarchy" had returned was well proved by the Spanish Civil War.

It was to this conflict that Leopold referred in giving his fifth cause, "the internal dissensions of certain states." The intervention of Italy and Germany in aid of Franco, and of Russia in favor of the Loyalist government, was an indirect threat to peace. If the dictatorships should decide to fight the matter out, France would be drawn into the conflict by the pact of assistance, and the play of alliance and interests would, it seemed, soon involve the rest of Europe. Should such a catastrophe occur, Belgium would need a strong army, well trained and well supplied, to deter any belligerent from seeking to use the easy highway between Germany and France.

The five reasons for building up the army were also five reasons for changing Belgian foreign policy. Probably the reason why the king did not so treat them was the fact that the subject under discussion was primarily the military, not the foreign, policy of the government. The next point of his speech dealt with the background of the new conscription law under consideration. For a full comprehension of the situation, however, some details regarding the early law of 1929 and the plans of defense drawn up later are necessary.

During the years immediately following the war, it had seemed quite possible that the Germans would attempt a war of revenge. To be ready to meet an attack the staff relied on the army law of 1913, providing for fifteen months with the colors for most conscripts, and twenty-one to twenty-four months for those in the cavalry and artillery. This prolonged period of service weighed heavily on the poor, and Socialists and Flemings united to force a revision of the law. This was done in 1923, the period of obligatory training being reduced to ten months for infantrymen, and twelve or thirteen months for those in special branches. This still seemed too long to those who were called to the colors, and agitation for a six months' training grew in strength. In 1927 the problem was submitted to a mixed commission composed of members of the general staff and other military technicians, and important party leaders. After a lengthy investigation, they produced a plan providing for eight months' service for infantrymen, with longer periods and slightly higher pay for men in those branches, such as artillery or engineering, which required special training.

The shorter period of conscription involved a reorganization of the strategic plans of the staff, in order to provide adequate frontier defense with a smaller number of effectives. On May 31, 1930, work commenced on the Albert Canal, keystone of the new system whose details, naturally, were not made public.[12]

In spite of the real need for fortifications, great difficulty was experienced by the government when it tried to secure funds for the proposed construction. The Socialists again were the backbone of the opposition, and they contended that the huge sums required would be better employed in a social security program.[13] The Flemings were likewise in opposition. As one of their number, Senator Lindekens, remarked, "Flanders does not want to be sacrificed for France. . . . Let France fortify its northern boundary, then Germany will leave Belgium alone."[14]

If Flemings and Socialists fought the new system on political and social grounds, the Liberals of Wallonia attacked it from the point of view of its inadequacy. According to the plan suggested by General Nuyten, chief of staff, the frontier area would be lightly held, with the bulk of the army stationed *en échelon,* using Liége, Namur, Antwerp, and Ghent as bases. The frontier districts naturally protested at thus being left to the invader. Defense minister

---

[12] *BPB,* no. 101, July 17, 1930, p. 7.

[13] *Cf.* Chambre, *CRA,* May 12, 1932, p. 612, and Sénat, *CRA,* Dec. 7, 1933, p. 78.

[14] Sénat, *CRA,* Feb. 8, 1934, p. 169.

Devèze then revised the plan so as to give strong protection to Wallonia. This scheme, however, was said by some authorities to rely for complete success on close coordination with the Maginot line, and thus to imply close union with France.[15]

On June 19, 1934, nevertheless, King Leopold announced the adoption of the Devèze proposals with the statement that "The territory will be defended in its integrity."[16] This pledge was repeated by premier de Broqueville on November 13, 1934, in his declaration of policy.

The dangerous situation of Europe makes it imperative for us not to endanger the security of the country by slackening the effort we have courageously made to assure its defense and to block an invasion at the frontier, if possible.[17]

The adoption of this policy necessitated a larger permanent army and stronger fortifications than were available under existing laws. This was apparent to the officers responsible for the defense of the nation, but not to the average citizen. Consequently in the spring of 1935, Devèze made a series of speeches to convince his fellow countrymen of the need for a new military policy. The members of the cabinet began to realize the situation, and, as premier van Zeeland described it, there were

Ministerial committees, discussions among competent ministers, the general staff, myself, a series of other services, a first government bill; discussion in parliament, acceptance of a temporary expedient; formation of a mixed commission, and, woven into all these, continual meetings among specialists, ministers, military leaders and those members of parliament particularly interested in these problems and representing all shades of public opinion.[18]

[15] Richard Dupierreux, "Belgique, 1934" *Europe Nouvelle,* XVII (1934), 1288; G. Charlyvel, "La nouvelle orientation de la politique étrangère belge; l'aspect militaire du problème," *Europe Nouvelle,* XIX, (1936), 1057.
[16] Charles Buchet, "Le rôle de la Belgique dans la défense des frontières de la France," *Revue de France,* XIV (1934), 32.
[17] Chambre, *Annales,* Nov. 13, 1934, p. 7.
[18] *Ibid.,* Dec. 2, 1936, p. 316.

The "temporary expedient" mentioned by van Zeeland was probably that adopted in April 1936, during the negotiations among the Locarno powers after Germany's remilitarization of the Rhineland. In the anxious days following March 8, Belgians realized that Devèze had spoken the truth about the army. The only way to raise enough troops to cover the eastern frontier was to keep the class of 1935 under arms until another group was fully trained.[19]

The mixed commission was formed after the rejection in February 1936, of the government's bill extending the term of service to eighteen months.[20] In expressing their opposition to the bill as it stood, members of the commissions of national defense of both houses insisted that they disapproved only on technical grounds, and were fully in accord with the government on the policy underlying the bill.[21] The mixed commission found its task complicated. There was, on the one hand, a conflict between the Flemish desire for complete isolation and the danger of antagonizing Hitler; and, on the other, the obvious fact that Belgium's defenses had to be planned to synchronize with those of the nations which would probably be fighting the same enemies. It was to awaken the public to these considerations that on August 4, 1936, the commission published an important resolution. Its most significant sentence stated that

. . . the military organization of the country, like the foreign policy of Belgium, pursues no other goal than that of assuring the defense of the territory against all aggression from whatever quarter it may come. . . .[22]

This declaration, which clearly united the nation's military and

[19] Robert Leurquin, "La nouvelle orientation de la politique étrangère belge; les conséquences pour la défense nationale de la Belgique,"*Europe Nouvelle,* XIX (1936), 1060.

[20] Chambre, *Documents,* Feb. 11, 1936, doc. no. 96, pp. 1-16.

[21] *Ibid.,* April 1, 1936, doc. no. 202, pp. 1, 4; G.N. Clarke, *Belgium and the War* (London, 1942), p. 14, gives the impression that the government's plan was rejected in its entirety; this is misleading.

[22] *BPB,* no. 123, Sept. 2, 1936, p. 7.

foreign policies, foreshadowed the position taken by Leopold in the third section of his speech, wherein he stated that the country must adopt an "exclusively and wholly Belgian policy." The idea was not a sudden inspiration of a young ruler, but had been matur-ing for some time, in the minds of his advisors. Since Locarno it had gained ground rapidly.

On July 20, 1936, at a breakfast of the *Union de la Presse étran-gère de la Belgique,* foreign minister Spaak had made a similar speech:

I wish that the foreign policy of Belgium be resolutely placed un-der the banner of realism. The very statement of this principle will make you understand at once that in my manner of envisaging our intercourse with foreign countries, I have decided to ignore com-pletely my own preferences for this or that political, economic or social system. . . . I want only one thing, a foreign policy that is exclusively and wholly Belgian. . . .

He then went on to say that if he were faced with the choice be-tween fighting for the right or preserving peace,

I would try above all to preserve peace. Because the basis of Right is essentially in motion, right is in perpetual evolution. . . . Is it not a mistake to found the principles of foreign policy solely upon Right, which is in perpetual evolution, and to risk the fate of men and of future civilization itself, for what is, after all, only passing?

In the decade after the armistice, he said, men tried to achieve the impossible by working to prevent war. He believed it would be wiser to proceed on the assumption that war was possible and must be kept from his country. To succeed in this, he continued, the Belgian foreign minister must always bear three facts in mind: the geographical position of his country, the existence of Flemish and Walloon groups, and the limited army.

We desire that this Belgium which has been, and still can be, an apple of discord in Western Europe, should by its loyalty, its clear and unequivocal attitude, be an element of appeasement and security for all.[23]

In general this speech met with approval in Belgium. As the *Standaard* wrote, "It is the attitude which we ourselves, the whole Flemish population, and the great majority of the Belgian people desire to adopt." The *Vingtième Siècle,* the *Nation Belge* and the Rexist *Pays Réel* likewise expressed their satisfaction, the last named wondering how Spaak could reconcile his policies with those of his party. For indeed the Socialists, who drew much of their strength from Wallonia, were not pleased with what they interpreted as an anti-French policy.[24]

On July 26 the General Council of the party asked the foreign minister for an explanation of his statements, which were a direct attack on the principles underlying the League of Nations and the ideal of collective security. Spaak retorted that Vandervelde had publicly declared that the League was a failure; and in that case a new policy had to be adopted. In spite of the remonstrances of such respected POB heads as Rolin and Louis de Brouckère, Spaak was not forced to retract.[25]

On the face of it, the Socialists strongly supported the League, but by allowing Spaak's defense to stand, and by not insisting on any rectification of his original statement, they gave him their silent approval. He had yet another group to satisfy on the subject of his speech: the foreign affairs committee of the Senate. To them he explained that he did not advocate a return to the old neutrality, but to an independent policy.[26]

That Spaak's statements were not merely the outcome of his own rather ebullient personality was shown on September 9, 1936, when premier van Zeeland made a somewhat similar statement. Describ-

[23] *Indépendance Belge,* July 21, 1936.
[24] *BPB,* no. 123, Sept. 2, 1936, p. 5.
[25] *Le Peuple,* July 27, 1936.
[26] *Indépendance Belge,* July 31, 1936.

ing his plans he said that the government was trying to avoid becoming entangled in wars where the country's vital interests were not at stake. The two means that were being used were a strong defense system, and freedom from commitments.

Except in the case of an ineluctable obligation we will take into account only considerations and purposes which are entirely and exclusively Belgian; we will not become the game of any diplomacy, of any group, of any tendency, whatever it may be.[27]

The premier's statement, like the king's a month later, was directed particularly at the Flemings. For sixteen years they had been warning the nation that by the Franco-Belgian military accord of 1920 it had become the "vassal" of its neighbor to the south. This had been one of the reasons for their consistent refusal to support military appropriations, which, they claimed, would only aid the "aggressive" French policy. Many of their spokesmen had, moreover, threatened that if war should come, they would not fight.[28] Even when, in March 1936, van Zeeland read to the Chamber the letters abrogating the alliance, there were Flemings who refused to believe in the change.[29] To forestall a similar attitude toward the policy he was advocating, the king showed that the government had come to believe that an alliance would not achieve its purpose of defending the country.

The fourth section of the speech was devoted to a demonstration of the necessity of maintaining a strong army if the nation wished to preserve its independent existence. Yet there is no indication that it ever occurred to the king that the nation might be called up-

[27] *Indépendance Belge,* Sept. 10, 1936.

[28] A typical statement was made in the Chamber by a Flemish Nationalist named Leuridan: "We Flemings will not fight, neither we nor our children. The day when you want to mobilize us for war we will refuse to march. . . . Towards Germany we wish to be a friendly neutral, in conjunction with Holland." Chambre, *CRA,* Nov. 28, 1934, p. 23.

[29] The Flemish Nationalist, de Backer, interrupted, "It is pure comedy." *Indépendance Belge,* March 12, 1936.

on to defend itself unaided. Once Belgium was attacked, he assumed that the other nations of Europe would hasten to its rescue.

In the concluding section he appealed for the support of all parties. This was pledged by the leaders and soon echoed by all groups. On October 27, Spaak gave an exposition of the new policy at the Socialist Congress. "I respect the ideal of the League of Nations," he said, "but I also respect facts." The League has shown itself powerless to protect Ethiopia, he continued; if Belgium, like the unfortunate African kingdom, placed its trust in collective security, it would suffer the same fate. For this reason he advocated the policy of independence. The Congress signified its approval by the adoption of a resolution stating it repudiated the old concept of neutrality, as well as any idea of failing to observe treaty obligations. At the same time it favored abandoning all military alliances except the League and expressed the hope that the Belgian government would actively carry out an independent policy, and would give every assistance for the strengthening of the League of Nations.[30]

Le Peuple, however, regretted that the new program, so praiseworthy in many respects, implied disloyalty to the ideal of collective security.[31]

Many Liberals approved of the royal speech because it dissipated their fear of being called upon to fight on the side of Soviet Russia. As the *Indépendance Belge* summed up their sentiments:

We will not be Stalin's soldiers. . . . When France by signing the Franco-Soviet pact, in a measure justified—if it did not provoke—the remilitarization of the Rhineland, by allowing Germany to believe that she was being encircled, Belgium resisted. . . . And let us add that the holy horror which almost all Belgians feel respecting Bolshevism has strengthened our reasons for dissociating ourselves from a policy which makes Stalin the arbiter of Europe.[32]

[30] *Indépendance Belge,* Oct. 27, 1936.
[31] *Le Peuple,* Oct. 27, 1936.
[32] *Indépendance Belge,* Nov. 17, 1936.

There was, however, opposition from one wing of the party. The Walloon Liberals were strongly Francophile by tradition, and they believed that king was in reality advocating a return to the neutrality of prewar days. They feared that this would eventually result in another invasion wherein Wallonia, strategically located at the Meuse bridgeheads, would be the first to suffer. One paper, *L'Action Wallon,* went so far as to insist that Leopold had exceeded his constitutional powers in attempting to dictate a policy.[33] The *Express,* of Liége, objected that "even by tripling its forces Belgium alone is incapable of resisting an attack from the East. The decision which has been taken will result in turning the whole Meuse valley over to destruction, and therefore will cause dissension in Belgium if war should break out."[34]

The Catholic press was unanimously in favor of the new program, and as was to be expected, Flanders gave it a warm welcome.[35] A Flemish deputy said later, "Everyone felt that we ought to return to a policy of independence and the royal speech warmed our hearts, above all those of us in Flanders."[36]

Even the Rexists approved, quieting their scruples at being in harmony with the hated cabinet by reflecting that the king was the true source of the new doctrine.[37]

The Belgians as a whole, then, received the policy outlined by Leopold with satisfaction. To them it seemed the method best calculated to safeguard peace, and, in the words of one commentator, "As in the dark days of 1914 there was union of all hearts in the great thought of national independence."[38]

---

[33] *Ibid.,* Nov. 16, 1936.

[34] René Pinon, "Le discours du roi Léopold III," *Revue des Deux Mondes,* XXVI (1936), 237.

[35] *BPB,* no. 124, Jan. 10, 1937, pp. 3-6; *Cf.* also "Le discours du roi," *Revue Général,* CXXXVI (1936), 532-539.

[36] Chambre, *CRA,* Dec. 1, 1936, p. 112.

[37] *Le Pays Réel,* Oct. 17, 1936.

[38] Pierre Goemaere and Raoul Crabbé, "Léopold III et l'indépendance de la Belgique," *Revue Belge,* XIV (1937), 485.

Outside Belgium, reaction to the new policy was not favorable. The comments of the French press showed surprise and disappointment. The *Echo de Paris* went so far as to say that the royal speech was "equal to the German act in remilitarizing the Rhineland."[39] Pertinax, writing in the *Europe Nouvelle,* regretted the Belgian defection, which he said was "a severe blow to French prestige among eastern countries."[40] There were also some anxiety expressed that Belgium was becoming pro-German, and was drawing away from the League.[41]

Many French politicians used the Belgian change of policy as an argument against their own political enemies. According to the *Petit Parisien* the Franco-Soviet pact was to blame; Pertinax said that the weakness of France at the time of the remilitarization of the Rhineland was responsible; and *L' Humanité* laid it at the door of Laval, who had sabotaged collective security.[42]

Some of the reaction to the Belgian policy, however, was based more on sentimental than on rational motives. A comment typical of the attitude opened with these words:

From the French point of view this repudiation of an alliance which was born of spontaneous enthusiasm rather than of diplomatic calculations, was painfully received by our people.[43]

On sober second thought many of these regrets gave way to a realization that a well armed Belgium was an invaluable aid to their own security.

Today, faced with the events which so deeply disturb the modern world, we understand the King's attitude better. . . . Like Switzer-

---

[39] *Indépendance Belge,* Oct. 16, 1936.

[40] Pertinax, "La nouvelle orientation de la politique étrangère belge; les répercussions diplomatiques," *Europe Nouvelle,* XIX (1936), 1056.

[41] *Cf.* Pierre Brossolette, "L'accord anglo-franco-belge," *Europe Nouvelle,* XX (1937), 411; Louis Dumont-Wilden, "La Belgique et le système locarnien," *Revue Politique et Littéraire,* LXXIV (1936), 740-743.

[42] *Indépendance Belge,* Oct. 16 and 17, 1936.

[43] René Pinon, "Le discours du Roi Léopold III," *loc. cit.,* 231.

land and the northern countries, Belgium has let it be known that to maintain her independence she will not allow the right of passage. This statement has no meaning which should arouse French susceptibilities.[44]

Official reactions in Paris were extremely reserved. A Havas dispatch of October 15 reported that foreign minister Delbos was "thoroughly studying" the royal speech in order to discover the underlying motives for the decision. This examination completed, Delbos would then ask van Zeeland to explain the way in which he intended to reconcile the new attitude with Belgium's obligations under the treaties of Versailles and Locarno. On October 15, the French senatorial committee on foreign affairs unanimously regretted "the unilateral denunciation of the Pact of Locarno."[45]

Within a week, however, the foreign affairs committee of the French Chamber had accepted Delbos' statement that Belgium had not modified its relation to France, and was still bound by the treaties. This change was the result of interviews between Delbos and Laroche, his representative in Brussels, and Baron Kerchove de Denterghem, Belgian ambassador in Paris.[46]

The British reaction to Leopold's speech was a quiet one. As an "informed source" stated, the exchange of notes regarding a new Locarno pact had already shown the foreign office that Belgium wished to return to a status resembling prewar neutrality.[47] On November 20, foreign secretary Anthony Eden, speaking to his constituents at Leamington on the purpose of British rearmament, stated that the armaments

may, and if the occasion arose, they would, be used in the defense of France and Belgium against unprovoked aggression in accordance with our existing obligations.[48]

[44] General Brécard, "Le Roi Léopold III," *Revue des Deux Mondes,* XLVII (1938), 925.
[45] *Indépendance Belge,* Oct. 16, 1936.
[47] *Ibid.,* Oct. 16 and 22, 1936.
[48] Anthony Eden, *Foreign Affairs,* (New York, 1939), p. 182.

This assurance of continued British support was repeated by Eden in proposing the toast "The Friendship of Nations, coupled with our friendship for Belgium, and with the name of Monsieur van Zeeland." After describing the ideals of both nations Eden added:

Let me therefore on this Anglo-Belgian occasion once again affirm that the independence and integrity of Belgium is a vital interest for this nation and that Belgium could count upon our help were she ever the victim of unprovoked aggression.[49]

This statement promising aid, yet asking for no further commitments, was very welcome in Belgium.[50]

The German reaction was less popular. The Nazi press, welcoming the announcement of the new policy "with interest and satisfaction," claimed that the move would lessen the danger of war, which in the past had come to Belgium from all sides.[51] Von Ribbentrop wrote to the Belgian paper *Le Vingtième Siècle*, "Henceforth be strong. Since the speech of your king, you are no longer a danger to us; you protect us."[52]

Italy also was pleased with the stand taken by Belgium, which could be interpreted as approval of the Italian unwillingness to negotiate another Locarno treaty.[53] This attitude was very marked in an interview given the following spring by Mussolini to *Le Vingtième Siècle* in which he said:

The new diplomatic position of Belgium has settled the problem of peace in the west. Belgium then took a logical attitude which bears witness to a remarkable sense of balance, and your sovereign has shown himself to be a 'chef d' Etat' careful of the true interests of his country.[54]

[49] *Ibid.*, p. 176.
[50] Chambre, *Documents*, Dec. 22, 1936, doc. no. 93, p. 4; *Annales*, Nov. 24, 1936, p. 189.
[51] *Indépendance Belge*, Oct. 16, 1936.
[52] Robert Leurquin, "La loi militaire belge," *Europe Nouvelle*, XIX (1934), 1262.
[53] *Indépendance Belge*, October 14, 1936.
[54] *BPB*, no. 126, July 3, 1937, p. 11.

The press of the traditionally neutral states of Europe welcomed the addition to their numbers. The *Handelsblad* of Amsterdam and the *Telegraaf* agreed that Leopold had proved the value of Holland's policy by adopting it, an action which both papers agreed would protect their own country as well. The Swiss were likewise pleased that they were pointed out as an example.[55]

In view of some of these comments, Spaak felt that further clarification was necessary, for there was a misunderstanding regarding Belgium's attitude toward the League, and a tendency to consider the step a return to prewar neutrality. On October 21, he explained to the Senate commission for foreign affairs that the government did not intend to return to neutrality; he reminded them that the word did not even appear in the speech. The mention of Holland and Switzerland referred not to their juridic status, but to their military preparations. He also asserted that the government expected to observe its obligations as a member of the League.[56]

A week later he repeated these assurances in answering an interpellation in the Chamber. He reminded the deputies that a speech could not dissolve solemn international agreements, and he assured them that the provisional understanding reached at London the previous March was still binding. He was, however, engaged in the negotiations preliminary to a new Locarno pact; when an understanding was reached it would be submitted to Parliament for approval.[57]

He gave further explanations in his speech during the discussion of the budget in the Senate. In the "new Locarno" Belgium would promise only "to defend ourselves against any invader and not to allow others to use us as a road."[58] At the same time premier van Zeeland, speaking on the military law, told the Chamber:

---

[55] *Indépendance Belge,* Oct. 16, 1936.
[56] *Ibid.,* Oct. 22, 1936.
[57] Chambre, *Annales,* Oct. 28, 1936, pp. 374-376.
[58] Sénat, *Annales,* Dec. 2, 1936, p. 143.

We will make no commitments, we will sign no treaties, we will
renew no agreement which might in law, in fact, or even in appearance, compromise the efficacy of the position of independence and
of balance which we are assuming.[59]

The most authoritative commentary on the new policy was that
made in February 1937, by Hymans, whom Spaak authorized to
speak for the government, in order to contradict the rumors of Belgo-German collaboration which had been in the air since Hitler's
speech of January 31 in the Reichstag. Reiterating Spaak's repudiation of obligatory neutrality, Hymans pointed out that the King
advocated full sovereignty and independence. This did not imply
a rupture with the policy pursued since the war; those who supposed
that it did based their conception on the mistaken idea that the
Franco-Belgian agreement of 1920 was a true military alliance,
binding its signatories to make war automatically under certain conditions. On the contrary, it had been merely a technical agreement,
stating the kind of military cooperation the two states would afford
each other if they should be fighting in a common cause. This understanding had been useful during the period before the rearmament of Germany and the remilitarization of the Rhineland, but
the events of the past three years had forced the government to
adapt its policy to meet realities. Such had been the purpose of the
royal declaration of "wholly Belgian policy." He closed with a
promise:

This policy of independence must, however, be orientated and directed. According to the royal words, it will try to prevent war. It
will be wholly Belgian, and Belgium will keep outside the great international competitions. Consequently our preferences, our friend-
ships, will never allow us to become attached to any other state,
nor to become vassal to its policy.[60]

Long before this statement, however, the new policy had begun to
bear substantial fruit.

[59] Chambre, *Annales,* Dec. 2, 1936, p. 318.
[60] Chamber, *Annales,* Feb. 11, 1937, p. 612.

CHAPTER TEN

The Immediate Results of the New Policy

THE REORIENTATION of Belgian policy so clearly described in the royal speech led to immediate and important results. The first of these was the passage of the defense bill, which on October 28, 1936, was introduced by the government. The Socialists managed to secure the adoption of an amendment reducing the average period to seventeen months, but otherwise they agreed that the measure was necessary. Only extreme Flemish Nationalists remained hostile; one of their number, who insisted that increased armaments would cause war, exclaimed, "I would prefer to become a Bolshevik rather than see my children killed."[1] The vast majority of Belgians, however, supported the bill, which the Chamber passed on December 2, by a vote of 137 to 43, with eight abstentions.[2] Three days later the Senate gave the bill an even more favorable vote, 122 to 19, with six abstentions.[3] These were the largest majorities ever accorded the government on a defense bill.[4]

The policy of "Independence" had won its first victory. The defeat of Degrelle by premier van Zeeland in the Brussels by-election, already referred to, was also in part a result of the policy which had brought increased prestige to the government, and discredited the rexist slogan: "Either Rex or Moscow."

[1] Chambre, *CRA,* Dec. 2, 1936, p. 129.
[2] *Ibid.,* p. 131.
[3] Sénat, *Annales,* Dec. 5, 1936, p. 150.
[4] Leurquin, "La loi militaire belge," *loc. cit.,* p. 1262.

With the nation united, the premier turned his energies to the task of securing acceptance of the change by other states. This had to a certain extent been done by the statements of Eden and Delbos, already mentioned. In a speech on foreign policy made in the Reichstag on January 30, 1937, Hitler announced: "The German government has also assured Belgium and Holland that it is prepared to recognize and guarantee the inviolability of their territories."[5]

This offer was not given a very enthusiastic welcome in Belgium. The *Nation Belge, Le Peuple,* and *Le Vingtième Siècle* for once agreed in their judgments, all three esteeming the promise of little worth. The *Libre Belgique* was more sanguine, and considered that in the last analysis the speech was "a success for the Belgian policy of independence."[6] The *Indépendance Belge* also was pleased with Hitler's offer, which seemed to it to "dissipate all equivocations" on the subject of Germany's intentions.[7] Nevertheless there was an undercurrent of anxiety, because many Belgians feared that the offer had been purchased at the price of some undesirable "understanding" with Hitler. This fear was some-what lessened on February 11, when Hymans gave his explanatory speech to Parliament.

Meanwhile Spaak continued to work for official and indisputable approval for the new policy, and to obtain a full release from all obligations under the Locarno pacts. On November 7, 1937, Great Britain sent to the governments of France, Italy, Germany and Belgium a series of questions bearing on the negotiations for a "new Locarno" treaty. On February 12, Cartier de Marchienne, Belgian ambassador to the Court of St. James, presented to Eden Spaak's reply. According to press reports this note stated that Belgium was unwilling to assume again the status of guarantor, as it had done in the Locarno treaty.[8]

---

[5] *Indépendance Belge,* Jan. 31, 1937.
[6] *BPB* no. 125, March 18, 1937, pp. 4-5.
[7] *Indépendance Belge,* Jan. 31, 1937.

This was not a new stand, for as early as the preceding October reports had been published that in its note of October 23, replying to a British memorandum of September 18, the Belgian government had stated that under existing circumstances the obligations laid down in 1925 were too heavy to be assumed by a small state.[9] In spite of the obvious determination of Brussels to make no alliance, British circles were—quite understandably—reluctant to relinquish the right to demand Belgian cooperation and to make staff arrangements to provide for the future.

On March 22 Baron Kerchove de Denterghem visited the Quay d'Orsay to explain his government's position. He was informed that Eden and Delbos had just agreed to give Belgium official assurances that it was no longer bound by the engagements contracted March 19, 1936, at London. As the Brussels cabinet was then engaged in waging war on the Rexist leader Degrelle, who was contesting a by-election with premier van Zeeland, King Leopold became his country's unofficial representative in the preliminary conversations held to determine the exact terms of the projected declaration.[10]

On April 24, 1937, Belgium was at last officially released from its obligations. The most significant clauses of the joint Franco-British note were couched in the following terms:

The said governments [of the United Kingdom and of the French Republic] have taken note of the views which the Belgian government has itself expressed concerning the interests of Belgium, and more particularly

(1) the determination expressed publicly and on more than one occasion by the Belgian government:—
   (a) to defend the frontiers of Belgium with all its armed force against any aggression or invasion, and to prevent Belgian territory from being used for purposes of ag-

---

[8] Chambre, *Documents,* March 3, 1938, doc. no. 132, pp. 3-4; Great Britain, *Parl. Deb.,* CCCXXIII, 308.

[9] Chambre, *Annales,* Oct. 28, 1936, p. 364.

[10] Toynbee, *Survey,* 1937, I, 357.

gression against another state either as a passage or as a base of operations by land, by sea, or in the air;

(b) to organize the defense of Belgium in an efficient manner for this purpose;

(2) the fidelity of Belgium to the Covenant of the League of Nations and to the obligations it involves for members of the League.

In consequence, taking into account the determination and assurances mentioned above, the government of the United Kingdom and the government of the Republic declare that they consider Belgium to be now released from all obligations towards them resulting from either the Treaty of Locarno or the arrangements drawn up in London on March 19, 1936, and that they maintain in respect of Belgium the undertakings of assistance which they entered into towards her under the above-mentioned instruments.[11]

On April 22, soon after this important act, Eden visited Brussels. On May 21 Delbos did the same. During their interviews with Spaak, it was decided that, in order to give the pledge contained in the joint note a more solemn character, it would be registered with the League Secretariat, as a treaty would have been. This was done on June 9, 1937, to the great satisfaction of the Belgians.

The press in general welcomed the Franco-British pledge. The *Indépendance Belge* wrote:

The policy defined by the Belgian government a little over six months ago and unanimously approved by public opinion, is now fully realized. Except for the League Covenant, to which she has expressed her attachment, Belgium rejoices in complete independence. She belongs to no defensive system, much less to an offensive one. Her position now resembles that of the Netherlands.[12]

The *Journal de Liége,* however, made the following observations:

The status of western Europe has been the object of a new Locarno

---

[11] Great Britain, *Parliamentary Papers,* 1936-1937, Cmd. 5437.
[12] *Indépendance Belge,* May 25, 1937.

negotiation. The hypothesis of a German guarantee to Belgium similar to that just given by France and England has been envisaged. But on what conditions would Germany give it? Would it oblige Belgium to renounce the obligations assumed as a member of the League? But the Franco-British guarantee was only given to Belgium on condition that she promise to use every means of defense, and remain faithful to the principles of solidarity of the Covenant.

The *Nation Belge* of May 26 expressed a similar anxiety.[13]

On April 29, Spaak appeared before the Chamber to explain the significance of the Anglo-French declaration. He opened his speech by reading the note in full, and then giving his reasons for desiring "to define and specify our international rights and duties in a new form." He pointed out that in 1925 Germany was disarmed, the demilitarized zone was a reality, and the League was strong. In 1937 all this had changed and there seemed to be no immediate prospects of a renewal of the safeguards provided by the Locarno treaties. He then proceeded to describe the principles on which his foreign policy was based. They were, first and foremost, to unite all sections of the people, then to rearm strongly enough to discourage invasion, and finally, to work for collective security and the codification of international law.

In conclusion he clarified two important points. With regard to Article 16 of the Covenant he said

. . . there are two conditions fundamental to affording the right of passage through our territory. The first is that on no hypothesis could passage be afforded without the consent of Belgium. The second is that Belgium could only give her consent in the case of joint action.

Secondly, he explicitly stated that

The Franco-British declaration of April 24th closes for us the period that might be described as the era of military agreements. . . .[14]

[13] *BPB,* no. 126, July 3, 1937, pp. 2-3.
[14] Chambre, *Annales,* April 29, 1937, pp. 1284-1286.

During the months since the royal speech, Belgian diplomats had been trying to secure a German declaration similar to that received from France and Great Britain. On October 13, 1937, the Reich gave the desired pledge. Hitler promised that:

Under no circumstances will it [the German government]impair this inviolability and integrity, except, of course, in the event of Belgium's taking part in a military action directed against Germany.[15]

The Belgian government in acknowledging the communication stated that it "took note of the German declaration" with "the greatest satisfaction."

In general, the Belgian press received the German pledge favorably. The *Libre Belgique,* the *Vingtième Siècle,* and the *Indépendance Belge* considered that it strengthened the security of their country. There were, however, some who thought otherwise, among them the *Nation Belge* and *Flandre Libérale.* The *Dernière Heure,* in expressing their common sentiments, was more prophetic than perhaps it knew:

Hitler invents nothing. The protective declaration which he deigns to grant us simply renews the old German policy which consists in stupefying its future victims, embracing them in order to stifle them more easily.[16]

Rumors began to spread to the effect that the German guarantee had been purchased at the price of some engagement, possibly even repudiation of the League obligations. These stories were refuted on October 21, 1937, by foreign minister Spaak. Speaking in the Chamber he told the deputies that the exchange of notes had been accompanied by commentaries from both governments. That of the Reich explained that the pledge would cease to bind should Belgium become involved in a military expedition against Germany,

---

[15] Chambre, *Documents,* doc. no. 132, March 3, 1938, Annex B.
[16] *BPB,* no. 127, Nov. 20, 1937, p. 6.

or should it allow other nations the right of passage. The Belgian commentary repeated that the nation was still bound by all the obligations flowing from the League Covenant.[17]

What Spaak did not say was that for some time he had been working for a revision of the Covenant which would diminish the responsibilities of member states. In this way only could the two guarantees be reconciled, since fidelity to the League might cancel Hitler's pledge, while a refusal to abide by the Covenant would free France and England from their promise, which was contingent upon Belgian observance of League obligations. The chief difficulty lay in the provisions of Article 16, which stipulated that members must grant the right of passage through their territory to troops sent against another nation by authority of the League; if the goal of such a march should be Germany, that country would no longer be bound by its promise to Belgium, made on the condition that the latter give no aid to Germany's enemies.

It became one of the major aims of Spaak and his successors to free their country from this League obligation, while at the same time retaining full membership. An opportunity to achieve this effect came in 1936, during a session of the Assembly. The relations between Belgium and Geneva from 1919 to 1936 have been traced in an earlier chapter. There it was shown that a period of skepticism as to the practical value of the new institution was followed by an era wherein the nation finally accepted collective security as offering a solid basis for peace. With the rise of Hitler, however, and the failure of the League to prevent the aggressions of Japan and Italy, confidence in its value again waned.

In 1936 the Assembly set up a committee to study means of strengthening the Covenant, and a questionnaire was sent to all member states asking for their suggestions. On November 13, Spaak replied in the name of Belgium. He said that the method of amendment provided for by the Covenant was too slow; it would be

[17] Chambre, *Annales,* Oct. 21, 1937, p. 164.

simpler and more effective to agree on interpretations to be given certain articles. A change was especially needed, he believed, in the clauses regarding the Council. The vote of a nation accused of an aggression should not be counted when action requiring unanimous consent of the Council was under consideration. Moreover, in a crisis, it should not be necessary to wait for a conference; certain measures should be automatic. And, finally

As to what concerns the repressive action of the League, it would be highly desirable to dissipate the uncertitude which still reigns as to the extent of the obligation which Article 16 of the Covenant imposes on the members of the League. It is indeed important that in so serious a matter the States should know as precisely as possible the extent of the charges incumbent upon them, and of the outside help which is assured them.[18]

This position was further explained by the premier on December 2, 1936, during the debate on the military bill. This statement was clarity itself.

Our will to be faithful to the League makes us desire that the engagements incumbent upon us in virtue of the Covenant should be defined, by being limited and at the same time precisely stated. Until that can be done: until such a definition has been given, we will accept no other interpretation than that which we ourselves will give in the fullness of our sovereignty.[19]

This interpretation was given by Spaak the following April, when he outlined the conditions under which Article 16 could be applied to Belgium; namely, that the nation should freely consent, and that it should be in pursuance of an action taken in common by all the members of the League.

In spite of this obvious lack of full confidence, in September 1937 Eden and Delbos suggested that Belgium reenter the Council. But the nation which ten years earlier had given up the coveted seat so

[18] Sénat, *Documents*, Nov. 24, 1936, doc. no. 28, Annex III.
[19] Chambre, *Annales*, Dec. 2, 1936, p. 318.

regretfully, was not anxious to recover it under the existing circumstances.[20] The government finally decided, however, that a refusal would injure the country's prestige, and accepted. By a vote of 47 to 0, with 5 abstentions, Belgium was awarded one of the three vacant seats.[21]

Every effort was made by its representatives to use the opportunity to secure the greatly desired revision of the Covenant. In a speech during the hundredth session of the Council, in January 1938, Spaak insisted that the Covenant must be so reformed as to restore full sovereignty to all the members, a remark which, in view of his earlier statements, all knew was aimed directly at the right of passage.[22] His endeavors to have the Council take the initiative in annulling Article 16, however, were fruitless. Consequently, Belgium continued to give its own interpretation to the obligations it had assumed as a member of the League. On March 16, 1638, Spaak said that since the principle of collective security was "in full decadence," he could not base his foreign policy upon it; and that if Great Britain and France, for example, should wish to aid Czechoslovakia by invading Germany through Belgium they would be treated as invaders.[23]

The Oslo powers, including Belgium, met in Copenhagen the following July. After discussing the whole problem of the repressive measures which the League might adopt against aggressor nations, on July 24 they announced that "they regard the sanctions system as having a non-obligatory character."[24]

The following September this declaration was repeated by Carton de Wiart, representing his country at the League Assembly. He added:

The Belgian government feels that, like the other members of the

[20] Pertinax, "La déclaration allemande à la Belgique et à l'Europe occidentale," *Europe Nouvelle,* XX (1937), 1028.
[21] Chambre, *Documents,* March 3, 1938, doc. no. 132, p. 8.
[22] League, *Official Journal,* 1938, II, 88.
[23] Chambre, *Annales,* March 16, 1938, p. 1146.
[24] Chambre, *Documents,* June 16, 1939, doc. no. 92, p. 9.

League, it has full power to decide whether circumstances enable it to consider the application of Article 16.

This statement had been made because some of the Great Powers on the Council insisted that sanctions were obligatory, and that the decision as to their application rested with the League.[25]

In this attempt to modify the constitution of the League the Belgian government had been fully in accord with public opinion in the country. The suggestions offered by different groups varied, but their purpose was the same. Some publicists simply pleaded for a more "realistic" conception of collective security.[26] Others advocated regional mutual assistance pacts to provide a means of enforcing sanctions within a restricted area; such a system would preclude the possibility of entangling the small European states in a Pacific war.[27] Another suggestion was that small states should be given a privileged position within the League, rejoicing in all its guarantees, but not obliged to allow the right of passage.[28]

When it became obvious that there was no immediate prospect of reforming the League, doubts were expressed as to the wisdom of continued membership. This question was discussed in the spring of 1939 by the foreign affairs committee of the Chamber, which eventually reached the conclusion that the country should remain in the League because the French and British guarantees were conditional on Belgium's fidelity to the Covenant.[29]

Thus, although no official revision of the Covenant took place

---

[25] Chambre, *CRA,* June 7, 1939, p. 159.

[26] *Cf.* J. Wullus-Rudiger, "La Belgique et les dangers de demain," *Revue Belge,* XII (1935), 215.

[27] Ernest Melot, "Société des nations, ou pactes d'alliance et d'assistance mutuelle," *Flambeau,* XVIII (1935), 193-214; and Jean de Failon, "La crise de la sécurité collective," *Revue Générale,* CXXXV (1936), 658-9.

[28] Raoul Crabbé, "La neutralité belge et la S. D. N.," *Revue Belge,* XIV (1937), 379-384; Louis de Lichtervelde, "La Belgique et la S .D. N.," *Revue Générale,* CXXXVIII (1937), 385-491.

[29] Chambre, *Documents,* June 6, 1939, doc. no. 92, p. 10.

during the years between the adoption of the "independent policy" and the outbreak of the war, Belgium gradually shifted its attitude toward the League. By insisting that Article 16 was optional, it tried to free itself from the most burdensome and dangerous of its obligations. At the same time it dealt yet another blow to the ideal of collective security, and possibly paved the way for its own downfall.

The new policy of independence which accelerated the country's shift away from the League as well as from its former allies at the same time resulted in an increasing friendliness toward the so-called "Oslo powers" of northern Europe, especially the Netherlands.

Only one major problem to disturb Belgo-Dutch relations still existed; this was the unsettled question of Antwerp's access to the sea. While apparently acquiescing in Holland's stubborn refusal to make concessions on this point, the Belgians, by constructing the Albert Canal, forged themselves a weapon with which to threaten the Dutch. Linking Antwerp to the Liége basin by a modern canal with few locks, this action would deprive Rotterdam of some of its business. The Netherlands government at length brought the case before the Permanent Court of International Justice, alleging that in virtue of a treaty of 1868 regulating the use of the waters of the Meuse, Belgium was not entitled to the volume of water necessary for the canal. Brussels was alarmed, for the canal was not only valuable for commercial reasons, but was essential to the new defense system.[30] On June 28, 1937, a decision was handed down in favor of Belgium.[31]

Some sections of the Brussels press advocated using this decision as a club to force the Netherlands to reopen negotiations for

---

[30] "Le problème de la Meuse," *Revue Générale*, CXXXVII (1937), 346-368.
[31] The Hague, Permanent Court of International Justice, Series A/B. Judgments, orders, and advisory opinions. Fasciscule 70, *The diversion of waters from the Meuse* (Leyden, n.d.), pp. 32-33.

an Antwerp-Moerdijk canal, but the government preferred to pursue a more friendly policy.[32]

Already in the preceding month Belgo-Dutch cooperation had made an advance. On May 28 at The Hague the original Oslo powers and Finland signed a convention whereby those signatory states already using the quota system agreed not to extend it, and those which had not hitherto adopted it undertook not to introduce it. All the states involved further pledged themselves not to raise their duties on goods imported from the other signatories. This agreement became unworkable, when the temporary improvement in trade which had occasioned it was checked. The following May the convention was regretfully abrogated.[33]

These negotiations had, however, one useful effect, for in July 1938 the Oslo states met in Copenhagen to discuss measures of political cooperation. The statement regarding the optional character of Article 16 which was the chief result of the conference has already been noted. It marked another step away from general security and toward regional understandings.

When, in November 1938, Leopold paid a state visit to the Netherlands, it seemed probable that further advances would be made in this direction by the signature of a military agreement. Belgian hopes were, however, frustrated, by the reluctance of the Dutch to abandon their old and successful policy of isolation. Premier Patijn, in an official statement to the Netherlands Estates General, commended the new direction of Belgian foreign policy, but at the same time he said that as long as fundamental relations between the nations of Europe remained uncertain, there could be no question of military collaboration.[34] From this time on, however, the

---

[32] Cf. BPB, no. 127, Nov. 20, 1937, p. 5.

[33] A. Randle Elliott, "The Oslo States and the European War," Foreign Policy Reports, XV (1940), 265.

[34] Chambre, Annales, June 8, 1939, pp. 452-453; Documents, June 6, 1939, doc. no. 92, p. 15.

diplomatic action of the two nations was closely united, and during the months before the invasion King Leopold and Queen Wilhelmina worked in close harmony to avert disaster. The measure of unity that was achieved, insufficient though it may have been, was yet an improvement over the distrust of the preceding decade.

The reorientation of Belgian policy was not a blunder, nor was it pro-German. It was an honest effort on the part of the King and his ministers to safeguard their country by freeing it from pledges made under very different conditions. It bore important results, first in the Franco-British declaration which recognized the changed circumstances; then in the German pledge, which, however, was not without dangers; and thirdly, in closer cooperation with the smaller nations of the North. More important than all of these was the closer union among the two great groups of Belgians, Walloons and Flemings, which enabled the government to build up its defenses and face the crises of the following years with a certain measure of assurance.

The concluding chapter will study the action of the government during the troubled years which followed, down to that tenth of May, 1940, which proved that "independence" was impossible for a small state located at the crossroads of Europe.

CHAPTER ELEVEN

The Failure of the New Policy

FORTIFIED BY a relatively strong internal unity, the Belgian government was in a better position to face the problems in the field of foreign relations which henceforth confronted it, than it would have been if still bound by the military alliance with France. The first opportunity to gauge the strength of this position was presented by the Spanish Civil War.

The Belgian government accepted the non-intervention plan sponsored by Great Britain and France. This required legislation forbidding the recruitment of volunteers for either the Loyalist or the Nationalist armies. Such legislation was submitted to Parliament, but was delayed by Socialist opposition until March 24, 1937, when a really effective act was passed.[1]

Meanwhile the murder in Spain of Baron Jacques de Borchgrave caused a breach between the two sections of the Socialist party which culminated in the resignation of Vandervelde from van Zeeland's cabinet.[2] Spaak and the younger men favored a strongly national

---

[1] Chambre, *Annales,* March 24, 1937, p. 1185.

[2] De Borchgrave had been working for the Belgian embassy in Madrid during the early days of the Civil War. His body was discovered after his disappearance had caused much agitation. The Socialists insisted that he was a garage keeper who was really in Nazi pay; the Catholics maintained that he was a loyal Belgian who had closed his automobile agency to aid the overworked embassy staff. The Madrid government, admitting that some reparation was due, offered apologies, but refused to pay the required indemnity of one million francs. Belgium

policy, and insisted that the Spanish Loyalist government pay an indemnity; Vandervelde and the older Socialists, on the other hand, more concerned with internationalism and the spread of Socialism, were in sympathy with the Loyalists, and wished to drop the matter. When Vandervelde left the cabinet, Spaak and his followers, with the approval of the POB, remained. Although the party council adopted a resolution soliciting help for the Spanish Republic, it specifically stated that the Belgian government ought to continue the non-intervention policy.[3]

As the Civil War continued and Franco's government at Burgos became increasingly important, the problem of recognition arose. The Catholics, at all times favorable to the Nationalists, now found some allies among the Liberals, who thought that representation at Burgos would enable them to win commercial contracts from Franco. Spaak refused to comply with their desires, basing his refusal on the stand that even *de facto* recognition would weaken the non-intervention policy, which was so useful, he felt, in limiting the conflict to one country.[4] In April, 1938, a Catholic Senator added to the budget an amendment providing for the appointment of a commercial agent to Nationalist Spain. Spaak opposed this, and when he made it a question of confidence, carried the day. Yet the vote was only 59 to 17; there were 58 senators who abstained from voting, all of them Liberals or Catholics who desired recognition of Franco, but refused to support the Rexists and Flemish Nationalists who were trying to use the issue as a means to overthrow the cabinet.[5]

The abstentions had been secured by Spaak in return for secret

carried the case to the World Court, but when Spain agreed to pay sixty thousand francs the compromise was accepted, and the matter dropped. The Hague, Permanent Court of International Justice, *Affaire Borchgrave* (*Désistement*), (Leyden, 1938), pp. 4-5.

[3] *Le Peuple,* January 26-27 and February 17, 1937.
[4] Chambre, *Documents,* March 3, 1938, doc. no. 132, pp. 10-11.
[5] Sénat, *Annales,* April 7, 1938, p. 1210.

assurances that as soon as possible, a commercial agent would be dispatched to Burgos. When a month passed without any action on the matter, the Senate foreign affairs commission asked for an explanation. Spaak answered that Franco refused to accept a simple commercial representative, and insisted on full recognition. The commission supported him in his refusal to grant this, and in return asked him to send an envoy to investigate the situation on the spot. This was done in June when M. Delcoigne was entrusted with the mission. In his report he stated that by not granting at least *de facto* recognition, Belgium had lost business, and that continued refusal would have even worse effects.

Upon the publication of these conclusions, Spaak announced that the cabinet had decided to withdraw from the non-intervention committee and to open negotiations with Franco. According to the foreign minister, this change of policy was chiefly due to the Anglo-Italian Naval agreement. Moreover, since all the European powers except Russia and France had already recognized Franco there seemed to be no valid reason why Belgium should not do so.[6]

Señor Ruy Funés, ambassador of the Spanish republic, lodged a protest against the negotiations with Franco, and on December 1, 1938, he was suddenly recalled. Spaak at once summoned his representative from Madrid.[7] On January 7, 1939, Spaak informed the British ambassador in Brussels that Belgium was withdrawing from the non-intervention committee. In order to pacify the Socialists, arrangements were at the same time begun to reestablish diplomatic relations with the Republic.[8] But by this time Franco's victory was merely a matter of weeks, and on February 24, 1939, Belgium, following France's lead, accorded full *de jure* recognition to the Nationalist government.[9]

[6] Sénat, *Annales,* Nov. 29, 1938, pp. 62-66.
[7] Chambre, *Annales,* Dec. 6, 1938, p. 161; Sénat, *Annales,* Dec. 13, 1938, p. 171.
[8] Chambre, *Annales,* Feb. 7, 1939, pp. 523-524.
[9] *Indépendance Belge,* Feb. 25, 1939.

Meanwhile Spaak's attention had been focussed on the danger resulting from the expanding power of Nazi Germany, coupled with the inability or unwillingness of France and Great Britain to restrain it. The first episode which clearly defined this twofold peril was the remilitarization of the Rhineland, already discussed. The next was the Anschluss, by which Austria was forcibly united to the Reich. Belgium did not follow the example of the other western Powers and register a formal protest in Berlin. The reason given was that the government was no longer under the obligation of participating in concerted diplomatic moves, and the League's failure to act freed its members from any duty to do so.[10] The true reason was, of course, fear of offering an excuse for aggression to a powerful neighbor. Many Belgians remembered that Austria too had received assurances from Hitler that he would not violate its sovereignty or territory, and that in *Mein Kampf* Hitler had proclaimed that when German interests were at stake, nothing would restrain him.[11] These reflections moved even some of the Flemings, who began to realize that if they wished any degree of "home rule," it could only be achieved within the framework of the Belgian state.[12]

Consciousness of the danger from the east accelerated work on the defense system. In September, 1938, the first test of the frontier plans was made. During the early days of the Czechoslovakian crisis no extraordinary precautions were taken, but on September 24 the engineer corps was mobilized.[13] Within twenty-four hours more

[10] Chambre, *Annales*, March 16, 1938, pp. 1043-1046.
[11] Raoul Crabbé, "La riposte au Führer," *Revue Belge*, XV (1938), 278; *cf.* also *Flambeau*, XXI (1938), 504.
[12] Pierre van Axel, "Le mouvement flamand et le retour à l'état belge," *Revue Générale*, CXL (1938), 376.
[13] An eye-witness' description of the popular reaction to the crisis is given by James M. Chapin, "Final Report," *Belgian-American Educational Foundation*, Nov. 4, 1938.

than 300,000 men were under arms, although technically the army was only on a "reinforced peace footing."[14]

Belgium was no longer present at the council tables of the Great Powers, and played no part in the negotiations leading to the break-up of Czechoslovakia. Carton de Wiart's declaration at Geneva on September 16, 1938, that his government did not consider Article 16 of the League Covenant to be obligatory may have helped strengthen Chamberlain and Daladier in their decision to concede Hitler's demands. With the road to Germany through Belgium closed to the British and French armies, military intervention would have been exceedingly difficult. That this determination of the Belgian government was real was shown during the September mobilization, when troops were posted on the French as well as on the German frontier.[15] Although this aroused some opposition within the country, in general it brought reassurance to those who were afraid of antagonizing Hitler.[16]

On October 4, 1938, a special session of parliament opened. It was marked by many manifestations of loyalty, and even the Rexists showed a more cooperative spirit than was their wont. They had recently agreed to demand a roll-call on every vote. At the opening of this session, however, they announced that for the time being they would forego this particular form of obstruction.[17] This attitude was typical of all parties, Flemings as well as Rexists, not to speak of the older groups, whose loyalty was taken for granted.[18] In glowing terms a Rexist Senator described the patriotic union of all Belgians: ". . . there was no longer any anti-patriotic national-

[14] Chambre, *Annales*, Nov. 3, 1938, p. 33.

[15] René Cercler, "France-Belgique," *Revue Politique et Parlementaire*, CLXX-VIII (1939), 238-240.

[16] *Cf.* Albert J. Lynd, "Preliminary Report," *Belgian-American Educational Foundation*, Jan. 1, 1939; *BPB*, no. 131, Jan. 21, 1939, pp. 7-8.

[17] Sénat, *Annales*, Oct. 4, 1938, p. 3.

[18] Victor de Laveleye, "Bilan intérieure d'une crise extérieure," *Revue Belge*, XV (1938), 373.

ism, no class struggle, no philosophic, economic, or regional quarrels. There was only an immense, tense crowd, ready to defend Belgium against any invader."[19]

As in other quarters, the selfish betrayal of a small state was forgotten in relief that peace still continued. On October 4 Spaak told the Chamber, "It seems to me that there is nothing nobler to be hoped for than to spare one's country the horrors of war, provided it can be done without breaking promises."[20] And the country agreed. The following spring the foreign affairs commission of the Chamber gave full approval to the government and praised the policy of Chamberlain and Daladier.[21]

There were realists in the country, however; they knew that the Munich pacts had merely obtained a reprieve. Foremost among these was King Leopold, who in October, 1938, made an important speech at the dedication by the French government of a memorial to his father. Omitting the customary banal phrases, he openly advocated an international conference to work for peace.[22] This conference was never called, and instead of devoting their energies to thinking out a plan for relieving the international tension, Belgian statesmen did the next best thing, and carefully strengthened their military preparations.

The quasi-mobilization of the preceding September had shown certain weaknesses, particularly in the supply system, the method of requisitioning transportation, and air raid protection. The government at once set about finding a remedy for these defects, especially the last named. A law providing for air raid protection was quickly voted, and in May, 1939, a first trial blackout was staged.[23]

---

[19] Sénat, *Annales,* Jan. 25, 1939, p. 380.

[20] Chambre, *Annales,* Oct. 4, 1938, p. 7.

[21] Chambre, *Documents,* June 6, 1939, doc. no. 92, p. 2.

[22] Jean de Richemont, *L'Europe devant l'indépendance belge,* (Paris, 1939), p. 138.

[23] Sénat, *Documents,* Dec. 21, 1938, doc. no. 63, Nov., 1938 doc. no. 10, pp. 15:30; Sénat, *Annales,* Jan. 25, 1939, p. 381, and June 13, 1939, p. 346; Chambre, *Annales,* Nov. 3, 1938, p. 33.

In addition to the technical weaknesses which the September crisis had revealed, three questions of military policy had emerged. A deputy from Wallonia brought up the first question in Parliament. After pointing to the fact that only demolition squads had been left in the southeastern provinces, he demanded that if this territory were not to be defended, the government make provision for evacuating the civilian population. In reply, the national defense commission repeated the promise that Limburg and Luxemburg provinces would not be abandoned, and that all Belgian territory would be defended.[24] In spite of this pledge, however, there was no longer any question of full frontier defense, and the general staff had decided to build a new line of fortifications extending from Antwerp to Namur, the Albert Canal line to be used only as an outpost. This decision was of course carefully kept secret.[25]

The second question was that of choosing which boundaries to defend. In September, 1938, some troops had been sent to guard the southern border, but the only permanent fortifications were to the east. The Flemish leader Declerq asked the minister of defense if he intended to fortify the Franco-Belgian frontier against possible invasion, and received an affirmative answer. This aroused anger in many quarters, many Belgians feeling that this would be an open insult to France. One Senator ironically remarked that consistency also required the erection of shore defenses to protect the country from the British fleet.[26] The national defense commission of the Chamber insisted that only the Belgo-German frontier be fortified, on the ground that "the only apparent danger is from that direction."[27]

[24] Chambre, *Annales,* Nov. 3, 1938, p. 44; *Documents,* May 9, 1939, doc. no. 26, p. 5.
[25] Belgium, Ministère des Affaires étrangères, *Belgium, the official account of what happened,* 1939-1940 (New York, 1942), pp. 15-16, 97-98. Hereafter cited as *D. D. 1939.*
[26] Senat, *Annales,* Nov. 30, 1938, p. 95.
[27] Chambre, *Documents,* May 9, 1939, doc. no. 26, p. 4.

So great did the peril from the east seem that the whole issue of foreign policy was revived. In March, 1939, Hitler's absorption of Czechoslovakia, in violation of the solemn pledges given at Munich, thoroughly alarmed his remaining neighbors. The internal disunion which facilitated the disintegration of Czecholovakia pointed the lesson of the dangers of such separatist tendencies as the Flemish movement. Even the influential *Standaard,* most of whose readers were staunch Flemings, advised them to "meditate on the lesson of Czecho-Slovakia." Another Flemish paper warned that "a federal Belgium is a Belgium destined for destruction."[28] With the Flemings awake to the danger of division, it seemed to some of their compatriots that it might be possible to return to the policy of military collaboration with France and Great Britain. This was the issue raised by the September crisis. The socialists led the way in asking for an immediate revision of foreign policy, but many Catholics and Liberals were of the same opinion.[29]

Some Senators had already asked that staff conversations be resumed, so that the "improvisations" of the first war could be avoided.[30] In the spring of 1939 this suggestion became increasingly popular. Several deputies expressed their opinion that eventually Belgium would be involved in the coming war, in spite of every effort to avoid provoking the invader. The only way to prevent a rapid surrender would be to make careful plans with the French and British staffs.[31] The military affairs committee of the Senate went even further, claiming that the independent policy included the right, which the committee hoped would never be renounced, of making staff contacts. Premier Pierlot, however, held to Spaak's theory, and insisted that if any such agreement were made, it would endanger Belgium's security by freeing Germany from its promise.[32]

---

[28] *BPB,* no. 132, May 10, 1939, pp. 3-4.
[29] *Le Peuple,* March 25, 1939.
[30] Sénat, *Annales,* Nov. 30, 1938, p. 94.
[31] Chambre, *Documents,* June 6, 1939, doc. no. 92, p. 7.
[32] Sénat, *CRA,* June 30, 1939, pp. 230, 249.

His caution was not without reason, for Hitler easily found excuses for threatening his smaller neighbors. This was evident from
his reaction to a suggestion made in April, 1939, by President
Roosevelt. The President asked the German and Italian dictators
to give assurances that their armies would never attack the territory
or the possessions of the independent states of Europe.[33] Before replying, the German government asked the smaller European states
if they considered themselves menaced. There was, of course, only
one safe answer. The Belgian reply of April 17 said that no invasion was feared because of the guarantees given in 1937 by Germany, France, and Great Britain.[34]

This diplomatic answer, the only one possible under the circumstances, was far from true. Since 1933 fears had been entertained
that the Germans would try to repossess themselves of the territory
lost under the provisions of the Treaty of Versailles. Since 1934
Nazi organizations had functioned in Eupen and Malmédy, to the
annoyance of loyal Belgians.[35] In 1937 these organizations began
to spread throughout the country, and by the summer of 1939 they
were so strong that the local gauleiters held regular meetings, distributed Nazi pamphlets, and reported any expression of anti-Ger-
man feelings to the Gestapo. Belgian branches of German business
enterprises were forced to discharge all Jews in their employ.[36]

It was natural, therefore that when the critical moment arrived
in August, 1939, Belgium should do everything possible to avert
the impending war. In the previous May there had been informal
talks between Belgian and Dutch diplomats and now King Leopold
took the initiative. On August 21 he called a conference of the Oslo
powers, to meet at once in Brussels to study the situation. Foreign
Minister Koht of Norway suggested that they offer to mediate be-

[33] Cordell Hull, *The Memoirs of Cordell Hull* (New York, 1948), I, 621-22.
[34] Chambre, *Annales,* June 7, 1939, p. 426.
[35] Elie Richard, "Terror on the Frontiers," *Living Age,* CCCLIV (138),
196-202.
[36] Chambre, *Annales,* June 13, 1939, pp. 191-194.

tween the German government on the one hand, and the British, French, and Polish governments on the other. The conference decided that this was inadvisable at the moment, and instead on August 23 King Leopold broadcast a plea for peace. After briefly summarizing the underlying causes of conflict—economic problems, mutual distrust, and militarism—he affirmed that a lasting peace could not be based on force. It could be based only on the moral order. In conclusion, he begged for further negotiation, "and may the disaster which threatens mankind be averted!"[37]

The British reply of August 24 was the first to reach Brussels. It expressed the "full sympathy" of the government with Leopold's sentiments, but went on to say that negotiations could not be successful under existing conditions.[38] Two days later the French government declared its willingness to help end the crisis, but repudiated any solution "imposed by violence or threats."[39] President Roosevelt assured Leopold that the people of the United States "wholeheartedly share the hopes and aspirations so eloquently expressed by Your Majesty."[40] But from Germany and Italy there was no reply.

Belgian statesmen made one more attempt to avert the war. On August 28 Premier Pierlot convoked the British, French, German Ambassadors, and the Polish minister, to make a formal offer of mediation on behalf of Queen Wilhelmina and King Leopold. This step, said to have been taken at the suggestion of the Vatican, failed to achieve its purpose.[41] The British foreign office replied that it welcomed the offer, and would "take advantage of it should the occasion present itself." The French and Polish governments gave

---

[37] D.D. 1939, pp. 68-69.
[38] Great Britain, *Parliamentary Papers,* 1939-1940, Cmd. 6106, p. 187, doc. no. 129.
[39] *Ibid.,* p. 187, doc. no. 130.
[40] Department of State *Bulletin,* I, Aug. 26, 1939.
[41] Great Britain, *Parliamentary Papers,* 1939-1940, Cmd. 6106, doc. no. 134, August 28, 1939. *Cf. Flambeau,* XXII (1939), 355.

equally indefinite replies. Once again, there was no answer from Hitler.[42]

The Fuhrer had, instead, given King Leopold a very different declaration. On August 26 King Leopold and Premier Pierlot received von Bulow-Shwante, the German Ambassador. He renewed the promises made two years earlier to respect the inviolability and integrity of Belgium, with the further condition that the Belgian government observe strict neutrality and oppose any violation thereof by a third Power.[43]

The following day the British ambassador repeated the pledges of 1937, and on August 28 the French government made a similar statement.[44]

The promises of the allies evoked little comment in the press; they were almost taken for granted. Hitler's guarantee, on the other hand, aroused skepticism. *La Libre Belgique* on August 28 assured its readers that such pledges must be received "with caution." Even the Flemings were not deceived. Three days before the outbreak of the war, *La Flandre Libérale* voiced their attitude: "In case of conflict, this Belgian nation will be neutral politically. But it will not be so at heart."[45]

That the government relied less on Hitler's promises than on its own military strength to preserve the country from war was shown by the protective measures taken at the outset of the crisis. On August 24 all soldiers on leave were recalled, and the following day the first stage of mobilization was decreed, to begin within twenty-four hours. The reserves were called up on September 1, after the beginning of hostilities. No further measures were taken until after the fall of Poland.[46] The complete mobilization ordered then was

---

[42] Cmd. 6106, doc. nos. 135, 136, 138, August 31, 1939.
[43] *D.D. 1939*, pp. 69-70.
[44] *Ibid.*, pp. 70-72.
[45] *BPB*, no. 133, Sept. 30, 1939, p. 13.
[46] *D.D. 1939*, p. 12.

smoothly carried out without panic. One factor which aided very much in the attainment of this success was the cooperation of the labor unions and of the Socialist party; the latter issued a statement to all its affiliates asking them to give every assistance to the government in order to "maintain the liberties of the people, national independence, and the integrity of the territory."[47]

On September 3, after the publication of the official declaration of neutrality, the cabinet was converted into a government of National Union by the inclusion of the Socialists. Among the five new ministers were Henri de Man, minister without portfolio, and Spaak, who returned to the ministry of foreign affairs. A special session of Parliament was called at once, to approve the cabinet changes and to vote special powers. Pierlot's reiteration of the policy of independence brought him a hearty ovation from all but the Communists. Speaking for the Catholics, Carton de Wiart paid homage to the King for "his generous and far-sighted effort to save the peace" and for "the wise directives" he had laid down for his people in a radio speech on September 3. He also approved the maintenance of the 1936 policy. The Socialist orator, Fischer, after pledging his party's support, admitted that although the POB knew that the war was aggressive, as Belgians "we understand that circumspection and calmness are necessary." Max, the famous burgomaster of Brussels in the days of the first war, expressed the same ideas in the name of the Liberals. The only advocate of intervention was the Communist deputy, Relecom. He favored an immediate attack on Hitler to save Poland. After him Degrelle and Romsée, speaking for the Rexist and Flemish nationalist parties respectively, made brief statements supporting the government.[48]

The full powers asked by Pierlot were then voted with little dis-

---

[47] *Flambeau*, XXII (1939), 354.

[48] Chambre, *Annales*, Sept. 5, 1939, pp. 5-10. Both Degrelle and Romsée later were active collaborators with the Nazis.

cussion, and the Senate gave its consent the following day.[49] For a
time, however, relatively few of these powers were needed.

When the dreaded invasion did not occur within the first weeks
of the war, the tension decreased. However, after the partition of
Poland, German troops were moved to the west, and anxiety once
more became acute. As reports of troop concentrations near Aachen
reached Brussels, the army completed its mobilization and intensified its efforts to develop a third line of defense behind the Albert
canal. At the same time, King Leopold requested Joseph Davies,
American Ambassador in Brussels, to ask President Roosevelt to
intervene in order to prevent a German attack on Western Europe.[50]

A few weeks later the Dutch foreign minister van Kleffens suggested that Queen Wilhelmina and King Leopold renew their offer of mediation made the previous August. Both rulers welcomed
the idea, and at once Leopold and Spaak drove to The Hague. By
the following morning, November 7, 1939, a draft had been agreed
upon, and was immediately transmitted to the heads of the belligerent nations. Its terms were simple; they offered to facilitate in any
way possible "inquiry into the factors likely to make for agreement."[51]

There was small likelihood that the offer would be accepted, as
France and Great Britain had just rejected Hitler's peace overtures,
and announced that his overthrow was their major war aim. On
November 9, two days after the publication of the joint note, Sir
Samuel Hoare told the House of Commons that the British government did not expect that Germany would make a satisfactory answer. Before making its own reply, the cabinet would consult with

[49] *Ibid.*, Sept. 5, 1939, p. 12; *Flambeau*, XXII (1939), 355.

[50] Hull, *Memoirs*, I, 710-711. Roosevelt and Hull declined to act, as they believed a peace offer would at the moment harm the allied cause. *Ibid.*, I, 711-12.

[51] *D.D. 1939*, pp. 14, 79. According to Ambassador Davies, the sovereigns had
acted because they had received information that a German invasion of their
territories was planned for November 9. Hull, *Memoirs*, I, 712.

the Dominions and with its allies.[52] The official British note was published three days later. It read in part:

... The larger purposes for which my peoples are now fighting are to secure that Europe may be redeemed ... from perpetually recurring fear of German aggression so as to enable the people of Europe to preserve their independence and their liberties, and to prevent for the future resort to force instead of the pacific means of settlement of international disputes.[53]

The French reply explicitly rejected any peace which did not include "reparation of the injustices forcibly done to Austria, Czechoslovakia, and Poland."

On November 15 Hitler's foreign minister von Ribbentrop informed Davignon, the Belgian Ambassador in Berlin, that after the blunt rejection of France and Great Britain, the German government considered the matter closed, and would give no formal answer.[54]

The royal appeal for peace was unpopular in Belgium, and criticism of it led to a reappraisal of the whole policy pursued since 1936. The Liberal periodical *Flambeau* declared that the Belgian people were "stupefied" to learn of the offer. In a lengthy editorial the review gave a full quotation from an article by a Catholic Deputy, Paul Struye, published in the *Libre Belgique* on October 10, four days after Hitler made his peace proposals. The sentiments of the writer, adopted by the *Flambeau's* editors, stigmatized any nation which supported peace proposals at that time as an accomplice of the aggressor. *Flambeau* also asked the government to proclaim "our absolute moral obligation and our unanimous resolution to defend Holland" in case of attack.[55]

The veteran Socialist deputy Hubin interpellating the government

---

[52] Great Britain, *Parl. Debates*, fifth ser., CCCLIII, 419-420.

[53] *Ibid.*, pp. 871-872.

[54] New York *Times*, November 13, 1939.

[55] Grégoire, "Une offensive morale," *Flambeau*, XXII (1939), 511-512.

on December 20, criticized the omission of Poland and Czechoslovakia from the offer, on the ground that this omission implied
acquiescence in their destruction. In a strong phrase he condemned
the government's policy: "We have raised national selfishness to
the rank of a virtue."[56]

Despite the rising chorus of protest, independence and neutrality
still seemed to most Belgians the wisest course to pursue. At the
opening of the regular session of Parliament on November 14, Frans
van Cauwelaert, President of the Chamber, spoke for the majority
when in his inaugural speech he congratulated the King and expressed "unshakable confidence in the triumph of his enlightened
action."[57]

The Chamber endorsed these sentiments; at the end of the budget debate on foreign policy, much shorter than usual, the government's line of action was almost unanimously voted, without even
the formality of a roll-call. During the discussion the policy of the
cabinet was clearly explained by Foreign Minister Spaak; describing
the views he and his colleagues held regarding neutrality, he said:
"No one has ever maintained that a neutral Belgium must be an
indifferent Belgium." He pleaded, in the next breath, for the sacrifice of "exaggerated utterances" in the press in order to strength-
en the hand of the government. After paying tribute to the "almost
irreproachable discussions in this Chamber," he explained the King's
part in the mediation offer: "My presence at The Hague was a
guarantee that the step taken by our Sovereign was strictly constitutional." He added:

. . . I feel I should thank the King in public for the magnificent efforts he has made for several years to spare our country the horrors
of war [Lively applause]; for the wise advice he has always given
to the various governments which succeeded one another in power;
for the strength of mind with which he performs his very heavy

[56] Chambre, *Annales,* Dec. 20, 1939, pp. 223-224.
[57] *Ibid.,* Nov. 14, 1939, p. 8.

task; for the example he has always set those with whom he comes in contact, an example which compels respect, admiration, and affection.

Turning then to the relations between Belgium and the Netherlands, he stated that "an independent and neutral Holland is of vital importance to Belgium" and that "if the situation in Holland changes, it would be madness to suppose that such an event would leave us indifferent." This remark was greeted with hearty applause.[58]

The reference to the press in the early paragraphs of the speech touched on one of the most troublesome problems then facing the government, that of censorship. Early in October an article in the *Nation Belge* attributed the war to the Allies' failure to partition Germany in 1919. Hitler at once sent for Ambassador Davignon and lectured him. The same day a note from von Ribbentrop listed a series of complaints against the Belgian government. According to the German memorandum, Pierlot had failed to repress the "insolent press," was not sufficiently enthusiastic in supporting Hitler's peace offer, and was acting as an "accomplice" of France and Great Britain by not protesting with sufficient vigor against the blockade. The day Davignon received the note several divisions of the German army were transferred from Emden to Treves, as if to underline the Nazi grievances.[59]

This affair forced Spaak to ask the press to adopt a more neutral tone. At once there was opposition from all sides. The Liberal *Soir* and *Gazette*, the Catholic *Libre Belgique*, the Socialist *Volksgazet* and *Le Peuple* for once agreed; none of them would accept censorship. Only de Man's *Lieding* favored severe repression of personal opinion.[60] The November issue of *Flambeau* openly criticized Leopold's mediation offer, with the result that the Minister of Edu-

[58] Chambre, *Annales,* Dec. 19, 1939, pp. 193-195.
[59] Henri Grégoire, "L'Europe de demain," *Flambeau,* XXII (1939), 710-711.
[60] Henri Grégoire, L'Interdiction du *Flambeau*: histoire d'une faute," *Flambeau,* XXIII (1940) 181.

cation cancelled the subscriptions of his department, thereby inflict-
ing severe financial hardship on the periodical. The editor of *Flambeau* published this news, with the remark that to consider that the
article was directed against the person of the King implied that the
mediation offer had been made without the approval of the cabinet.[61] This editorial caused the suppression of the review on the
ground that the royal person had been attacked. At once there were
strong protests from both Liberal and Catholic press. Even the *Vingtième Siècle,* Pierlot's organ, joined in the condemnation. Three
weeks later, on February 27, the descree of suppression was rescind-
ed, but at the same time Declerq's *Volk en Staat,* a violently extremist Flemish paper, was likewise permitted to resume publication.[62]

The incident is significant, not only as illustrating the views of
a large and well informed section of public opinion, but also as
partially revealing the anxieties of the government. The offer made
by Wilhelmina and Leopold had been an attempt to forestall a German invasion which at the time seemed imminent. Public criticism
of their offer might provoke the dreaded conflict—hence the censorship. In January, 1940, at the time *Flambeau's* defiant reply to
official censure caused its suppression, another threat to Belgium's
security had appeared.

On January 10, 1940, a German plane made a forced landing at
Mechelen, in Belgium, near the Dutch boundary a few miles north
of Maestricht. Some confidential documents which the German officers in the plane tried to destroy were saved by their captors. The
rescued papers proved to be instructions to the squadron leader of
the Second Air Fleet giving detailed directions for invading Belgium in the Maestricht district, and for landing airborne troops between the Sambre and Meuse rivers.[63] The army at once called up

---

[61] Henri Grégoire, "Le *Flambeau* de guerre," *Flambeau,* XXII (1939), 621-
629.
[62] Henri Grégoire, "L'Interdiction du *Flambeau*"; *loc. cit.,* p. 205.
[63] *D.D. 1939,* pp. 14-15; 85-91.

more men, raising the total under arms to 600,000; at the same time parts of Eupen and Malmédy were evacuated and Brussels was blacked out.[64]

The Netherlands, France, and Great Britain were at once notified by Belgium, since the plan of attack involved them. Prime Minister Chamberlain replied that if the invasion occurred, the Franco-British guarantee would at once become operative. He also informed the House of Commons that the army had made careful plans to meet the situation.[65] The last remark contained a veiled allusion to the "staff agreements" which were so important for successful military collaboration. As early as September 20, 1939, there had been secret negotiations between General Gamelin and General van den Bergen, Belgian chief of staff, culminating in an arrangement whereby the latter agreed to keep his army fully mobilized, and to strengthen further the second line of defense from Namur to Antwerp.[66] In spite of the deepest secrecy, rumors of such concerted plans spread throughout Belgium.[67] Some confirmation was given these reports when it became known that General van den Bergen, who was believed to be opposed to cooperation with the Allies, was succeeded as chief of staff by General Michiels, known to favor it. Defense Minister Denis, when questioned on the subject in Parliament, admitted that van den Bergen had resigned because his strategy differed from that of the minister, who was known to be pro-Ally.[68] A week later, on February 7, 1940, those who wished closer military union between the western powers were pleased to learn from Denis that "The responsible Belgian authorities will neglect no steps to enable the Powers which have guaranteed Belgium to fulfill their obligations towards us!"[69] The Belgian High

---

[64] Great Britain, *Parl. Debates,* fifth ser., CCCLVI, 36-37.
[65] Great Britain, *Parl. Debates,* fifth ser., CCCLVI, 580.
[66] Winston Churchill, *The Second World War,* (Boston, 1948), I, 482-83.
[67] Henri Grégoire, "La politique belge," *Flambeau,* XXIII (1940), 126.
[68] Chambre, *Annales,* Feb. 1, 1940, p. 470.
[69] *Ibid.,* Feb. 7, 1940, p. 560.

Command, moreover, received from General Gamelin assurances that "he had at his disposal everything necessary to ensure that the help to Belgium would be rendered without delay."[70] This closer understanding had long been desired by many of van den Bergen's subordinates, but he and the government opposed it for fear that it might give Hitler a pretext for war.[71]

The change in policy aroused violent attacks from the Flemings. Declerq wrote in his *Volk en Staat*: ". . . the road we have entered upon leads not only to the complete destruction of our national economy, but likewise to a military dictatorship."[72] This passage caused the paper to be suppressed until February 27, when it and the *Flambeau* were again allowed to circulate.

While freedom of the press was occupying public attention, the cabinet had other worries. Declerq's prophecy of destruction of the national economy was based on sober fact. During the week from February 19 to 24, a total of 213,483 men were unemployed, forty percent of this number living in the province of Antwerp, showing the loss in the transit traffic due to the blockade.[73] At the same time that provision had to be made for these men and their families, 600,000 more were standing guard at the frontier. They too had to be paid, and their families given relief. As a result, the budget deficit from the coming tax year was estimated to be close to 7,408,000,000 francs, although new taxes to the amount of

[70] *D.D. 1939*, p. 22. According to Churchill, however there was a division of opinion in the Allied High Command as to whether the second and main line of Belgian fortifications, extending from Namur to Antwerp via Louvain, should be held, or whether the third line along the Scheldt should be the allied line of defense in case of an invasion of Begium. Some even favored surrendering all of Belgium, and concentrating on prepared positions within France. Churchill, *Second World War,* I, 481-3.

[71] Col. Requette, "The Low Countries and the European War," *Atlantic,* CLXV (1940), 695.

[72] Chambre, *Annales,* Feb. 22, 1940, p. 735.

[73] *Ibid.,* March 1, 1940, p. 842. It was doubly dangerous to have the Antwerp men out of work, as in their discontent it was only too probable that they would join the ranks of the Flemish extremists.

1,381,000,000 francs were voted in February.[74] There was a strong possibility that even this high estimate might prove too moderate, for in January, 1940, several of the bridges over the Albert canal showed large cracks, and had to be closed to traffic. This was not the first time that the canal, the first line of defense, had given anxiety. In March, 1938, a bridge at Hasselt collapsed, and in June, 1939, a dike near the same city gave way, causing much damage. The following August two more bridges, strategically located near Liége, also collapsed. By the first months of 1940 seven other bridges were in bad condition, giving much worry not only because of the expense entailed in their repair, but even more because of the possibility that the damage was the result of deliberate sabotage. A group of engineers was sent to study the situation, but their report was never published.[75]

Other anxieties harassed Pierlot and his colleagues during the uneasy months preceding the invasion. There was the vital matter of importing food. This was no easy task, as Great Britain was determined to preserve the efficacy of the blockade by preventing Ger-

[74] Chambre, *Annales,* Feb. 29, 1940, p. 807. The summary given to the Chamber is eloquent:

Receipts

Ways and Means	11,150,000,000 francs
New taxes	1,381,000,000
Total	12,531,000,000

Expenditures

Ordinary budget	12,000,000,000
Extraordinary budget (proper)	2,302,000,000
Supplementary credits	279,000,000
Mobilization budgets	
Ordinary	4,161,000,000
Extraordinary	649,000,000
Anti-aircraft defenses	450,000,000
Total	19,940,000,000 francs

[75] Chambre, *Annales.* Feb. 1, 1940, p. 477; March 1, 1940, p. 814. It seems doubtful that the faults in the bridges were due to German sabotage. The Germans in 1940 were greatly helped by the failure of the retreating Allies to destroy the bridges.

many from obtaining supplies through neutral neighbors. In September, 1939, the Belgian government had on hand only a month's reserves of foodstuffs, but every effort was made to increase these during the autumn, and to guarantee their fair distribution by imposing the ration system.[76]

This problem was closely linked with that of preserving neutral rights in face of the blockade. On November 28, 1939, an Order-in-Council entitled "Reprisals restricting German commerce" decreed that all ships sailing in the North Sea must stop at a British port for examination. All enemy goods, or even goods merely suspected of an ultimate enemy destination, were to be confiscated, Belgium at once protested against this extension of the law of blockade, but to no avail. At the same time the German government censured Spaak for acquiescing in Britain's "starvation policy."[77] As the United States could not obtain a change in the British conception of neutral rights, it was hardly likely that the small states could be more successful.[78]

Although in general the policies of the government, both domestic and foreign, were accepted by the bulk of the population, opposition came from the Flemings, the Rexists, and the Communists. The last two named were severely treated, but the danger that the application of strong measures against the Flemish extremists would alienate the moderates, forced the adoption of what might be termed "appeasement" in their regard. This was evidenced by the difference in treatment accorded the Liberal periodical *Flambeau* and that given Declerq's *Volk en Staat*. Moreover, no action was taken to suppress an inflammatory pamphlet, "The Catechism of the Vigilant Flemish Soldier," which circulated among the troops. The following extract shows its tone:

[76] *D.D. 1939*, pp. 10-11; Elliott, "Oslo States and European War," *loc. cit.*, p. 271.

[77] New York *Times*, Nov. 29, 1939.

[78] Hull, *Memoirs*, I, 733-736.

Q. What should the Flemish soldier do if he is given orders in French?

A. He cannot disobey under pain of severe punishment. But he can carry out the order backwards [*tout de travers*], since he does not understand it.[79]

To please the Flemish section of the population certain administrative changes were adopted. During the winter of 1939-1940 the central office of each national department was divided into two sections, one French, one Flemish. The only bond of unity between them was the Secretary General, the permanent official at the head of each department. This measure, closely resembling complete administrative separation, was not enough to satisfy Declerq's followers, but it was all that the rest of Belgium was willing to accept.[80]

Communists and Rexists received harsher treatment. On November 17, 1939, the *Voix du Peuple,* the chief Communist organ, was permanently suspended, and all other publications of the party were suppressed before March. None of the party members themselves, apparently, were molested, though they were several times shouted down in the Chamber.[81]

At first the Rexists were unmolested, as they seemed to have become comparatively harmless. Degrelle expressed his agreement with the government during the debate on foreign policy in September. Three months later, in December, 1939, in the discussion of the budget, he categorically denied that he would accept German hegemony in Europe.[82] But during the January crisis his paper, *Le Pays Réel,* advocated making terms with Hitler, incidentally claiming that this was the royal policy.[83] When this propaganda contin-

---

[79] Chambre, *Annales,* Dec. 19, 1939, p. 193.

[80] Wullus-Rudiger, *Défense de la Belgique,* p. 113; Grégoire, "La politique belge," *loc. cit.,* p. 248.

[81] Chambre, *Annales,* March 12, 1940, p. 1010. The Communists were loudly booed during a discussion of the Russo-Finnish War, Chambre, *Annales,* Dec. 19, 1939, pp. 194-195.

[82] Chambre, *Annales,* Dec. 15, 1939, p. 181.

[83] Grégoire, "La politique belge," *loc. cit.,* p. 126.

ued, the government took alarm, and in March, 1940, introduced a bill for "the Defense of National Institutions." The first article provided penalties to be inflicted on the leader of any group "working for the destruction of the independence, liberties, or constitutional institutions" of Belgium. Milder sentences were to be inflicted on the members of such organizations, or those who worked alone for similar ends. The terms of the second article made it illegal for anyone engaged in politics to receive from a foreign power instructions or information which might harm Belgium. The bill aroused slight discussion. Members of the older parties agreed that under the circumstances the law would not be unconstitutional, and as de Lavelye, a Liberal, said, it was directed "only against the forerunners of the invasion." The Rexists, Flemish Nationalists, and Communists were bitter in their opposition, and accused the Socialists of hypocrisy for supporting the proposal. A few members of the majority had constitutional scruples, so when, on March 12, 1940. the law was voted by 136 to 24, 15 deputies abstained.[84]

In virtue of this law Degrelle and several of his followers were arrested in April, after the invasion of Norway demonstrated the dangers which beset a nation with a well organized fascist party.[85]

In spite of the relative calm on the Western frontier, broken only once when in early March a German reconnaissance plane crossed the frontier and shot down three planes of the Belgian air patrol, the Belgian government was not deceived.[86] As early as April 1 Spaak told American Ambassador Cudahy that he expected an attack about the middle of the month.[87] When Norway proved to be

---

[84] Chambre, *Annales,* March 12, 1940, p. 1001.

[85] Degrelle, together with some Flemish Nationalists arrested on May 10, was taken to France, but after the armistice all were freed and returned to Belgium, where they worked in close collaboration with the Nazi officials. Motz, *Belgium Unvanquished,* p. 37.

[86] Berlin at once disavowed this action and offered reparation, *D.D. 1939,* p. 95.

[87] Hull, *Memoirs,* I, 761.

the next victim, the foreign minister, perhaps to keep the record clear in case his country's turn would follow, made a long declaration to the Senate, largely a summary of his foreign policy. He showed that since 1936 all those who held his office had sought but one aim, "to preserve our country from the scourge of war." The means used had been absolute independence of foreign alliances, a strong army, and complete frankness. The government had repudiated all idea of an alliance with any power, and would continue to do so, for such an agreement would only lead to war.

The second part of the speech was intended for Spaak's domestic audience. He tried to convince those who favored closer union with the Allies that this would only bring the war to their homeland. In that case, "Our fate would be worse than that of any other country. This alone is sufficient justification for our efforts, and I am not ashamed of the egoism, the sacred egoism which inspires me when I am fighting to spare Belgium an ordeal which she has not deserved."[88] After this speech and the ensuing debate the Senate registered its support of the government in a vote of 131 to 3 (the three were Communists), with 2 abstentions.[89]

Meanwhile, across the frontier the last preparations were being made. On May 4 the Netherlands government received from its intelligence service warning that an attack would come within a few days. The Belgian authorities were also on the alert, expecting to receive an ultimatum before the week was out.[90] On the evening of May 9, 1940, secret reports reached Brussels of extensive movements on the German side of the boundary. From Luxemburg came word that the National Socialists of the grand duchy had

---

[88] *D.D. 1939*, pp. 91-96.

[89] *Ibid.*, p. 24. However, only two days later King Leopold informed Ambassador Cudahy that he expected invasion very shortly, and asked if President Roosevelt would warn Hitler that American public opinion would not be indifferent to such aggression. Hull and Roosevelt agreed that at the moment American intervention would do little good. Hull, *Memoirs*, I, 762.

[90] Hull, *Memoirs*, I, 763.

been warned to prepare for an immediate invasion. The Belgian cabinet realized the gravity of the situation, but not until news arrived at four in the morning of May 10 that planes were flying over various parts of Holland was a state of siege proclaimed. At the same time suspected persons in the eastern provinces were taken into custody.

At five o'clock that morning came official reports of the bombing of two Dutch airfields, the violation of the Belgian frontier, and the attack on the stronghold of Eben-Emael, north of Liége. While this information was being checked, the Brussels air raid sirens blared, and German planes bombed the city and the neighboring air field. At eight-thirty the German ambassador, von Bulow-Schwante, appeared at the ministry of foreign affairs. Before he could speak, Spaak indignantly protested against the aggression. Then the Ambassador read the declaration in which the government of the Reich tried to justify its deeds by claiming that Great Britain and France were planning to attack Germany through Belgium and the Netherlands. If Belgium would cooperate with the German High Command, its possessions and dynasty were guaranteed. Otherwise complete destruction and loss of independence were threatened. Spaak repeated that "Belgium is determined to defend herself," and closed the interview.[91]

Later that day Spaak described the scene in a note to the Allied powers, and reviewed the German promises made in the declarations of October 13, 1937, and August 26, 1939, as well as the efforts of King Leopold and Queen Wilhelmina to bring about peace through mediation. The note concluded with an appeal to France and Great Britain to fulfil their promises of armed aid.[92]

The Allied armies were already moving northward. The British

[91] D.D. 1939, pp. 26-29.
[92] Ibid., pp. 100-101.

advance was successful, that of the French less so, especially at the strategic Meuse crossing at Dinant where they did not establish a strong position. This fact did not become apparent at once.[93]

Immediately on learning of the attack, King Leopold went to General Headquarters to assume command of his army.[94] Not waiting to address parliament, he released a proclamation in which he reminded his people of the first invasion, and invited them to repeat their noble stand. He informed them that their Allies were already on the way to help them, and prophesied final victory.[95]

While the King assumed direct command of the army, his ministers appeared before parliament to explain the situation, ask for a vote of confidence, and present some urgent legislation, including a law providing for the government of the country in case of a German occupation. This was passed, and the cabinet was given a unanimous vote of confidence.[96]

From that hour forward, the story of Belgium's part in the war became one of almost constant defeat. On May 10 the Germans crossed the Meuse near Maestricht and the Albert Canal near Hasselt. The following day fort Eben-Emael, key to the Liége defense system, surrendered. During the night of May 11-12 the Belgian forces withdrew to the Antwerp-Namur line, which the British

---

[93] Churchill, *Second World War*, II, 38-40.

[94] In this connection it is well to note that the King's title of Commander-in-Chief was not purely nominal. In 1935, when defense plans were being drafted, they were submitted to him first; only after receiving royal approbation, not always accorded, was a proposal conveyed to the cabinet.

[95] *D.D. 1939*, p. 102.

[96] The authoritative Belgian account is that given by the Belgian foreign ministry in *D.D. 1939*, pp. 32-52. Another much briefer Belgian narrative is Belgian-American Foundation, *The Belgian Campaign and the surrender of the Belgian Army, May 10-28, 1940* (New York, 1940); this contains the statement of General Michiels. Churchill gives a clear and detailed study from the British point of view, *Second World War*, II, 27-28. A good summary of events on the entire western front, drawn from newspapers and private sources is still Armstrong, "The Downfall of France," *Foreign Affairs*, XIX (1940) 55-144.

had considered the first line of defense. At a conference with the Allied commanders held at Casteau on May 12, King Leopold agreed to place his armies under Generalissimo Gamelin, who was to be represented at Belgian Headquarters by General Billotte. This unity of command remained a dead letter, however, because soon the rapid retreat made communications nearly impossible, and General Billotte, who might be presumed to know his commanding officer's mind, was killed in an automobile accident. The German breakthrough around Sedan soon threatened the Allies' right flank, while the Dutch surrender on May 15 exposed their left. Under these circumstances further retirement was imperative, and on the night of May 16-17 it was carried out.

The Germans had by this time driven a wedge between the forces in Belgium and the main army in France. A counter-attack to reunite them was planned, but it was broken before it had barely begun, leaving the Allied center thinly defended, and forcing retirement from the last prepared position on the Scheldt, to an improvised line on the Yser.

The conditions of the battle were appalling for the retreating troops; they were strafed by low-flying planes and bombed by diving Stukas, while underfoot were milling hordes of refugees from the eastern provinces. Driven back beyond their last defenses, the Belgians had no supplies and were running short of food and water. To them the situation seemed hopeless.

On May 24-25, in an all-night session with Pierlot, Spaak, Denis, and Vanderpoorten, the only cabinet ministers in the vicinity, King Leopold announced and defended his decision to surrender in order to prevent unnecessary slaughter. Although they admitted that there was no possibility of saving the army, the premier and his colleagues begged the king to accompany them to Paris. This he stubbornly refused to do, as he believed that his place was with his soldiers. He finally agreed to delay the capitulation until the

French and British could be informed. The ministers then left their king, who notified London of his intentions.

The next day brought no improvement in the situation. At Menin the Germans succeeded in forcing a wedge between the British left and the Belgian right. When this gap was widened on May 27, Leopold warned General Gort, commander of the British Expeditionary Forces, that he would soon be forced to capitulate. He sent a similar message to the French commander.[97]

Two hours later the King notified the French and British liaison officers with him that he intended to ask for an armistice at once. This message was telegraphed to Generalissimo Weygand, Gamelin's successor, and to London, but for a few hours it was impossible to locate Generals Gort or Blanchard, the local British and French commanders.

General Derousseaux, deputy chief of staff, was immediately sent to German Headquarters to ask for terms. At ten o'clock that night he returned with Hitler's ultimatum: "unconditional surrender." An hour later the King capitulated, and at four o'clock in the morning of May 28, 1940, the Belgian army ceased firing. The terms of the protocol signed on May 28 by General von Richenau for the German Army, and General Derousseaux for the Belgian army were simple:

The Belgian Army shall unconditionally lay down its arms at once and shall from that time onwards regard itself as prisoner of war. An armistice was entered into this morning at 5 A. M., at the request of the Belgian Command. The German operations against the British and French troops will not be suspended.
Belgian territory will at once be occupied, including all the ports. No further damage shall be done to the locks or coastal fortifications.

[97] *D.D. 1939*, pp. 48-49.

Additional Protocol.

1. As a mark of honourable surrender, the Officers of the Belgian Army shall retain their weapons.
2. The Château of Laeken shall be placed at the disposal of His Majesty the King in order that he may reside there with his family, his military attendants and his servants.[98]

In view of the desperate military situation, it was evident that the action of King Leopold saved the lives of many of his people, both soldiers and civilians. At the time it left the northern flank of the retreating British—who had exposed themselves to come to Belgium's rescue—undefended. King Leopold may not have felt that his men should sacrifice themselves for the Allies, as the existing strategy required, but under the circumstances it was impossible to expect anything but the most bitter criticism. Premier Reynaud of France excoriated the surrender, slightly twisting the truth as he did so: "Now in the midst of battle King Leopold III without warning General Blanchard and without word to the French and British soldiers who had come to the aid of his country in answer to an anguished appeal—King Leopold III of Belgium said, 'Lay down your arms.' This event is without precedent in history."[99]

Churchill, who at first spoke moderately of the surrender, later, at Reynaud's request, gave a harsher judgment of what he termed "this pitiful episode."[100] Even Premier Pierlot, in a broadcast over the French radio, denounced the capitulation and declared it illegal.[101] Only President Roosevelt and his advisers did not indulge in public recriminations—their armies were not involved.[102]

The King's decision to remain a prisoner in Belgium instead of

---

[98] *D.D. 1939*, p. 51. The discrepancy of an hour between the time given in this document for the armistice and that given elsewhere in the text can be explained by the difference between German and Belgian time.

[99] New York *Times*, May 29, 1940.

[100] Great Britian, *Parl. Debates*, fifth ser., CCCLXI, 421 and 789. See also, Churchill, *Second World War*, II, 95-96.

[101] Belgian American Foundation, *The Belgian Campaign*, p. 18.

[102] Hull, *Memoirs*, I, 773.

escaping with his ministers appeared at first to place his country's eventual independence in jeopardy. Gradually, however, it appeared that this would not be the case, and from London a miniature Belgian cabinet was able to direct the government of the Congo and aid those of their fellow citizens who escaped to England. The four ministers who managed to reach Great Britain after the fall of France were Vleeschauwer, minister of colonies; Gutt, minister of finances; Spaak, minister of foreign affairs, and Pierlot. By a decree of May 28, 1940, they assumed the sovereign power, as the King was considered to be incapable of ruling.[103] They stated as their fundamental aim: "The liberation of Belgium and the liberation of our King who is a prisoner of war; the restoration of our country's territorial integrity and of her independence."[104]

It is not within the province of this study to describe the fulfillment of these aims. Belgium once more is an independent sovereign state, and because it possesses a wealthy colony, is moderately prosperous. Nevertheless events have made it abundantly clear that so small a nation cannot stand alone, and it is not without significance that Spaak has been a leading personality in the United Nations.

During the twenty years which separated the two great world wars, Belgian statesmen tried various expedients to strengthen their security. After the first world war they repudiated guaranteed neutrality, substituting for it a policy of collective security which was not given a fair trial; in 1936 they turned to isolation and "independence." The invasion of May, 1940, showed the weakness of this self-reliance, and today the pendulum has swung back to collective security, though in a new form. Belgian acceptance of the United Nations, the Benelux agreements, the Atlantic Pact, and Western European Union are all signs that Belgium has learned the big lessons of the past thirty years.

[103] Great Britain, *Parl. Debates,* fifth ser., CCCLXIII, 761-62.
[104] Joel Cang, ed., *The Who's Who of the Allied Governments* (London, 1941), p. 62.

Appendix

The Belgian Cabinets, 1919-1940

November 22, 1918, to November 7, 1919.

Prime Minister and Minister of Finances: Delacroix.
Minister of Foreign Affairs: Hymans
Minister of Justice: Vandervelde
Minister of the Interior: de Broqueville
Minister of Science and Arts: Harmignie (to Sept. 21, 1919)
  de Broqueville (after Sept. 21, 1919)
Minister of Agriculture: Ruzette
Minister of Public Works: Anseele
Minister of Industry, Labor, and Supply: Wauters
Minister of Railways, Navy, Post, and Telegraphs: Renkin
Minister of Colonies: Franck
Minister of War: Masson
Minister of Economic Affairs: Jaspar

December 9, 1919, to November 7, 1920.

Prime Minister and Minister of Finances: Delacroix
Minister of Justice: Vandervelde
Minister of Foreign Affairs: Hymans (to August 28, 1920)
  Delacroix (after August 28, 1920)
Minister of the Interior: Renkin (to June 2, 1920)
  Jaspar (after June 2, 1920)
Minister of Sciences: Destrée
Minister of Agriculture: Ruzette
Minister of Public Works: Anseele
Minister of Industry, Labor, and Supply: Wauters
Minister of Railways, Navy, Post, and Telegraphs: Poullet
Minister of Colonies: Franck
Minister of War: Masson (to February 4, 1920)
  Janson (February 4, 1920, to September 30, 1920)
  Jaspar (ad interim)
Minister of Economic Affairs: Jaspar (to June 2, 1920)
  de Wouters d'Oplinter (after June 2, 1920)

November 20, 1920, to December 6, 1921

Prime Minister and Minister of the Interior: Carton de Wiart
Minister of Justice: Vandervelde (to November 19, 1921)
Minister of Foreign Affairs: Jaspar

Minister of Finances: Theunis
Minister of Sciences and Arts: Destrée
Minister of Agriculture: Ruzette
Minister of Public Works: Anseele (to November 19, 1921)
Minister of Industry, Labor, and Supply: Wauters (to November 19, 1921)
Minister of War: Devèze
Minister of Railways, Post, and Telegraph: Neujean
Minister of Economic Affairs: Van de Vyvere

December 6, 1921, to Feb. 27, 1924.

Prime Minister and Minister of Finances: Theunis
Minister of Justice: Masson
Minister of Foreign Affairs: Jaspar
Minister of the Interior: Berryer
Minister of Arts and Science: Hubert (To October 16, 1922)
   Leclerc (October 16 to November 8, 1922)
   Nolf (After November 8, 1922)
Minister of Agriculture and Public Works: Ruzette
Minister of Industry and Labor: Moyersoen
Minister of Railways, Post, Telephone, Telegraph: Neujean
Minister of Defense: Devèze
Minister of Colonies: Franck
Minister of Economic Affairs; Van de Vyvere

March 11, 1924, to April 5, 1925.

Prime Minister and Minister of Finances: Theunis
Minister of Foreign Affairs: Hymans
Minister of Justice: Masson
Minister of the Interior and Health: Poullet
Minister of Science and Arts: Nolf
Minister of Agriculture and Public Works: Ruzette
Minister of Industry and Labor: Tschoffen
Minister of Railways, Post, telephone, Telegraph: Neujean
Minister of Defense: Forthomme
Minister of Colonies: Carton
Minister of Economic Affairs: Van de Vyvere

May 13, 1925, to May 22, 1925.

Prime Minister and Minister of Finances: Van de Vyvere
Minister of Justice: Theodore
Minister of Foreign Affairs: Ruzette
Minister of the Interior and of Health: Poullet
Minister of Sciences and Arts: Theodore
Minister of Agriculture and Public Works: Ruzette
Minister of Industry and Labor: Tschoffen
Minister of Post, Telegraph, Telephone: Tschoffen
Minister of Defense: Lt. General Hellebaut

Minister of Colonies: Carton
Minister of Economic Affairs: Moyersoen

June 17, 1925, to May 20, 1926.

Prime Minister: Poullet
Minister of Foreign Affairs: Vandervelde
Minister of Economic Affairs: Poullet (to December 10, 1925)
Liederkerke (to February 24, 1926)
Office then suppressed
Minister of Justice: Tschoffen (to December 10, 1925)
Poullet (to May 20, 1926)
Minister of the Interior and of Health: Rolin-Jacquemyns
Minister of Science and Arts: Huysmans
Minister of Finances: Janssens
Minister of Agriculture: Van de Vyvere (to February 24, 1926)
Liederkerke (to May 20, 1926)
Minister of Public Works: Laboulle
Minister of Industry and Labor: Wauters
Minister of Railways, Post, Telephone, Telegraph: Anseele
Minister of Defense: Lt. General Kestens (to January 16, 1926)
Poullet (after Jan. 16, 1926)
Minister of Colonies: Carton

May 20, 1926, to November 21, 1927.

Prime Minister, Minister of the Interior and of Health: Jaspar
Minister of Foreign Affairs: Vandervelde
Minister of Justice: Hymans
Minister of Science and Arts: Huysmans
Minister of Finances and Colonies: Houtart
Minister of Agriculture and Public Works: Baels
Minister of Industry and Labor: Wauters
Minister of Railways, Post, Telegraph, Telephone: Anseele
Minister of Defense: de Broqueville
Minister Without Portfolio: Francqui

November 24, 1927, to May 19, 1931.

Prime Minister, Minister of Colonies: Jaspar
Minister of Foreign Affairs; Hymans
Minister of Foreign Affairs: Hymans
Minister of Defense: de Broqueville
Minister of the Interior: Carnoy
Minister of Finances: Houtart
Minister of Science and Arts: Vauthier
Minister of Industry and Labor: Heyman
Minister of Agriculture: Baels
Minister of Railways: Lippens

June 11, 1931, to May 19, 1932.

Prime Minister and Minister of the Interior: Renkin
Minister of Justice: Cocq
Minister of Foreign Affairs: Hymans
Minister of National Defense: Denis
Minister of Finances: Houtart (to February 17, 1932)
    Renkin (February 17 to May 19, 1932)
Minister of Sciences and Arts: Vauthier
Minister of Industry and Labor: Heyman
Minister of Agriculture: Van Dievoet
Minister of Transport: Van Isacker
Minister of Colonies: Charles
Minister of Posts and Telegraph: Bovesse
Minister of the Interior (After February 17, 1932): Carton
Minister of Public Works: Van Caneghem

May 24, 1932, to October 18, 1932.

Prime Minister: Renkin
Minister of Justice: Cocq
Minister of Foreign Affairs: Hymans
Minister of Defense: Forthomme
Minister of Finances: Renkin
Minister of Science and Arts: Petitjean
Minister of Industry and Labor: Heyman
Minister of Agriculture: Van Dievoet
Minister of Railways: Van Isacker
Minister of Colonies: Tschoffen
Minister of Posts: Bovesse
Minister of the Interior: Carton
Minister of Public Works: Sap

October 22, 1932, to December 12, 1932.

Prime Minister and Minister of Agriculture: de Broqueville
Minister of the Interior and of Health: Poullet
Minister of Justice: Janson
Minister of Science and Arts: Lippens
Minister of Posts, Telegraph, and Telephone: Bovesse
Minister of Transport: Forthomme
Minister of Foreign Affairs: Hymans
Minister of Finances: Jaspar
Minister of National Defense: Theunis
Minister of Colonies: Tschoffen
Minister of Public Works: Sap
Minister of Industry and Labor: Heyman
Minister of the Treasury: Francqui

December 17, 1932, to June 7, 1934.

Prime Minister: de Broqueville
Minister of Foreign Affairs: Hymans
Minister of Justice: Janson
Minister of National Defense: Devèze
Minister of Transport: Forthomme
Minister of Public Instruction: Lippens
Minister of the Interior and of Posts: Poullet (to January 9, 1934)
    Pierlot (after January 10, 1934)
Minister of Finances: Jaspar
Minister of Colonies: Tschoffen
Minister of Industry and Labor: Van Isacker
Minister of Social Prevention and Health: Carton de Wiart (to January 9, 1934)
    Van Cauwelaert (after January 10)
Minister of Public Works and Agriculture: Sap

June 12, 1934, to November 13, 1934.

Prime Minister: de Broqueville
Minister of Defense: Devèze
Minister of Foreign Affairs; Jaspar
Minister of Justice: Bovesse
Minister of the Interior: Pierlot
Minister of Public Instruction: Maistriau
Minister of Finances: Sap
Minister of Agriculture and Economic Affairs: Van Cauwelaert
Minister of Public Works: Forthomme
Minister of Labor: Van Isacker
Minister of Transport: Dierckx
Minister of Colonies: Tschoffen
Ministers without Portfolio: Igenbleek and Van Zeeland

November 20, 1934, to March 19, 1935.

Prime Minister: Theunis
Minister Without Portfolio: Francqui
Minister of Foreign Affairs: Hymans
Minister of Defense: Devèze
Minister of Agriculture and Public Works: Van Cauwelaert
Minister of Justice: Bovesse
Minister of the Interior: Pierlot
Minister of Public Instruction: Hiernaux
Minister of Finances: Gutt
Minister of Economic Affairs: Van Isacker
Minister of Labor: Rubbens
Minister of Transport: du Bus de Warnaffe
Minister of Colonies: Charles

March 25, 1935, to May 26, 1936.

Prime Minister and Minister of Foreign Affairs: Van Zeeland
Ministers Without Portfolio: Vandervelde, Poullet, Hymans
Minister of Defense: Devèze
Minister of Justice: Soudan
Minister of the Interior: du Bus de Warnaffe
Minister of Public Instruction: Bovesse
Minister of Finances: Gérard
Minister of Agriculture: de Schrijver
Minister of Public Works: de Man
Minister of Economic Affairs: Van Isacker
Minister of Labor: Delattre
Minister of Transport: Spaak
Minister of Colonies: Rubbens

June 13, 1936, to November 24, 1937.

Prime Minister: Van Zeeland
Minister of Health: Vandervelde (to January 27, 1937)
    Wauters (after January 28, 1937)
Minister of Public Works: Merlot
Minister of Foreign Affairs: Spaak
Minister of Labor: Delattre
Minister of Finances: de Man
Minister of Posts, Telephone, Telegraph: Bouchery
Minister of Economic Affairs: Van Isacker
Minister of Justice: Bovesse (until April 14, 1937)
    de Laveleye (after April 14, 1937)
Minister of Colonies: Rubbens
Minister of Agriculture: Pierlot
Minister of the Interior: de Schrijver
Minister of Transport: M-H. Jaspar
Minister of National Defense: Denis
Minister of Public Instruction: Hoste

November 21, 1937, to May 13, 1938.

Prime Minister: Janson
Minister of Public Health: Wauters
Minister of Public Works: Merlot
Minister of Foreign Affairs: Spaak
Minister of Labor: Delattre
Minister of Finances: de Man (to March 4, 1938)
    Soudan (after March 4, 1938)
Minister of Post, Telephone, Telegraph: Bouchery
Minister of Economic Affairs: Van Isacker (to February 7, 1938)
    De Smet (after February 15, 1938)
Minister of Justice: du Bus de Warnaffe
Minister of Colonies: Rubbens

Minister of Agriculture: Pierlot
Minister of the Interior: Dierckx
Minister of Transport: Marck
Minister of National Defense: Denis
Minister of Public Instruction: Hoste

May 16, 1938, to January 15, 1939.

Prime Minister and Minister of Foreign Affairs: Spaak
Minister of Transport, Posts, Telegraph, Telephone: Marck
Minister of Public Instruction: Dierckx
Minister of Finances: Gérard
Minister of Justice: Pholien
Minister of the Interior and Health: Merlot
Minister of National Defense: Denis
Minister of Economic Affairs and Agriculture: Heymans
Minister of Labor: Delattre
Minister of Public Works: Balthazar
Minister of Colonies: Vleeschauwer

February 8, 1939, to February 22, 1939.

Prime Minister: Spaak
Minister of Foreign Affairs: P-E. Janson
Minister of Transports, Posts, Telephone, Telegraph: Marck
Minister of Public Instruction: Dierckx
Minister of Finances: Janssen
Minister of Justice: Van Dievoet
Minister of the Interior: Merlot
Minister of Health: Jennissen
Minister of Defense: Denis
Minister of Economic Affairs: Barnich
Minister of Agriculture: d'Aspremont-Lynden
Minister of Labor: Delattre
Minister of Public Works: Balthazar
Minister of Colonies: Vleeschauwer

February 22, 1939, to February 27, 1939.

Prime Minister: Pierlot
Minister of Justice: de Schrijver
Minister of Public Works and Transport: Marck
Minister of Foreign Affairs: Soudan
Minister of the Interior and of Health: Eckelers
Minister of Labor: Wauters
Minister of Finances: Gutt
Minister of Economic Affairs and Agriculture: Richard
Minister of Public Instruction: Blanquart
Minister of National Defense: Denis
Minister of Colonies: Heenen

April 18, 1939, to September 3, 1939.

Prime Minister and Minister of Foreign Affairs: Pierlot
Minister of Communications: Marck
Minister of Agriculture: d'Aspremont-Lynden
Minister of Economic Affairs: Sap
Minister of Colonies: Vleeschauwer
Minister of Labor: Delfosse
Minister of Justice: P-E. Janson
Minister of the Interior: Devèze
Minister of Health: M-H. Jaspar
Minister of Public Works: Vanderpoorten
Minister of Finances: Gutt
Minister of Defense: Denis
Minister of Public Instruction: Duesberg

September 3, 1939, to January 5, 1940.

Prime Minister: Pierlot
Minister of Communications: Marck
Minister of Agriculture: d'Aspremont Lynden
Minister of Economic Affairs: Sap
Minister of Supply: Delfosse
Minister of Colonies: Vleeschauwer
Minister of Foreign Affairs: Spaak
Minister of Labor: Balthazar
Minister of Information: Wauters
Minister of Justice: Soudan
Minister of the Interior: Devèze
Minister of Public Works: Vanderpoorten
Minister of Health: M-H. Jaspar
Minister of Finances: Gutt
Minister of Defense: Denis
Minister of Public Instruction: Duesberg
Ministers Without Portfolio: de Man, Janson

January 5, 1940, to May, 1940.

Prime Minister: Pierlot
Minister of Justice: Janson
Minister of Foreign Affairs: Spaak
Minister of Defense: Denis
Minister of the Interior: Vanderpoorten
Minister of Public Instruction: Soudan
Minister of Finances: Gutt
Minister of Colonies: Vleeschauwer
Minister of Public Works: Matagne
Minister of Economic Affairs and Supply: de Schrijver
Minister of Agriculture: d'Aspremont-Lynden

Minister of Labor: Balthazar
Minister of Communications: Delfosse
Minister of Health: M-H. Jaspar

Government-in-Exile

Prime Minister: Pierlot
Minister of Foreign Affairs: Spaak
Minister of Finances: Gutt
Minister of Colonies: Vleeschauwer

BIBLIOGRAPHY

MANUSCRIPT.

Logan, James A. "Memorandum for Professor Adams. The London Conference." Paris, September 5, 1924.

Logan, James A., comp. *Secret Dawes Report; the Reparation Question.* Vol. I-III. [Paris, 1924] A collection of typewritten, mimeographed, and confidential printed materials on the reparation question.

GOVERNMENT DOCUMENTS.

Allied Powers. Agent General for Reparation Payments. *Report of the Agent General for Reparation Payments, May 30, 1925 - May 21, 1930.* Berlin, 1925-1930.

Allied Powers, Reparation Commission. *Agreement regarding the distribution of the Dawes Annuities (14th January 1925).* Paris, 1925.

Belgium. *Moniteur Belge, Journal Officiel.* 88e année. June 30, 1918 - Dec. 31, 1918.

Belgium constitution. *La Constitution belge revisée 1921.* Brussels, 1923.

Belgium, corps législatif, Chambre des représentants. *Annales Parlementaires de Belgique.* Sessions législatifs ordinaires et extraordinaires de 1919-1927, 1934-1940. Brussels, 1919-1927, 1934-1939.

——————— *Compte rendu analytique de la Chambre des Représentants.* Sessions législatifs ordinaires et extraordinaires de 1927-1939. Brussels, 1927-1939.

———————*Documents parlementaires imprimés par order de la Chambre des Représentants.* Sessions législatifs ordinaires et extraordinaires de 1919-1928, 1934-1939.

Belgium. Corps législatif, Sénat. *Annales parlementaires de Belgique.* Sessions législatifs ordinaires et extraordinaires de 1919-1927, 1934-1939. Brussels, 1919-1927, 1934-1939

——————— *Compte rendu analytique du Sénat.* Sessions législatifs ordinaires et extraordinaires de 1934-1939. Brussels, 1934-1939.

——————— *Documents parlementaires imprimés par order du Sènat.* Sessions ordinaires et extraordinaires de 1919-1928, 1934-1939. Brussels. 1919-1927, 1934-1939.

Belgium. Ministère de l'intérieur et de l'hygiène. *Annuaire statistique de la Belgique et du Congo Belge.* 1934-1939.

Belgium. Ministère des affaires étrangères. *Belgium; the Official Account of What Happened, 1939-1940.* London,1941.

———————*Documents diplomatiques relatifs à la révision des traités de 1839.* Brussels, 1929.

——————— *Documents diplomatiques relatifs aux réparations.* (*Du 26 décembre au 27 août 1923*). Brussels, 1923.

——————— *Documents diplomatiques relatifs aux réparations.* (*Conférence de Londres du 16 juillet au 16 août 1924*). Brussels, 1924.

Committee of experts entrusted with the preparation of the conference of finance ministers to be held on January 6, 1925. . . . *Annexes to report* [London, 1925] (Great Britain, Foreign Office, confidential, 12614a.)

——————— "Memorandum of British experts on Belgian war debt. 31. 10 24." [Paris, 1924].

——————— "Note by the British experts: Belgian priority. 31. 10. 24." [Paris, 1924]

——————— . . . *Report* . . . [London, 1925]. (Great Britain, Foreign Office, confidential, 12614, amended copy).

Conference of Ambassadors. "Notes of a Meeting" . . . CA, 1-101, January 26, 1920 - January 12, 1921 [Paris, 1920-1921.] 101 nos.

Conference of Finance Ministers held at Paris, January 7-14, 1925. *Documents relatifs à la conférence des ministres des finances tenue à Paris du 7 au 14 janvier 1925.* [Paris, 1925]

Council of Five (Foreign Ministers). "Secretary's notes of a conversation . . ." FM 1-29, March 27 - July 2, 1919. [Paris, 1919]. 29 numbers.

Council of Four. "Minutes". . . IC 171D - 181F, April 19 - May 7, 1919. [Paris, 1919]. 49 nos.

Council of Four. "Notes of a Meeting" . . . CF 1 - 99A, May 8 - June 28, 1919. [Paris, 1919]. 123 nos.

Council of Heads of Delegations. "Notes of a Meeting of the Heads of Delegations of the Five Great Powers. H.D. 1-125, July 7, 1919 - January 10, 1920. [Paris, 1919-1920]. 125 nos.

Council of Ministers of Foreign Affairs. "Notes of a Meeting of the Ministers of Foreign Affairs." CM 1-3, January 10 - January 21, 1920. [Paris, 1920]. 3 nos.

Council of Ten. "Secretary's Notes of a Conversation . . ." BC A-63, January 12- July 5, 1919. [Paris, 1919]. 67 nos.

France. Comité d'études. *Travaux.* 2 vols. Paris, 1918. French preparations for the peace conference. The first volume is entirely devoted to Alsace Lorraine and the north-eastern frontier of France.

Germany. Auswärtiges amt. *Documents concernant la consultation populaire dans les cercles d'Eupen et Malmédy.* Berlin, n.d. Publication of the documents and protests presented to the League Council.

Great Britain. Foreign Office, historical section. *Handbooks prepared under the direction of the historical section of the foreign office, no. 26, Belgium.* London, 1920. Prepared for the use of delegates to the peace conference.

Great Britain. Parliament. *Parliamentary Debates. Commons.* 5th series. 1926-1940. London, 1920-1940.

Great Britain, Parliament. Parliamentary Papers, 1919 [-1939/40]. London, 1919-1940.

1919, Cmd. 221 "Treaty respecting assistance to France in the event of unprovoked aggression by Germany, signed at Versailles June 28, 1919."

1921, Cmd. 1325 "Protocol and correspondence between the Supreme Council and the Conference of Ambassadors, and the German Peace delegation between January 10, and July 17, 1920, respecting the execution of the treaty of Versailles of June 28, 1919."

1923, Cmd. 1812 "Inter-Allied Conferences on Reparations and inter-Allied debts Held in London and Paris December 1922 and January 1923."

Cmd. 1943 "Correspondence with the Allied Governments respecting reparations payments by Germany."

1924, Cmd. 2169 "Papers respecting negotiations for an Anglo-French Pact."

Cmd. 2184 "Correspondence concerning the Conference which it is proposed to hold in London on July 16, 1924 to consider the measures necessary to bring the Dawes plan into operation."

Cmd. 2258 "Minutes of the London Conference on Reparations, August 1922."

Cmd. 2270 "Proceedings of the London Reparation Conference July and August 1924."

Cmd. 2315 "Commercial convention between Canada and the economic union of Belgium and Luxemburg, signed at Ottawa, July 3, 1924."

1925, Cmd. 2435 "Papers respecting the proposals for a Pact of Security made by the German government on February 9, 1925."

Cmd. 2468 "Reply of the German Government to the Note handed to Herr Stresemann by the French Ambassador at Berlin on June 16, 1925 respecting the proposals for a Pact of Security."

1929/1930, Cmd. 3343 "Report of the Committee of Experts on Reparation."

Cmd. 3417 "International agreement on the evacuation of the Rhineland territory, The Hague, August 30, 1929."

1930/1931, Cmd. 3947 "Report of the International Committee of Experts respecting suspension of certain intergovernmental debts falling due during the year ending June 30, 1932, together with Protocols and Declarations signed at London, August 11 and 13, 1931."

1932/1933, Cmd. 4126　　"Final Act of the Lausanne Conference, Lausanne, July 9, 1932."

1935/1936, Cmd. 5071　　"Documents and proceedings of the League of Nations."

Cmd. 5134　　"Text of proposals drawn up by the Representatives of Belgium, France, the United Kingdom of Great Britain and Northern Ireland, and Italy. London, March 19, 1936."

Cmd. 5143　　"Correspondence showing the course of certain Diplomatic Discussions directed towards securing an European Settlement, June 1934 to March 1936."

1936/1937, Cmd. 5300　　"International committee for the application of the agreement regarding non-intervention in Spain; the legislative and other measures taken by the participating governments to give effect to the agreement regarding non-intervention in Spain, and by the Swiss government to prohibit the export, etc., of arms and war material from Switzerland to Spain."

"Documents exchanged between His Majesty's Government in the United Kingdom and the French Government and the Belgian Government concerning the international position of Belgium, Brussels, April 24, 1937."

1939/1940, Cmd. 6106　　"Documents concerning German-Polish relations and the outbreak of hostilities between Great Britain and Germany on September 3, 1939."

Great Britain, Parliament. *Parliamentary Papers,* 1925, 1932 - [1934/35]. "Financial statement of the Chancellor of the Exchequer." London 1925, 1933-1935.

The Hague. Permanent Court of International Justice. Series A/B. Judgments, orders and advisory opinions. Fascicule 73. *Affaire Borchgrave (Désistement).* Leyden, 1938.

————— Fascicule 70. *The diversion of water from the Meuse.* Leyden, n.d.

Inter-Allied Conference of Prime Ministers. "Notes of a meeting". . . ICP 18-23, January 16-20, 1920. [Paris, 1920], 6 nos.

League of Nations. Assembly. *Official Journal.* Records of the Assembly, ordinary and extraordinary sessions, 1920-1939. Geneva, 1920-1939.

League of Nations. *Council Minutes.* Fifth, eighth, ninth, and tenth meetings. May-November, 1920. Geneva, 1921.

London Reparation Conference, July-August, 1924, *Proceedings.* 2 vols. [London 1924]. (Great Britain, Foreign Office, 12530-12531). Bound in James A. Logan, *Secret Dawes Report, The Reparation Question,* vol. IIB.

Netherlands. Department van buitlandsche zaken. *Bescheiden in zake de Tusschen Nederland en België hangende vraagstukken door de wederzydsche regeeringen gewisseld sedert de verwerping van het verdrag van 3 April 1925.* The Hague, 1929. The same documents were published by the Belgian Foreign Office at the same time.

United States. American Commission to negotiate Peace. "S-H Bulletin." February 2 - December 7, 1919. [Paris, 1919], 1428 nos.

United States. Bureau of foreign and domestic commerce (Department of Commerce). *The Reparation Problem, 1918-1924.*Washington, 1924.

United States. Committee of experts on reparations, nominated January 10, 1929. *Report of committee of experts on reparations with annexes and concurrent memorandum; also settlement of Belgian mark claim.* Washington, 1929.

United States. Department of State. *Bulletin.* Washington, 1939-1943.

——————— *Papers relating to the Foreign Relations of the United States, 1919-1930.* Washington, 1934-1945.

Papers relating to the Foreign Relations of the United States. The Lansing Papers, 1914-1920. Washington, 1940. 2 vols.

———————*Papers relating to the Foreign Relations of the United States. 1919. The Paris Peace Conference.* 13 vols. Washington, 1924-1947.

———————*Press Releases,* 1934-1939. Washington, 1934-1939.

United States. Department of the Treasury. *Annual Report of the Secretary of the Treasury on the state of the finances for the fiscal year ended June 30, 1933.* Washington, 1933.

United States Embassy, Paris, comp. "ESH Bulletin." December 12, 1919 - January 3, 1921. [Paris, 1919-1921]; 1358 nos.

United States. Office of commissioner of accounts and deposits. *Memorandum covering the indebtedness of foreign governments to the United States and showing the total amounts paid by Germany under the Dawes and Young plans.* Washington, 1939.

United States. World War Foreign Debt Commission. *Combined Annual Reports, 1922-1926.* Washington, 1927.

——————— *Minutes, 1922-1926.* Washington, 1927.

NEWSPAPERS.

France. Ministère de la guerre et des affaires étrangères, *Bulletin périodique de la presse belge.* Paris, 1919-1940.

L'Indépendance Belge, 1919-1939. Brussels. The leading Liberal organ.

New York Times, 1934-1940. New York.

Pays Réel, 1936-1937. Brussels. The Rexist periodical.

Le Peuple, 1919-1938. Brussels. Organ of the Socialist party.

Rex, 1936-1938. Brussels. Rexist journal.

PERIODICALS.

Current History, 1918-1940. New York.
Europe Nouvelle, 1918-1939. Paris. A well-documented weekly, giving careful attention to both international affairs and internal developments in European countries.
Flambeau, 1919-1940. Brussels. A monthly of pronounced Liberal views.
Revue Belge, 1924-1940. Brussels. Neutral in tone.
Revue belge des livres, documents et archives de la guerre 1914-1918, 1924-1940. Brussels.
Revue de droit international, 1920-1939. Paris.
Revue de Paris, 1920-1939. Paris.
Revue des Deux Mondes, 1920-1939. Paris Conservative periodical.
Revue Générale, 1924-1939. Brussels. Catholic literary and historical periodical.

COLLECTED DOCUMENTS, LETTERS AND SPEECHES.

Berber, J. *Locarno; a collection of documents*. London, 1936.
Belgian American Foundation. *Final Reports*, 1922-1939. Reports of students profiting from the Educational Foundation. Some of these, the work of students of history, give penetrating analyses of conditions in Belgium.
Buffin, Baron Camille, ed. *Mémoires et Documents inédits sur la révolution belge et la campagne de dix-huit jours* (1830-1831). 2 vols. Brussles, 1912.
Burnett, Philip Mason. *Reparation at the Paris Peace Conference from the standpoint of the American Delegation*. 2 vols. New York, 1940. Includes not only minutes of the more important committee meetings, Council of Four, etc., but important memoranda from the private papers of Colonel House.
Eden, Anthony. *Foreign Affairs*. New York, 1939. Speeches delivered while the writer was Foreign Secretary, and some from the period of his retirement.
Gay, George I. and H.H. Fisher. *Public Relations of the Commission for Relief in Belgium. Documents*. 2 vols. Stanford University, 1929.
Langenhove, Fernand van., ed. *Le dossier diplomatique de la question belge; recueil des pièces officielles, avec notes*. Paris, 1917. Compiled by a permanent official of the Belgian Ministry of Foreign Affairs.
Luckau, Alma. *The German Delegation at the Paris Peace Conference*. New York, 1941.
Terrail, Gabriel [Mermeix]. *Le Combat des Trois; notes et documents sur la conférence de la paix*. Paris, 1922.

DIARIES.

D'Abernon, Edgar Vincent. *An Ambassador of Peace: pages from the diary of Viscount D'Abernon (Berlin, 1920-1926)*. 3 vols. London, 1929-1930.
Dawes, Charles G. *A Journal of Reparations*. London, 1939.
Miller, David Hunter. *My Diary at the Conference of Paris, with Documents*.

21 vols. New York, 1924. An invaluable mine of source material; there are some discrepancies between the documents as published by Miller, and those in the files of the State Department. The documents in the Hoover Library at Stanford University agree with Miller's versions.

Nevins. Allan, ed. *The Letters and Journal of Brand Whitlock chosen and edited with a biographical introduction.* 2 vols. New York, 1936. Very interesting when compared with Whitlock's *Belgium,* which is full of praise for all things Belgian. The postwar comments reflect the inevitable letdown in the mood of exaltation which accompanied victory. Excellent thumb-nail sketches of Belgian personalities.

Riddell, George A. *Lord Riddell's intimate diary of the peace conference and after, 1918-1923.* New York, 1934.

Seymour, Charles, ed. *The Intimate Papers of Colonel House, arranged as a narrative,* vol. IV. Boston, 1928.

Sutton, Eric, ed. *Gustav Stresemann, his diaries, letters, and papers.* 3 vols. New York, 1935-1940. The publication of this work strengthened French and Belgian intransigence, for Stresemann is revealed as thoroughly nationalistic, despite his apparent friendship for the Allies.

REMINISCENCES AND AUTOBIOGRAPHY.

Allen, Henry T. *The Rhineland Occupation.* Indianapolis, 1927. By the General commanding the American Army of Occupation.

Baruch, Bernard Mannes. *The Making of the Reparation and Economic Sections of the Treaty.* New York, 1920. By one who was on the Reparations Commission, and who was an influential adviser of the American delegation.

Churchill, Winston. *The Second World War.* 2 vols. Boston, 1948-1949.

Dawes, Rufus C. *The Dawes Plan in the Making.* Indianapolis, 1925.

Haskins, Charles Homer and Robert Howard Lord. *Some Problems of the Peace Conference,* Cambridge, 1920. By two eminent historians who served as advisers to the American delegation. Treats the Belgian position very sympathetically.

House, Edward Mandell and Charles Seymour. *What really Happened at Paris; the story of the peace conference, 1918-1919.* New York, 1921. Each chapter is written by one of the American advisers most closely in touch with the topic under discussion.

Hull, Cordell. *The Memoirs of Cordell Hull,* 2 vols. New York, 1948.

Hymans, Paul. *Fragments d'histoire; impressions et souvenirs.* Brussels, 1940. By the distinguished Belgian diplomat who represented his country at the Peace Conference, on the League Council, at several conferences, and who was for years Foreign Minister.

Lloyd George, David. *Memoirs of the Peace Conference.* 2 vols. New Haven, 1939. Not too reliable; everything good emanated from him, according to this version, and everything unwise was the brain child of Wilson and Clemenceau.

——————————— *The Truth about Reparations and War-Debts.* New York, 1932. Tries to show their close interconnection.

——————————— *The Truth About the Peace Treaties.* 2 vols. London 1938.

Miller, David Hunter. *The Drafting of the Covenant.* 2 vols. New York, 1928. By the legal adviser to the American delegation, who actually did a large share of the drafting.

Snowden, Philip. *An Autobiography.* 2 vols. London,1934. Shows Snowden's absolute self-confidence, as well as the important position he played in international and national affairs. Interesting sidelights on the London and Hague Reparations Conferences.

Shotwell, James T. *At the Paris Peace Conference.* New York, 1937.

Tardieu, André. *The Truth About the Treaty.* Indianapolis, 1921. The conference from the point of view of Clemenceau's right-hand man.

Vandervelde, Emile. *Souvenirs d'un militant socialiste.* Paris, 1939. Is more concerned with the history of the Belgian Socialist party than with foreign affairs.

Whitlock, Brand. *Belgium, a personal narrative.* 2 vols. New York, 1919. Omits any material which might dim the glory of "martyred Belgium."

BIOGRAPHY.

Ashley, Evelyn. *The life and correspondence of Henry Temple, Viscount Palmerston.* 2 vols. London, 1879.

Baker, Ray Stannard. *Woodrow Wilson and World Settlement; written from his unpublished and personal materials.* 3 vols. New York, 1922.

Cammaerts, Emile. *Albert of Belgium, defender of Right.* New York, 1935. An "official" biography.

Denuit, Désiré. *Albert, roi des Belges.* Brussels, 1934.

Dumont-Wilden Louis. *Albert I er, rois des Belges.* Paris, 1934.

Galet, Lt. General. *Albert, King of the Belgians, in the Great War. His military actions and experiences set down with his approval.* Tr. from the French by Major General Sir Ernest Swinton. Boston, 1931.

Hamilton, Mary Agnes. *Arthur Henderson, a biography.* London, 1938.

Lane-Poole, Stanley. "Temple, Henry John, third Viscount Palmerston."*Dictionary of National Biography.* LVI, 16-33 (New York, 1898) .

Maurice, Frederick. *Haldane, the life of Viscount Haldane of Cloan, K.T., O.M.* London, 1939.

Petrie, Charles. *The Life and Letters of the Right Hon. Sir Austen Chamberlain, K.G., P.C., M.P.* 2 vols. Toronto, 1939-1940.

Tarbell, Ida M. *Owen D. Young, a new type of industrial leader.* New York, 1932.

MONOGRAPHS AND SPECIAL STUDIES.

Alia, Antonino d'. *La Belgique intellectuelle, économique, politique.* Tr. from the Italian by Pierre Poirier. Brussels, 1923.

Batsell, Walter Russell. *The Debt Settlements and the Future.* Paris, 1927.

Bergmann, Karl. *The History of Reparations*. London, 1927.

Binkley, Robert Cedric. "Reactions of European public opinion to Woodrow Wilson's statesmanship from the Armistice to the treaty of Versailles." Unpublished doctoral dissertation in Stanford University Library, 1927. Based on a thorough study of the newspapers in the Hoover Collection.

Blount, D.L. *Belgium's Recovery; an example of what industry and political stability can accomplish*. Brussels, 1920. By the former director of the Information Office of the Belgian Ministry of Economic Affairs.

Brand, Carl. F. *British Labour's rise to power*. Stanford University, 1941.

Clough, Shepard Bancroft. *History of the Flemish Movement in Belgium, a study in nationalism*. New York, 1930. Thorough study of the movement, which is traced from its beginnings in nineteenth-century romanticism.

Delzell, Charles F. "The military occupation of Belgium, 1914-1918." Unpublished master's thesis in Stanford University Library, 1943.

Descamps, Edouard. *La Neutralité de la Belgique au point de vue historique, diplomatique, juridique, et politique: Etude sur la constitution des états pacifiques à titre permanent*. Brussels, 1920.

Franck, Louis. *La Stabilisation monétaire en Belgique*. Paris, 1927. By one of the bankers who helped Francqui carry out the stabilization program.

Hall, John. *England and the Orleans Monarchy*. New York, 1912.

Henry, A. *Le Ravitaillement de la Belgiue pendant l'occupation allemande*. Paris, 1924.

Hoch, Charles. *The Neutral Territory of Moresnet*. Tr. by W.W. Tucker from *Un Territoire oublié au centre de l'Europe*. Cambridge, 1882. An interesting explanation of the interesting case of this tiny area left to itself by chance after the Congress of Vienna.

Juste, Theodore. *Histoire du Congrès National de Belgique ou de la fondation de la monarchie belge*. 2 vols. 2 ed. Brussels, 1861.

Lingelbach, William E. "Belgian Neutrality: its origin and interpretation." *American Historical Review*, XXXIX, 48-72 (October, 1933.)

Mahaim, Ernest. *La Belgique Restaurée; étude sociologique*. Brussels, 1926.

Massart, Charles Mathieu. *La Belgique socialiste et communiste*. Paris, 1922. By a Belgian Communist, trying to show the deficiencies of the Belgian Socialists.

Moore, Mary Margaret. "Public opinion in Belgium in 1919." Unpublished Master's thesis in Stanford University Library, 1942.

Moulton, Harold G. and Leo Pasvolsky. *War Debts and World Prosperity*. New York, 1932.

Nothomb. M. *Essai historique et politique sur la révolution belge*. 2 vols. 4 ed. Brussels, 1876.

Piérard, Louis. *Belgian Problems since the War*. New Haven, 1929.

Pirenne, Henri. *La Belgique et la guerre mondiale*. New Haven, 1928.

Richemont, Jean de. *L'Europe devant l'indépendance belge*. Paris, 1939. A French conservative tries to show the causes and the probable results of the royal speech.

Ridder, Alfred de *La Belgique et la guerre* Vol. IV. 2 ed. Brussels, 1928.

Rowntree, B. Seebohm. *Land and Labour; lessons from Belgium*. London, 1911.

Roussel le Roy, André. *L'abrogation de la neutralité de la Belgique, ses causes et ses effets. Etude d'histoire diplomatique et de droit public international*. Paris, 1923.

Scott, Charles Craven. "Belgian diplomatic relations, 1875-1887; a study in the diplomacy of neutrality." Unpublished doctoral dissertation in Stanford University Library, 1940. Based on material in the Belgian archives. The year 1887 was the terminal date because the archives of the foreign office are closed for fifty years.

Shepherd, Henry Longdon. *The Monetary Experience of Belgium 1914-1936*. Princeton, 1936. A thorough, clear study, based chiefly on published government documents.

Siotto-Pintor, Manfredi. "Le Régime international de l'Escaut." *Académie de Droit International: Recueil des Cours*, XXI, 277-369 (1928).

Solansky, Adolph. *German Administration in Belgium*. New York, 1928.

Wheeler-Bennett, John Wheeler. *Information on the reparation settlement; being the background and history of the Young plan and the Hague agreements, 1929-1930*. London, 1930.

_____ *The Wreck of reparations, being the political background of the Lausanne agreement, 1932*. New York, 1933.

Wullus-Rudiger, J. *La Défense de la Belgique en 1940*. Villeneuve, France, 1940.

GENERAL WORKS.

Barnouw, Adraan J. *Holland under Queen Wilhelmina*. New York, 1923.

Cammaerts, Emile. *A History of Belgium, from the Roman invasion to the present day*. London, 1921.

Ensor, R.C.K. *Belgium*. New York, 1915.

Essen, Léon van der. *A Short history of Belgium*. University of Chicago, 1915.

Kalken, Frans van. *La Belgique contemporaine (1870-1930)*; *histoire d'une évolution politique*. Paris, 1930.

_____ *Histoire de Belgique*, 2 ed. Brussels, 1924.

Linden, H. Vander. *Belgium; the making of a nation*. Tr. by Sybil Jane from *Vue générale de l'histoire de Belgique* (Paris, 1918). Oxford, 1920.

MacDonnell, John de Courcy. *Belgium, her kings, kingdom and people*. London, 1914.

Pirenne, Henri. *Histoire de Belgique*. 7 vols. Brussels, 1909-1932.

Toynbee, Arnold J. ed. *Survey of International Affairs, 1920-1938*. London, 1925-1940.

PERIODICAL ARTICLES.

A. BELGIAN INTERNAL POLITICS, COMMENTS BY LEADING POLITICIANS.

Carton de Wiart, Henry. "Les grands partis belges et les élections." *Flambeau*, IV, 155-165 (October, 1921).

Janson, Georges. "Emile Francqui, l'homme d'état." *Flambeau*, XVIII, 677-700 (December, 1935).

Jaspar, Marcel-Henri and Henry Janne. "Les jeunes libéraux belges." *Europe Nouvelle*, XIX, 848-850 (August 22, 1936).

Lichtervelde, Louis de. "Albert I er." *Revue Générale*, CXXXI, 261-274 (March, 1934).

Man, Henri de. "La Résorption du chômage." *Europe Nouvelle*, XIX, 425-427 (April 25, 1936).

Tschoffen, Paul. "Le parti Catholique." *Flambeau*, IV, 166-170 (October, 1921).

B. BELGIAN POLITICS, COMMENTS BY POLITICIANS AND JOURNALISTS.

Axel, Pierre Van. "Le Mouvement flamand et le retour à l'état belge." *Revue Genérále*, CXL, 375-384 (September, 1938).

Bruyne, Edgard De. "Le Mouvement flamand et les tendances fédéralistes." *Revue Générale*, CXXXVII, 451-472 (April, 1937). By a Flemish professor at the University of Ghent.

Denuit, Désiré. "En Flandre avec les Dinasos." *Revue Générale*, CXXXIV, 454-465 (October, 1935). A description of the plans and methods of the Flemish Extremists.

Francisci-Gerbino. G. de. "La réconstruction financière de la Belgique; un nouveau projet d'amortissement de la Dette Publique." *Flambeau*, VIII, 21-40 (September, 1925)

Geyle, P. "Beginnings of administrative separation in Belgium." *Contemporary Review*, CXLI, 725-732 (June, 1932).

Grégoire, Henri. "Le 'Flambeau' de guerre." *Flambeau*, XXII, 621-629 (December, 1939). By its editor.

———————— "L'Interdiction du 'Flambeau': Histoire d'une faute." *Flambeau*, XXIII, 181-205 (February, 1940). A plea for freedom of the press.

Jaspar, Marcel-Henri. "Chronique des mauvais jours; les élections du 5 avril et le ministère Poullet-Vandervelde." *Flambeau*, XI, 320-341. (December, 1928).

Laveleye, Victor de. "Bilan intérieur d'une crise extérieure." *Revue Belge*, XV, 372-375 (November 15, 1938). Summary of the reactions of Belgium to the Munich crisis.

Piérard, Louis "Les arrêtés-lois du gouvernement de Broqueville." *Europe Nouvelle*, XVII, 879-880 (September 1, 1934).

———————— "La Belgique, terre de compromis." *Flambeau*, XVIII, 651-674 (June, 1935). The author praises the Belgian Socialists and their wise compromise with van Zeeland over Man's *Plan du Travail*.

———————— "Un plan quinquennal belge." *Europe Nouvelle*, XVII, 5-7 (January 6, 1934).

Ydewalle, Pierre d'. "Au delà du flamingantisme: le Verdinaso." *Revue Générale*, CXXXVII, 694-710 (June, 1937).

C. BELGIAN POLITICS, FOREIGN COMMENT

Dupierreaux, Richard. "La nouvelle équipe de M. van Zeeland." *Europe Nouvelle*, XVIII, 307-309 (March 30, 1935).

Garson, Jules. "La situation politique en Belgique." *Revue Politique et Parlementaire*, CLXXXI, 247-253 (November, 1939).

George, Robert H. "Eupen and Malmedy." *Foreign Affairs*, V, 332-335 (January, 1927).

Jouvenel, Bertrand. "Henri de Man, l'homme du Plan." *Europe Nouvelle*, XVII, 1216. (December 8, 1934).

Langerock, Hubert. "The Flemish Demand for Autonomy." *Current History*, 789-794 (August, 1923).

Laurent, Henri. "Belgium under a new leader." *Current History*, XLII, 481-487 (August, 1935).

Leurquin, Robert. "Après les élections communales belges: le Rexisme et le nationalisme flamand refoulés." *Europe Nouvelle*, XXI, 1186-1187, October 29, 1938).

_____ "Les Bruxellois contre le dictature." *Europe Nouvelle*, XX, 373-374 (April 17, 1937).

_____ "La loi militaire belge." *Europe Nouvelle*, XIX, 1261-1262 (December 19, 1936).

Lynd, Albert. "Death of a Socialist." *Commonweal*, March 17, 1939, pp. 566-568.

Marès, Roland de. "La crise belge." *Revue de Paris*, April 1, 1939, pp. 661-672.

Norton, H.K. "Belgium at Work." *Current History*, XIX, 428-434 (December, 1922).

"Le plan de travail de Man." *Europe Nouvelle*, XVII, 286-291 (March 17, 1934).

"Réforme bancaire en Belgique." *Europe Nouvelle*, XVII, 870-871 (September 1, 1934).

Roger Charles. "Les modalités de la réforme monétaire." *Europe Nouvelle*, XIX, 421-424 (April 25, 1936).

Rotvand, Georges. "Problèmes belges." *Europe Nouvelle*, XVIII, 396-398 (April 27, 1935).

Rouland, E. "La crise politique en Belgique." *Journal des Economistes*, CIX, 180-184 (March-April, 1939).

Schwob, Phillippe. "Les dévaluations, la production et les échanges." *Europe Nouvelle*, XVIII, 1206-1208 (December 14, 1935).

Verax. "Silhouettes Etrangères - M. Paul van Zeeland." *Revue des Deux Mondes*, 8° partie, XXXII, 520-532 (April, 1936).

D. BELGIAN FOREIGN POLICY: ARTICLES BY STATESMEN.

Broqueville, Charles de. "Pourquoi j'ai parlé en mars 1934." *Revue Générale*, CXLI, 289-298 (March, 1939).

Dortens, Hans. "The Rhineland Movement." *Foreign Affairs*, III, 398-410 (April, 1925). Included here as being the authorized statement of the man most responsible for the movement, and in a position to judge Belgian actions.

Hymans, Paul. "Belgium's Position in Europe." *Foreign Affairs*, IX, 34-64 (October, 1930).

Janson, Paul Emile. "Lophem." *Flambeau*. IX, 257-294 (March, 1926).

Jaspar, Henri. "La Belgique et la politique occidentale depuis le traité de paix." *Revue Belge*, II, 385-410 (June, 1924).

——————— "Cannes et Locarno." *Revue Générale*, LIX, 1-16 (January, 1926).

——————— "La conférence de Cannes de 1922." *Revue Générale*, CXX-VIII, 129-147 (August, 1937).

——————— "Les directives de la politique extérieure de la Belgique." *Esprit International*, VII, 3-22 (January, 1933).

——————— "Locarno et la Belgique." *Revue Belge*, II, 157-169 (November, 1925).

Lamont, Thomas W. "The Final Reparations Settlement." *Foreign Affairs*, VIII, 336-363 (April, 1930).

Langenhove, Fernand van. "La politique commerciale de la Belgique." *Flambeau*, IX, 55-70 (January, 1926). By the commercial director of the Foreign Ministry.

Lichtervelde, Louis de. "La Belgique et la S.D.N." *Revue Générale*, CXXXV-III, 385-491 (October, 1937).

——————— "Les cantons de l'Est." *Revue Générale*, CXXXVIII, 156-172 (August, 1937).

Theunis, George. "Belgium Today." *Foreign Affairs*, IV, 264-277 (January, 1926).

Tirard, Paul. "Comment nous avons occupé la Ruhr." *Revue des Deux Mondes*, 7° partie, LX, 122-148; 319-344 (November, 1930). Although not by a Belgian, it is included here because it gives a trustworthy description of the methods used by the Franco-Belgian MICUM in the occupation.

Vandervelde, Emile. "Belgian Foreign Policy and the Nationalities Question." *Foreign Affairs*, XI, 657-670 (July, 1633).

Zeeland, Paul van. "Aims of Recent Belgian Foreign Policy." *Foreign Affairs*, XVIII, 140-147 (October, 1939).

E. BELGIAN FOREIGN POLICY; COMMENTS BY BELGIAN POLITICIANS AND JOURNALISTS.

Cammaerts, Emile. "The Belgian Problem." *Contemporary Review*, CLI, 658-666 (June, 1937).

Crabbé, Raoul. "La Neutralité belge et la S.D.N." *Revue Belge*, XIV, 379-384 (May, 1937).

——————— "La riposte au Führer." *Revue Belge*, XV, 272-278 (May, 1938).

Crokaert, Jacques. *L'accord belgo-luxembourgeois.* Brussels, 1921.

"La déclaration allemande et la politique extérieure de la Belgique." *Revue Générale*, CXXXVIII, 524-539 (November, 1937).

Détry, G. A. "La Belgique et les 'Papiers de Stresemann." *Revue Belge des Livres, Documents, et Archives de la Guerre 1914-1918*, VIII, (August-November, 1932,) 498-503.

"Le discours du Roi." *Revue Générale*, CXXXVI, 532-539 (November, 1936).

Failon, Jean de. "La crise de la sécurité collective." *Revue Générale*, CXXXV, 650-659 (June, 1936).

——————— "La guerre d'Afrique et la paix de l'Europe." *Revue Générale*, CXXXIV, 544-556 (November, 1935).

Goemaere, Pierre, et Raoul Crabbé. "Leopold III et l'indepéndance de la Belgique." *Revue Belge*, XIV, 485-498 (December, 1937).

Grégoire, Henri. "L'Europe de demain." *Flambeau*, XXII, 710-711, December, 1939.

————— "Une offensive morale." *Flambeau*, XXII, 509-517 (November, 1939). This article, strongly disapproving Leopold's mediation offer, caused the imposition of severe censorship regulations in Belgium.

————— "La politique belge." *Flambeau*, XXII, 352-358 (September, 1939).

————— "La politique belge." *Flambeau*, XXIII, 115-128 (January, 1940).

Laveleye, Victor de. "La dette belge envers les Etats-Unis." *Revue Belge*, XII, 1-14 (January, 1935). Surprisingly pro-American.

————— "La politique extérieure de la Belgique." *Flambeau*, XIV, 284-304 (March-April, 1931).

Melot, Ernest. "La conférence de Locarno." *Revue Générale*, LVIII, 511-517 (September, 1925).

————— "Société des Nations, ou pactes d'alliance et d'assistance mutuelle." *Flambeau*, XVIII, 193-214 (August, 1935).

Ombiaux, Maurice Des. *La Politique belge depuis l'armistice; la grande peur de la victoire*. Paris, 1921. Violent nationalistic diatribe against any appeasement of Germany.

"Le problème de la Meuse." *Revue Générale*, CXXXVII, 346-368 (March, 1937).

Wullus-Rudiger, J. "La Belgique et les dangers de demain." *Revue Belge*, XII, 215-229 (November, 1935). Feels that Belgium should support Italy's Ethiopian venture in order to have an ally in case of future trouble.

F. BELGIAN FOREIGN POLICY: FOREIGN COMMENT.

Armstrong, Hamilton Fish. "The Downfall of France." *Foreign Affairs*, XIX, 55-144 (October, 1940).

Brécard, General. "Le Roi Léopold III." *Revue des Deux Mondes*, 8° partie, XLVII, 921-925 (October, 1938).

Brossolette, Pierre. "L'accord anglo-franco-belge." *Europe Nouvelle*, XX, 411-413 (May 1, 1937).

Buchet, Charles. "Le rôle de la Belgique dans la défense des frontières de la France." *Revue de France*, XIV, 27-47 (November, 1934).

Buttgenbach, André. "Le mouvement rexiste et la situation politique de la Belgique." *Revue des Sciences Politiques*, LIX, 511-554 (October, 1936).

Cercler, René. "France-Belgique." *Revue Politique et Parlementaire*, CLXXVIII, 238-248 (February, 1939).

Charlyvel, G. "La nouvelle orientation de la politique étrangère belge: l'aspect militaire du problème." *Europe Nouvelle*, XIX, 1056-1058 (October 24, 1936).

Dumont-Wilden, Louis. "La Belgique et le système locarnien." *Revue Politique et Littéraire*, LXXIV, 740-743 (November, 1936).

Dupierreux, Richard. "Belgique, 1934." *Europe Nouvelle*. XVII, 1287-1288 (December 29, 1934).

Elliott, A. Randle. "The Oslo States and the European War." *Foreign Policy Reports*, XV, 258-272 (January 15, 1940).

Fodor, M.W. "Blitzkrieg in the Low Countries." *Foreign Affairs*, XIX, 193-206 (October, 1940).

George, Robert H. "The Scheldt Dispute." *Foreign Affairs*, VI, 155-157 (October, 1927).

Jouvenel, Bertrand de. "La nouvelle orientation de la politique étrangère belge: les raisons intérieures." *Europe Nouvelle*, XIX, 1061-1062 (October, 24, 1936).

Leurquin, Robert. "La nouvelle orientation de la politique étrangère belge: les conséquences pour la défense nationale de la Belgique." *Europe Nouvelle*, XIX, 1059-1061 (October 24, 1936).

Pertinax. "La déclaration allemande à la Belgique et à l'Europe occidentale." *Europe Nouvelle*, XX, 1027-1029 (October 23, 1937).

——————— "La nouvelle orientation de la politique étrangère belge: les répercussions diplomatiques." *Europe Nouvelle*, XIX, 1055-1056 (October 24, 1936).

Pinon, René. "Le discours du roi Léopold III." *Revue des Deux Mondes*, 8° partie, VI, 230-237 (November, 1936).

Requette, Lt. Col. "The Low Countries and the European War." *Atlantic Monthly*, CLXV, 695-699 (May, 1940.)

Richard, Elie. "Terror on the Frontiers." *Living Age*, CCCLIV, 196-202 (May, 1938).

Whittier, Richard. "Belgium Emphasizes Security." *Contemporary Review*, CLI, 29-37 (January, 1937).

PAMPHLETS.

Batavus. *Belgian Ports and Dutch Waterways*. London, 1919.

Belgian-American Educational Foundation. *The Belgian Campaign and the surrender of the Belgian Army, May 10-28, 1940*. New York, 1940.

Clark, George Norman. *Belgium and the War*. New York, 1942. Oxford pamphlets on World Affairs.

Motz, Roger. *Belgium Unvanquished*. New York, 1942.

Struycken, Antonius A.H. *Holland, Belgium, and the Powers*. The Hague, 1919.

Index

A

Aachen, German troop concentrations, 272

Aaland Islands Case, Hyman's solution, 209

Aberdeen, George Gordon, earl of, and proposed Conference of London, 14; resignation, 15

Abrogation of Treaty of 1839, 105

Abyssinia. See Ethiopia

Action Wallon, opposes royal speech, 241

Activists, 25, 35; join Front party, 36; traitors released, 44. See also Flemish movement

Activist trials, 35

Adelaide, Grand Duchess of Luxemburg, 177

Administrative separation, early demands, 21; first steps, 37-38; completed, 45, 281; See also Flemish movement

Air Locarno, 213; suggested by Hitler, 221

Aix-la-Chapelle, Rhineland separatist movement, 124

Albert I, accession, 23; at La Panne, 24; refuses to incorporate army with French, 28; refuses to discuss economic treaty of 1916, 28; reply to Wilson's peace note, 28; speech of Nov. 22, 1918, 31; in Belgian politics, 29, 37, 41 n, 42, 43, 44 n, 55 n; meeting with Council of Four, 65 n; favors revision of 1839 treaties, 71; Eupen - Malmedy, 98-99; intervenes at Brussels Conference, 114; visit to London in 1921, 184; personal direction of Belgian policy, 160,

197; death 46, 205

Albert Canal, work begun, 234; and Belgian Dutch relations, 257; defense outpost, 266; defective bridges, 279; German crossing, 285

Allied Conference in Paris 1917, Belgium asks revision of 1839 treaties, 70

Allied Military Commission, suppressed, 203

Alsace and Lorraine, retrocession 99

Amis de l'Exploité, expelled from POB, 38

Amnesty, granted to Flemish traitors, 44

Anglo-Belgo-French Military agreement, 223; abrogation, 249-250

Anglo-Dutch treaty of commerce, 198 n

Anglo-French entente, Belgium works to reestablish, 125; Belgian policy, 133

Anglo-French treaty of alliance, tentative draft at Cannes, 185

Anglo-Italian Naval Agreement, and Belgian recognition of Spain, 262

Annexationist policy. See Belgo-Dutch relations.

Anschluss, Belgian reaction, 263

Anseele, Edouard, at Lophem, 29; leader of Flemish Socialists, 35; and *fusil brisé* incident, 39

Antwerp, development, 36; and occupation of the Ruhr, 122; Russian trading company, 218; unemployed, 278 n; approaches to controled by Netherlands, 57, 74, 257 (see also Wielingen Pass); neutrality, relief prevented by 1839 treaties, 77-78; neutrality abrogated, 83-84, 105;